Independence in Spanish America

Diálogos

A series of course adoption books for Latin America

Tangled Destinies: Latin America and the United States—Don Coerver, TCU, and Linda Hall, University of New Mexico

The Century of U.S. Capitalism in Latin America—Thomas O'Brien, The University of Houston

The Faces of Honor: Sex, Shame, and Violence in Colonial Latin America—Edited by Lyman L. Johnson, The University of North Carolina at Charlotte, and Sonya Lipsett-Rivera, Carleton University

¡Que vivan los tamales! Food and the Making of Mexican Identity—Jeffrey M. Pilcher, The Citadel

Heroes on Horseback: A Life and Times of the Last Gaucho Caudillos—John Chasteen, University of North Carolina at Chapel Hill

The Life and Death of Carolina María de Jesús—Robert M. Levine, University of Miami, and José Carlos Sebe Bom Meihy, University of São Paulo

The Countryside in Colonial Latin America—Edited by Louisa Schell Hoberman, University of Texas at Austin, and Susan Migden Socolow, Emory University

Independence in Spanish America: Civil Wars, Revolutions, and Underdevelopment, Second Revised *Diálogos* Edition—Jay Kinsbruner, Queens College

Senior advisory editor: Professor Lyman L. Johnson, University of North Carolina at Charlotte

Independence in Spanish America

Civil Wars, Revolutions, and Underdevelopment

Second Revised *Diálogos* Edition

Jay Kinsbruner

University of New Mexico Press
Albuquerque

Library of Congress Cataloguing-in-Publication Data

Kinsbruner, Jay.
   Independence in Spanish America : civil wars, revolutions, and
underdevelopment / Jay Kinsbruner. — 2nd rev. Diálogos ed.
     p. cm. — (Diálogos)
   Includes bibliographical references (p.   –   ) and index.
   ISBN 0-8263-2177-1 (pbk. : alk. paper)
   1. Latin American—History—To 1830. 2. Self-determination,
National—Latin America—History. I. Title. II. Series: Diálogos
(Albuquerque, N.M.)
F1412.K56 2000
980'.02—dc21   99-38403
                                               CIP

Dedicated to the memory of my father, Mac Kinsbruner,
and to my friend, Allen Yanoff

Contents

Illustrations		ix
Preface to the Second *Diálogos* Edition		xi
Preface to the First *Diálogos* Edition		xiii
Acknowledgments		xix
Chronology		xxi
Life Span of Some Leaders of Independence		xv
1.	By Way of Introduction	1
2.	The Causes of Independence	7
3.	The Late Colonial Revolts and Protests	24
4.	The First Phase of the Independence Movements	43
5.	The Second Phase of the Independence Movements	72
6.	The Independence Leaders as Liberals	108
7.	The Problems of Independence	130
8.	Conclusion	154
	Notes	159
	Selected Bibliography	169
	Index	183

✝

Illustrations

Figures

Simón Bolívar   39
José de San Martín   40
Bernardo O'Higgins   41
Antonio José de Sucre   42

Maps

The Spanish Colonies in America Prior to Independence   8
Military Campaigns in the Wars of Independence   71
Spanish America at the End of the Wars of Independence 109
Mexico and Central America at the End of the Wars of
    Independence   148
Viceroyalty of the Río de la Plata   150

Preface to the Second *Diálogos* Edition

This new edition is revised and enlarged based on my reading of the literature published since 1993, as well as my rereading of some older studies. In some instances changes replaced the original material. Here and there I rethought some things, and in several instances went further with my exploration of Simón Bolívar. In the Selected Bibliography I added more than forty items, some with comments. We have redone some of the maps, and added a birth/death graphic of leaders of independence.

I would like to thank Lyman L. Johnson, editor of *Diálogos,* and David V. Holtby, my editor at the University of New Mexico Press, for working with me so well once again. I would especially like to thank UNMP for its willingness to repaginate this edition, a rarity among publishers these days. Fidel Iglesias kindly sent me some of his not yet published material about the clergy, and I thank him. I would like to thank once again all those colleagues, students, and especially doctoral candidates and recent Ph.D.s who went out of their way to say kind things about the book.

❖

Preface to the First *Diálogos* Edition

This is a revised and enlarged version of *The Spanish-American Independence Movement*. During the two decades since I wrote the first edition a massive amount of literature has appeared dealing with the independence period, considered broadly. In general this literature is of a superior quality with regard both to its technical and conceptual nature. While my emphasis continues to be on the *active citizenry* (the oligarchy in the colonial period, and the oligarchy and the people on the way up from the middle and lower ranks of society in the national period), the new social history and the techniques of quantification make it possible to consider groups of people largely unknown to us during the dark days of presocial history. We now can include in our analysis bureaucrats, merchants, artisans, grocery-store owners, free people of color, and many others. And while we knew something about women in Spanish American society, we know much more now. We also know much more about the economy, the great landed estates and small estates, mines and miners, Indians and Indian communities. And we know much more now about rebellion and insurgency. Regions previously only lightly studied now receive far more attention from scholars; therefore, my own understanding of Spanish America from the last decades of the eighteenth century through the first decades of the nineteenth has been much enriched, and so too, I trust, has the new edition. In fact, too much of my discussion in the first edition was based on my knowledge of Chile. The new literature, as well as my own studies in Mexico, Venezuela, Argentina, and Puerto Rico, have made it possible to broaden my perspective and refine the discussion.

The corpus of this research has not led to a credible new general theory of Spanish American independence. Current research has now buttressed, however, a theory of Chilean independence espoused by the Marxist historian Hernán Ramírez Necoechea more than thirty years ago.[1] This Marxist interpretation maintained that the Chilean economy had matured, even with its weaknesses, to the point that its future evolution was thwarted by Spanish colonialism. One need not be a Marxist to share this interpretation. Research during the past several decades permits us to generalize this interpretation to all of Spanish America. However, the interpretation suffers from a fundamental flaw: it does not account for loyalism, or, as it is known in Spanish American history, royalism. Before a new general theory of independence can claim serious attention we must have much more research in this area of little appeal, royalism.

It is extremely difficult to produce precise and systematic data about royalists, but we Latin Americanists have lagged behind similar efforts in the United States. John Adams had put loyalist support during the American war for independence at one-third of the population. Later estimates place the number at between 15 and 36 percent of the white population. In 1780 there were eight thousand loyalists among the British troops, at a time when Washington's army counted about nine thousand patriot soldiers.[2] But these figures disguise the regions that were mainly loyalist, and not only those where the British were garrisoned. What, then, of Spanish America? If Spanish Americans needed to direct their own economies, why did they chose royalism? It seems fair to speculate that one-third of Spanish Americans were royalists. Entire regions fought bitterly against the patriot forces, whether within the Spanish regular army or as guerrilla bands. Though this issue of royalism remains opaque, we know enough to discern that support for the royalist cause was often a matter of self-interest, reflective of logic that confounds general theories of action. Even so, it is in this terrain, perhaps especially, that brave souls must tread, though I fear that historians shall not progress far until we learn to substitute *loyal* for *royal*, *loyalism* for *royalism*. Such a beginning is long overdue.

In 1972 I noted that it probably would be salutary if someone would write a book about the independence movement without ever mentioning the great liberators. To me a study of the independence movement would be significant to the degree that it illuminated the nature of early nationhood. To comprehend independence from this perspective, we needed to focus, for example, upon bureaucrats and the economy. The new literature satisfies this need and permits a more refined appreciation of the era, but it has led me in an unanticipated direction. In writing this second edition, I found myself interested again in the great liberators, men like Bolívar, San Martín, O'Higgins, Sucre, and early politicians like Rocafuerte, as much as bureaucrats, artisans, and storekeepers. Now more than ever, the greatest of the liberators, Simón Bolívar, appears to me a tragic figure. The greatest failure of the independence movement was its inability to deliver a hemispheric political federation and common market. The only person who might have served as midwife to such an entity was Bolívar, but in the end he, too, had feet of clay. A character with flaws of heroic proportion, Bolívar was incapable of overcoming the deficiencies inherent in the Spanish colonial system; in particular, a regionalism similar to Spain's and reinforced by a statism that did not encourage, even discouraged, an integrated infrastructure, a means whereby goods and words could be exchanged efficiently. This regionalism sometimes spilled over into a protonationalism in the late colonial period, but this was uncommon, at least until independence, when it too marred attempts by Bolívar and others like Rocafuerte to create a supragovernment for the former colonies. Apparently no one could have brought together successfully the disparate—and often passionately so—parts and interests. But this does not prevent me from being a little disappointed in Bolívar. Thus, the present edition devotes more attention to the great personalities of the period.

This edition differs from the first in another, even more fundamental way. Previously, I stressed that the independence movement was a civil war rather than a revolution. Although I emphasized the regional nature of the movement, I realize now that I should have underlined that there were many independence movements rather than a single independence movement. But more importantly, it is no longer tenable to consider the independence movements exclusively as civil wars. They were also, to varying degrees, revolutions.

Before taking up the matter of revolution, however, it is worthwhile to reaffirm that the independence movements were indeed civil wars. They were civil wars because those who started and led the independence movements sought to govern themselves rather than be governed by Spain. These leaders of independence did not contemplate or condone vast social change along the lines that occurred in France or in Saint-Domingue (later Haiti). They were civil wars also because Spanish American patriots fought against each other, over matters such as control of territory or ports and their customshouses. Furthermore, soldiers and officers sometimes switched sides, as did whole regions and their inhabitants.

Nevertheless, the wars were also revolutionary. I came of age as a historian at a time when many, and perhaps most, influential professors of American history denied that the American war for independence was a revolution. This was a pointed rebuff of J. Franklin Jameson's remarkable *The American Revolution Considered as a Social Movement*.[3] Jameson argued—persuasively, it seems to me now—that American independence was revolutionary because it unleashed social changes, even if such was not the intent of the main proponents of independence. The generation of historians who taught me disdained the significance of this theory and stressed that the American independence movement was a civil war fought over home rule, not a revolution to decide who should rule at home. (Historians of *my* generation probably will recognize the origin of those good words.) This theory made good sense especially to those of us who had come under the influence of a generation of historians determined to reconceptualize the phenomenon of revolution and to assert that revolution always conveyed vast social change, achieved through massive violence. For my own part, it seemed necessary to stress that Spanish American independence was a civil war (or civil wars) since the mass of the population gained relatively little socially or politically.

It is time to step back from this position and view Spanish American independence from a different perspective. For several years I have been following changes in interpretation about the American independence movement, especially in the work of Gordon S. Wood. Wood has argued that American independence was indeed revolutionary because it set in motion long-term changes in fundamental social relationships. Wood refined his thoughts in his 1992 prize-winning *The Radicalism of the American Revolution,*[4] and it would be perilous for anyone to consider Spanish American independence without taking into consideration Wood's exquisite argument.

Indeed, from this broader, more reflective, and more generous view, Spanish American independence was also revolutionary. It too set into motion both short and long-term changes in social arrangements and relationships that would have been impossible under Spanish imperialism. During the war years thousands of slaves were freed, although at the price of service in the patriot (or royalist) armies. No longer subject to debilitating legislation that severely limited their opportunities for social and economic mobility and confined them to a stigmatized caste, free people of color found unprecedented opportunities for advancement during the wars and the decades that followed. Some became military officers, even generals, and thus shared handsomely in the rewards of victory. Because many officers were given landed estates, sometimes impressively large ones, officers of color sometimes found themselves in an economic position they rarely achieved under the king. Where the use of racial classification was abolished, as in Mexico and Venezuela, people of color gained access to universities and became physicians, lawyers, and priests. Poverty, prejudice, and hindrances to basic education kept their numbers low, but this should not deflect our attention from the fundamental fact that ever so slowly greater numbers began to take advantage of these newer opportunities.

In independent Spanish America, men of color became government officials and even presidents of countries, while nothing of the sort occurred in Cuba or Puerto Rico, which remained Spanish colonies until the end of the nineteenth century. While racism continued to blemish the benefits of independence and nationhood, and slavery endured longer than it should have, racism against free people of color was no longer institutionalized or as insurmountable as it would have been if independence had not occurred. Consider the words of Governor Prim of Puerto Rico. In 1848 newly emancipated slaves on the French islands of Martinique and Guadeloupe were involved in destructive activities, and Prim wanted to make sure that nothing of the kind occurred in Puerto Rico. Considering the "ferocious stupidity of the African race," Governor Prim decreed that all crimes committed by people of the African race, whether they were free or slave, would henceforth be judged by a military court. Any free colored person who used arms against a white, no matter how justified, would have his right hand cut off. If the white was wounded, the person of color would be executed by a firing squad.[5] In contrast to such virulent, pernicious racism, Spanish American independence was revolutionary.

Independence was revolutionary also for Indians. During the colonial period Indians were wards of the crown and treated as minors, and they were subject both to protection and to burdens. During the early national period colonial protective devices were dismantled, but burdens like tribute were often continued. Thus, during Spanish American independence men who were clearly of Indian descent became generals, and later some became presidents. One, a full-blooded Indian, born somewhere near the lower reaches of society and early orphaned, rose to become governor of his state of Oaxaca, minister of justice, and then president of Mexico. In the same way that Abraham Lincoln might be considered the quintessential American near the middle of the nineteenth century, Benito Juárez was the quintessential Mexican, and the similarities between the two were not lost upon Juárez. It is simply impossible to imagine colored or Indian captains general or viceroys of nineteenth-century Spanish American colonies had independence not occurred.

Long-term revolutionary change also touched those members of society who were neither free colored nor Indian. The constitutions of independence defined citizenship broadly, and citizenship conveyed the right to vote. Restrictions, such as the ability to read and write, eliminated the majority of the adult male population from the franchise, although not permanently. In the long run, however, millions of adult males became eligible to vote and finally brought about reform. Slowly, the "active" citizenry broadened enough to become simply *the* citizenry.

In light of the preceding discussion, one can understand why I changed the title for this edition.

Acknowledgments

It is with pleasure that I acknowledge those who have helped me in the preparation of this edition of the book. My greatest debt is to Lyman L. Johnson, editor of *Diálogos,* and David V. Holtby, editor at the University of New Mexico Press, who encouraged this project in many ways. Both got me to move in directions that I had not originally envisioned, and they did so with remarkable sensitivity and respect for my own concerns. Professor Johnson brought his extraordinary knowledge and fine intelligence to bear on the several critical readings he willingly gave the drafts. I would also like to thank the two anonymous readers for their intelligent and demanding critical readings. Any errors in fact and judgment that may appear in the book are, of course, my own responsibility.

I would also like to thank Philip C. Curtin and Franklin Knight for taking the time to discuss with me mortality figures for the Haitian Revolution. During the past decades, my colleagues, Jay Gordon and Frank Merli, have joined with me once or twice a week in a "seminar" during which many historical matters relating to this book were discussed. I have benefitted greatly from these discussions, which seem almost always to have found their way back to early modern Europe. My colleague David Syrett generously answered many questions about military matters.

Once again I would like to thank the staff of the Queens College Library, especially the Inter-Library Loan department. The staff of the Columbia University Libraries were particularly helpful, as was the staff of my favorite place of all, the New York Public Library (the Forty-Second Street Library to so many of us), now restored to its glory.

Of great help was the staff of the Computer Lab of the Monroe-Woodbury High School, who answered questions about computers and made sure that I had one to work on when the need arose. Candi Uhelsky kindly saw to the electronic conversion of the first draft from Apple to DOS.

Chronology

1765   Rebellion of the Barrios, Quito.

1767   Expulsion of the Jesuits.

1780–83 Rebellion of Túpac Amaru.

1781   Revolt of the Comuneros.

1791   Saint-Domingue revolution.

1804   Independence of Haiti declared.

1806   British invasion and occupation of Buenos Aires.

1807   French troops enter Spain. British occupation of Montevideo.

1808   Charles IV abdicates in favor of Napoleon, and Ferdinand abdicates in favor of Charles; both are removed by Napoleon, who places his brother Joseph on the Spanish throne. War of reconquest begins; local juntas appear and then Junta Central (the *suprema*) of Seville.

Peninsular coup in Mexico City.

Free trade declared in Buenos Aires.

1809   Revolts in Chuquisaca and La Paz.

1810   Junta established in Caracas, Venezuela.

Junta established in Santiago, Chile.

Council of Regency replaces the *suprema* in Spain; Cortes of Cádiz convenes.

Grito de Dolores.

Hidalgo sacks Guanajuato.

Miranda and Bolívar return to Caracas from England.

1811   Venezuela declares independence.

Junta established in Asunción, Paraguay; Paraguay declares independence.

Hidalgo killed; replaced by Morelos.

1812   Constitution of Cádiz proclaimed.

1814   Ferdinand VII reinstated and proclaims absolutism and
        rescinds constitution.
        Chilean patriots defeated at Rancagua.
1815   Morillo arrives in Venezuela.
        Morillo lands at Cartagena.
        Bolívar to Jamaica.
        Morelos captured and executed.
1816   Morillo victorious in New Granada.
        Argentina declares independence.
1817   Army of the Andes defeats royalists at Chacabuco and patriots
        take Santiago; O'Higgins becomes Supreme Director of Chile.
1818   Chile declares independence.
1819   Congress of Angostura; writes constitution and proclaims
        creation of Republic of Colombia; Bolívar elected president.
        Patriot victory at Boyacá.
1820   Revolt of Riego at Cádiz and reinstatement of Liberal
        constitution of 1812; Ferdinand accepts it.
        Departure of combined Argentine-Chilean expeditionary force
        from Chile to Peru.
1821   Iturbide proclaims *Plan de Iguala* in Mexico, declaring
        Mexican independence; Captain General O'Donojú arrives
        and signs Treaty of Córdoba, creating Mexican empire.
        Bolívar wins at Carabobo and enters Caracas.
        Congress of Cúcuta adopts constitution and Bolívar elected
        President.
        Peru declares independence.
        Guatemala [Central America] declares independence.
1822   Central America joins Mexican empire.
        U.S. recognition of Chile, Argentina, Peru, Colombia, and
        Mexico.
        Sucre defeats royalists at Pichincha and enters Quito.
        Iturbide becomes emperor of Mexico.
        Bolívar and San Martín meet at Guayaquil.
        San Martín leaves Peru for self-imposed exile in Europe.
1823   O'Higgins begins self-imposed exile in Peru.
        Iturbide abdicates and is exiled.
        United Provinces of Central America declares independence.
1824   Bolívar defeats royalists at Junín (August), and Sucre wins at
        Ayacucho (December).

British recognition of Mexico, Colombia, and Argentina at end of December—announced in the new year.

1825   Bolivia declares independence.
1828   Uruguay declared independent.
1829   Venezuela out of Republic of Colombia.
1830   Ecuador declares independence.
        Ecuador out of Republic of Colombia, leaving only New Granada. Bolívar dies.

Life Span of Some Leaders of Spanish American Independence

	1750	1760	1770	1780	1790	1800	1810	1820	1830	1840	1850	1860	1870	1880
Artigas												(1764–1850)		
Bolívar											(1783–1830)			
Flores													(c.1800–1864)	
Francia											(1766–1840)			
Hidalgo										(1753–1811)				
Miranda										(1750–1816)				
Morelos										(1765–1815)				
O'Higgins												(1778–1842)		
Paez													(1790–1873)	
Santander										(1790–1840)				
San Martín											(1778–1850)			
Sucre										(1795–1830)				

Independence in Spanish America

1

By Way of Introduction

During the late eighteenth century the Atlantic world was convulsed by change. First the French lost much of their empire in America, then the British lost thirteen of their North American colonies. Saint-Domingue would soon suffer a cataclysmic revolution on its way to becoming independent Haiti. As the Enlightenment reached its zenith, the French Revolution shook Europe at its very foundations, producing remarkable intellectual and constitutional change, and great destruction. Over approximately two decades, the spinning jenny, the frame, the mule, and a steam engine capable of powering other machines were invented. These initiated the industrial revolution and changed the nature of economies and humankind. Shortly the cotton gin was invented, and it too changed both economies and humankind.

It was in this era of ferment, in this swirl of ideas and events, that Spain's empire in America would soon cleave, leaving only Cuba and Puerto Rico loyal to the crown. Where four viceroyalties had stood under the command of the king, there would be 16 independent nations, responsible for the well-being of perhaps 16 million people.

While this book focuses on the great turmoil of the independence movement, it is also largely about the active citizenry who brought about the transition from colony to nation, and it is about the problems that followed that transition. To understand the character of this active citizenry, considered in the broadest possible sense to include even those who were just working their way into its ranks, to appreciate their values and thoughts, and ultimately the nations they defined, it is necessary to know something about the late colonial economy.

The generation that waged the struggle for independence came of age in an economy that was fundamentally preindustrial commercial capitalism. Spanish American economic life in the late colonial and early national periods was based upon a market economy that functioned, to varying degrees of maturity, by means of money, credit, bills of exchange, private property, and the profit motive.[1]

Nonetheless, it was a capitalism that suffered from many contradictions. The empire's economic rationale was mercantilism, which by definition was statism. The state, Spain, intervened and interfered in many areas of the colonial economy, but not always in ways that were beneficent. The most flagrant flaw was the limited direction and support for improving infrastructure. Spanish America's topography was, and is, difficult to traverse, and transportation costs greatly added to the region's economic burden, increasing the costs of both primary products and consumer commodities.[2] Spanish America lacked a system of inland waterways comparable to that of England or the United States, and in most places canals could not have been constructed. Transportation generally meant overland roads, but the crown did not support road construction or maintenance effectively.

What follows are three representative examples of transportation problems, drawn from an interminable list. Toward the end of the eighteenth century, the Mining Deputation of the important regional city of Guanajuato, Mexico, estimated that the city was supplied by producers of corn (maize) from a distance no farther than 10 leagues (approximately 26 miles). Corn produced at the far end of the supply zone was burdened by transportation costs amounting to 40 percent of its sale price. The Deputation noted that an improved road system, to say nothing about even cheaper water transportation, would have added greatly to "the development of markets and the growth of productivity."[3] Even water transportation, normally less burdensome than overland transportation, could be costly. The small river boats that transported goods from Asunción, Paraguay, downriver to Buenos Aires took two months and added as much as 25 percent to the cost of their cargoes. The return trip upriver took much longer and added to greater retail costs.[4] This is one of the fundamental reasons why the European countries enjoyed a trading advantage with Spanish America. In the 1830s it cost 13 times as much to move a ton of goods from Salta, Argentina, to the port of Buenos Aires as it did to ship a ton from Buenos Aires to Liverpool, England![5]

The development of Spanish American capitalism was also seriously hindered by costly administrative burdens. Added to the excessive cost of transportation and communication were sales taxes and regional customs tariffs, both of which further diminished the possibility of extended markets, regional specialization (the division of labor), and increased productivity.

Another more subtle flaw was Spain's immature system of public finance, which raised money for its military and bureaucratic expenses by autocratic methods of confiscation, forced loans, and donations.[6] This system contrasted sharply with the more mature capitalism of northern Europe, especially Holland and England, where governments were able to raise funds routinely through issuing interest-bearing financial instruments that paid their benefits systematically and promptly. Not until nearly the end of the eighteenth century did Spain attempt to develop a modern system of public finance. Spain's irregular and punitive methods of public finance slowed the growth of national capital markets capable of underwriting development at a reasonable cost, thus placing the future nations of Spanish America at a serious disadvantage when they entered the world capitalist marketplace under their own guidance.

At the pinnacle of the colonial economy were the import-export merchants. They were often peninsulars (born in Spain), but by the last decades of the colonial period many wealthy merchants were creoles (born in America). Spain's economic system was governed by the *Casa de Contratación,* which enforced and often created the very detailed and encompassing regulations that served the mercantilist rationale. In the colonies the *Casa* was aided by the merchant tribunals, the *consulados.* From the early eighteenth century, trade between Spain and the colonies was conducted under tight supervision and to the unquestionable advantage of the merchants in Cádiz, Spain. They and the merchants of the colonial *consulados* enjoyed clear benefits from the restricted trading system. Many merchants became inordinately affluent and invested in mines, landed estates, and even retail stores.

Nearly as affluent as the import-export merchants were the owners of the large landed estates, and sometimes these agrarians were also merchants or were related to them. Titled aristocrats in Mexico City owned landed estates in different ecological zones of Mexico, where crops or animals could be raised according to varying market demands. Some of the wealthiest members of the agricultural elite owned *pulque*-producing estates near Mexico City. (*Pulque* is an alcoholic drink fermented from the maguey plant.) They also owned *pulquerías,* or taverns, in the capital, leasing them out with the understanding that the *pulque* served would come from their estates. Some aristocrats grew wheat and ground it in flour mills they owned; some raised sheep and even owned textile mills to process the wool.[7]

Although late colonial Spanish America was overwhelmingly rural and agricultural, and the value of agricultural production was greater than that of any other sector of the economy including mining, many people still lived in towns or cities. For instance, in the important agricultural region of Guanajuato, northwest of Mexico City, toward the end of the colonial period approximately half the population resided in towns of at least 5,000 inhabitants.[8] At the same time, there were 6 cities of more than 10,000 inhabitants within a radius of 300 kilometers of Mexico City.[9] The daily needs of those living in towns or cities were met by many wholesale and retail merchants. In the larger cities hundreds of merchant shops lined streets, some even able to specialize due to the size of the immediate market.

A central characteristic of the Spanish American economy was entrepreneurialism. That is, people participated in the market economy by investing capital at risk. The degree of risk varied, as did the degree of business skill and acumen required for success. But in the broadest and most realistic sense, they were entrepreneurs.

This entrepreneurialism was widespread. Even many artisans were entrepreneurs. Some master craftsmen branched out into other areas of the economy. In 1789, for instance, Don José Ancelmo García, a master dyer of Mexico City, owned simultaneously a dye shop, a silk shop, and a retail grocery store.[10] Many master craftsmen not only did "bespoken" work, they purchased finished items from other artisans to sell in their own shops or in distant markets.

Entrepreneurialism clearly existed even at the level of small storekeeping. Grocery stores were normally capitalized at anywhere from a few hundred to several thousand pesos, and since most, if not all, of the inventory was acquired through credit, many men and women of modest means were able to become storekeepers. Some small stores were administered by clerks, some of whom worked their way into partnerships. Many grocery stores were administered by partners who for a share of the profits put into the arrangement their skill and labor. Frequently, widows inherited a store from their deceased husbands, and sometimes they expanded the store. Many grocers did not last very long in this precarious business; some endured only a few months or a year or two, but others lasted 10 or 20 years. While there were many bankruptcies, some grocers thrived, even opening more than one store. In the great commercial center of Mexico City in 1781, for instance, seven people each owned two grocery stores; two owned three stores; and one owned four of them. In Buenos Aires in 1825, twenty grocers each owned at least two grocery stores. The brothers Don Tomás and Don Nicolás Giraldes each owned five grocery stores in that important port city.

This entrepreneurialism functioned throughout the Spanish American economy in a marketplace circumscribed by the state. At the end of the eighteenth century, when Spain liberalized trade within the empire (to be discussed in Chapter 2), it also established new monopolies. Town councils traditionally granted monopolies for the supply of fresh meat; they controlled the price of bread, and often other foods. Town councils established public markets that directly competed with the small retail grocery stores. Generally the grocers were prohibited from entering the public markets to purchase items for resale in their stores until the general public had reasonable opportunity to make such purchases themselves. However, much the same may be said about contemporary Britain and the United States, where monopolies and market restrictions were common as well as traditional. Town councils in colonial North America, for example, routinely granted monopolies to millers, granted loans and subsidies, controlled wages, established the maximum price of bread, prohibited retail grocers from entering the competing public markets until the general public had time to make its purchases, and prohibited grocers from selling certain items. In both the United States and Spanish America the marketplace was restricted, yet people participated in it, succeeding or failing according to their talents, resources, and sometimes not a little luck. This was, in short, commercial capitalism.[11]

Spanish American society was divided by statute and custom into racial castes, the famous *sistema de castas,* which comprised, broadly speaking, whites, free people of color (free people of African descent), Indian and white mixtures (mestizos), Indians, and black slaves. The castes were subject to differing rights and responsibilities. For instance, free people of color were not permitted to become physicians, lawyers, or notaries, or to enter the various civil, Church, or military bureaucracies. When the colonial militia was created, free people of color were permitted to serve, but only in segregated units. By the last decades of the colonial period the term *casta* was a pejorative reference to those of mixed blood. Yet where the economy grew expansive and miscegenation became widespread, as in Mexico City, Guadalajara, and Oaxaca economic performance rather than race tended to determine one's place in society.

If Spanish American society was no longer essentially a caste system, was it a society of classes? To Karl Marx, there were many classes and fractions of classes. Thus, among the elite the interests of agrarian exporters of grain may be fundamentally different from those of manufacturers, or different from various branches of each. One of the classes or fractions becomes dominant (what social scientists often call *hegemonic*), asserting broader class leadership. For Marx, those whose "mode of life" results in shared circumstances still require hostility toward and competition with other classes in order for a class of their own to develop. Yet even when that occurs, there must be a "community," a "national bond," and a "political organization among them," for a class to evolve.[12] Here, E. J. Hobsbawm's comment on "class" is instructive: "Class in the full sense only comes into existence at the historical moment when classes begin to acquire consciousness of themselves as such."[13] By this logic there were undoubtedly politically conscious classes or class fractions in Spanish America by the end of the colonial period. That is, many people with mutual economic interests joined together to pursue political advantage. Sometimes rich merchants entered into such an alliance, as did agrarians, small retail grocers, all types of artisans, and even cartmen. Thanks to Spanish America's corporatist nature, many of these "classes" even had political organizations. The many Spanish Americans who belonged to a corporate body, such as a guild, a lay sodality, or an Indian community with its own town council, automatically possessed the potential for political organization.

Since we rarely speak in terms of an infinite number of classes, it is worth considering whether there had evolved by the end of the eighteenth century two or three great classes. The answer is no. Society was comprised of many socioeconomic *gradations* (a term Marx used), what some would call *strata* (a term he also used).[14] Socioeconomic gradations sometimes coalesced temporarily to form politically conscious classes during the final decades of the colonial period, but mainly these were, at best, only potential or incipient classes. Furthermore, for many, society was still *ascriptive* (one in which a child's place in society was determined by that of the father). For instance, the child of an artisan probably would become an artisan, although in a city he or she might enter a different and more prestigious craft. The child of a small farmer probably would become a small farmer, unless he or she migrated to a city, which often happened. The child of an Indian peasant would almost certainly become an Indian peasant. But with commercial capitalism and the spread of urbanism more and greater opportunity arose, and with opportunity came increased socioeconomic movement.

It was this society, structured as a caste system but evolving toward socioeconomic classes, that the active citizenry would guide to independence. By the end of the eighteenth century it was a society that was deeply troubled in many respects and in need of reform. What it got was a series of bloody and destructive civil wars, but also revolutionary beginnings and promise.

2

The Causes of Independence

The Spanish American independence movements were by-products of the Napoleonic seizure of the Spanish throne in 1808. In accordance with traditional Spanish political theory, and in some cases propelled by a concurrence found in the Enlightenment, and following the example of Spain itself, many of the colonies began to govern themselves in the name of the deposed king. When Ferdinand was restored to the throne and proclaimed the return of royal absolutism in 1814, many colonists decided to seek more formal and truer independence. It was clear now that the imperial state could not accommodate the requirements of colonial economies whose growth rates were irregular, and in some instances retarded. After several years of actual self-government and the enjoyment of many locally determined reforms and freedoms, including instances of political liberty, the thrust toward independence grew irresistible. In an age of change and turmoil, in which compelling examples of revolution and independence preceded them, many colonists experienced little trouble in finding both political and economic reasons for a break with the mother country.

Four causes of Spanish American independence are often cited: the Enlightenment, the Bourbon reforms, the creole-peninsular controversy, and the late colonial revolts and protests. This chapter is concerned with the first three causes, those aspects of the late colonial period that led some Americans, such as Francisco Miranda and Bernardo O'Higgins, to become active advocates of independence prior to the Napoleonic invasion of the Iberian peninsula and that encouraged others to embrace independence once the invasion had taken place. We shall also attempt to find clues to the nature of the new nations.

The Enlightenment

By the middle of the eighteenth century the European Enlightenment had resulted in the glorification of rationalism—a rationalism based not on

**THE SPANISH COLONIES IN AMERICA
PRIOR TO INDEPENDENCE**

the study of revelation and the ancient didactic tracts, but rather on the direct observation of nature. Scholars seem to focus most on the political aspects of the Enlightenment—the ideas of John Locke, the Baron de Montesquieu, Jean-Jacques Rousseau, and many others—and less on other aspects of the movement. The Enlightenment was concerned, for instance, with philosophy and economics, and, very obviously, with science. As Carl Becker observed, the Enlightenment was "an international climate of opinion."[1] Yet except for the underlying fundamentals of a rationalism founded on the scientific method and a respect for man and his perfectibility, the Enlightenment did not produce general agreement on many things. In politics, for example, there was strong support not only for both limited monarchy and enlightened despotism, but also for republicanism, representative government, and the protection of individual rights. Some thinkers were impressed with Locke's conception of a society of individuals whose rights to property were protected, while others stood by Rousseau's conception of a society of the people governed by the general will. In practical terms the difference between these two political theories could not have been greater; the Liberal constitutions of the late eighteenth and early nineteenth-century Atlantic world found their logic in Locke, and in others of similar thought, rather than in Rousseau.

The European Enlightenment provides an important context in which to view the fall of the empire and the rise of the new nations since the Enlightenment caused many alterations in the imperial system. The Enlightenment effectively entered Spain when the Bourbon dynasty occupied the throne at the beginning of the eighteenth century. Thereafter, two broad stages are evident. The first one extended to about the middle of the eighteenth century, and its most prominent figure was the Benedictine monk, Benito Jerónimo Feijoó. The second stage extended to the end of the century, and its most prominent and influential figure was Gaspar Melchor de Jovellanos. The central political difference between the two periods is that the first accepted the concept of limited monarchy as it had developed over the centuries in Spain, while in the second this tradition lost ground to theories of enlightened despotism that sought to strengthen royal prerogatives. The second phase of the Spanish Enlightenment reached its highest development during the reign of Charles III (1759–1788) and was personified by his ministers the Count of Aranda, the Count of Campomanes, and the Count of Floridablanca; by writers like Jovellanos; by economists such as Jerónimo de Uztáriz; and by a prestigious group of scientists. The second phase was popularized, and made accessible to many people, through the famous *Sociedades Económicas de Amigos del País,* whose first

branch had been established in 1765. These economic societies were devoted to the rational pursuit of knowledge, even in fields somewhat removed from economics. Significantly, the societies were committed to the
development and dissemination of practical technologies.

The Enlightenment's supporters in Spain were reformers, and they were
quite effective. They sought to change the economic system, the political
system, the schools, the Church, and the sciences. The economics they followed was increasingly derived from the Liberal economics of the French
physiocrats and Adam Smith. Thus, Jovellanos could argue in 1795 against
entailed estates—lay or religious—and the equally powerful institution of
corporate privilege, the sheep raisers' guild (the *Mesta*); and at the same
time advocate the development of scientific agriculture. Adam Smith's
Liberal economics followed naturally from John Locke's individualist,
property-oriented conception of state and society. The articulation of
Smith and Locke, along with an admixture of ideas from several other
Enlightenment thinkers, resulted in the Liberalism of the late eighteenth
and early nineteenth centuries that inspired constitutions in Spain and in
the Americas.

As a climate of opinion, Enlightenment thinking could not be kept out
of Spanish America by royal fiat, as the crown would have liked, or by such
artificial barriers as the Inquisition and censorship. The colonists who comprised the active citizenry not only read the same books as their counterparts in Europe (although often clandestinely and sometimes by means of
a single, much-used, and prized copy), but they discussed the same philo-
sophic and practical issues. Spanish bureaucrats, foreign travelers, sailors
from foreign ships making distress calls, sailors from neutral ships, members of foreign scientific expeditions permitted to visit the colonies during
the late colonial period, Spanish and foreign merchants—all were potential
sources of Enlightenment knowledge.

Enlightenment thinking was very much a part of the colonial system by
the end of the eighteenth century. It was evident in the vigorous efforts by
royal officials as well as local reformers to stimulate economic and scientific
development. Near the end of the eighteenth century, Spain sent botanical
and mining missions to Mexico, New Granada, and Peru, all of which
conveyed the ideas of modern science. Among the renowned scientists the
crown sent to the colonies, were the Spanish brothers Fausto and Juan José
Elhuyar. Fausto, born in 1757, was the more distinguished scientist. He
studied in France, England, Germany, Sweden and Norway. When he was
summoned to go to Mexico, he was studying mining techniques in Austria.
Fausto arrived in Mexico in 1788 with several German mining specialists.

In Mexico, he established and directed the influential College of Mines. Juan José led a mission to New Granada. Although the effort to improve mining revenues was not always successful, scores of young scientists were trained by instructors celebrated for their work in the latest scientific techniques and methods. To them the methodology of medieval scholasticism was every bit as alien as it was to the European scholars.

The pursuit of economic progress also contributed significantly to the dissemination of Enlightenment thinking. Between the early 1780s and 1812 several economic societies, *Sociedades Económicas de Amigos del País,* modeled after the Madrid Society, were established in the colonies. Not all of them lasted long or were impressive in their accomplishments. But the more successful societies advocated rationalism and progress in their pursuit of economic development, and they were actively concerned with scientific progress. Perhaps most importantly, however, their membership was comprised largely of merchants, large landowners, and bureaucrats, rather than scientists, economists, and political theorists; and they brought the Enlightenment home to a broad spectrum of the elite. Yet not all of the societies would favor independence; both life and the Enlightenment were too complex for that to have occurred. In fact, the first and in some ways the most "progressive" of these societies was the Havana society, located in a colony that remained loyal to the crown.

Colonial universities and even high schools, or *colegios,* were sources of new ideas. During the eighteenth century their curricula were modernized, and while they might not have been teaching Rousseau, they were teaching René Descartes and Isaac Newton, whose critical perspectives were just as provocative and dangerous in the long run. However, the colonies were not in the vanguard of intellectual change. It took nearly a century after the death of Descartes for Cartesianism to find an open and secure place in the curricula, although Newton's teachings were incorporated shortly after his death. Once these changes were instituted and educational modernization became a reality, other new ideas were more quickly adopted. In many cases, government officials encouraged this process. During the final phase of the colonial period, some viceroys directly influenced the reform of curricula, including the incorporation of modern writers, and the establishment of Enlightenment institutions. By the last decades of empire there was practically no intellectual distance between Europe and the colonies.

By the end of the colonial period all of the ingredients of the European Enlightenment were to be found in Spanish America, and many influential proponents of independence clearly were moved in that direction by the Enlightenment. Yet not all colonists who came under the influence of the

Enlightenment favored independence; in some instances, in fact, the opposite was true. Once colonists were aware of what was occurring in the revolutionary Atlantic world, however, it was unnecessary to focus on the Enlightenment, since an inflammatory revolutionary doctrine existed right in the heart of the Spanish political tradition. Both the contractual theory and the concept of popular sovereignty were integral components of Spanish medieval scholastic thought, and both were popularized in Spain especially by the Jesuit Francisco Suárez (1548–1617). These ideas were important centuries before the Enlightenment came into vogue, and they continued to be influential while Locke, Montesquieu, and Rousseau were having their day.

To Suárez, the polity, or the *corpus politicum mysticum,* was created by individuals to secure the general good, the *bonum commune.* Power had been transmitted, though not absolutely, to the king through the principle of *translatio.* Royal authority was therefore legitimate only so long as the king did not rule tyrannically; in such a case, the people had the right to oust the tyrant. Furthermore, had the king been unable to govern, the people had the right to replace him.[2] This right was of great importance to the independence movement since it meant that sovereignty reverted to the people. Even laws lost their legitimacy when they became unjust or too severe, or were disavowed by a majority of the people. Clearly, in the right context this might provide the spark for revolt; it was simply traditional Spanish Late Scholastic political theory, invoked time and again during violent outbreaks in the late colonial period and later during the independence movements.

The Bourbon Reforms

The military disasters Spain suffered at the hands of the British during the Seven Years' War, culminating in the temporary loss of Havana in 1762, caused the crown to expand and revitalize its imperial defenses, which, in turn, required an increase in royal revenues. To increase revenues and to provide for the defense of the empire the crown undertook a series of reforms and initiatives known collectively as the Bourbon reforms (or Caroline reforms). Keenly aware of the administrative rationalization being carried out by their French cousins, the Spanish Bourbons were determined to revamp and centralize the colonial system. The reforms were designed to protect the empire from foreign encroachment, and to enhance royal prerogatives as well as further royal absolutism. Simultaneously, the crown hoped to satisfy some of the complaints voiced by the colonists, which it feared might lead to insurrection.

Military Reforms

One of the consequential Bourbon reforms created creole regular army units and expanded the militia, both with creole officers. Garrisoning the colonies with peninsular troops to defend them against the eventuality of foreign invasion or of local social unrest would have required an enormous outlay of money, and just at the time that the crown was reforming the imperial system to produce increased revenues. No doubt the crown would have felt more secure with an all-peninsular army and officialdom, but its weakened financial position limited its options. Colonial armies were created, and militia units were greatly enlarged, incorporating tens of thousands of part-time soldiers. Those in the militia were entitled to the same corporate privileges enjoyed by regular army personnel, especially the coveted *fuero* (the privilege of special military jurisdiction for themselves and their families).

Many creoles may have joined the militia for no other reason than to take themselves outside the purview of the civil courts, but there were other attractions as well. The creoles were honored by the new policy; and many, for whom it was a form of recognition and enhanced status, were quick to take advantage of it. The uniform was frequently as great an attraction then as it is now. In the principal urban centers, creoles were proud to be finally admitted into the ranks of military officialdom and to share a broad range of obvious privileges with their peninsular colleagues and sometime competitors. In the many frontier and near-frontier regions, creoles were pleased to see the formation of local militia units, with themselves as the officers. If additional peninsular troops and officers had been placed in these regions, the creoles would have faced increased competition in the quest for social dominance. Peninsular officers, after all, were very attractive figures, especially to the young creole ladies. A potential social impediment had been eliminated in many places. The creole army and militia were also institutions of upward socioeconomic mobility for many poor whites and castes (a term used here in the popular sense, meaning those of mixed blood), who found in the expanded military career opportunities that were not always available elsewhere.

Vexations, however, did exist. Men in the crafts and commerce were heavily burdened when a militia unit was mobilized for service at a distant garrison. The more affluent hired replacements. Others could not afford to do so, like most small retail grocers who were troubled by having to parade on Sundays, when they should have been in their stores. Soon the attraction diminished and it became difficult to recruit personnel and to muster the required numbers. Many militia units were poorly equipped, and functioned at a level far below standard. Furthermore, the militia was frequently deployed for political rather than military purposes, as, when it was called upon to serve as a domestic police force, a demand that was not universally appreciated.

While it enacted a reform essential to the preservation of the empire, the crown unwittingly prepared elements of the future patriot armies. By the early nineteenth century thousands of organized troops—sometimes fairly ragtag, poorly armed, and undisciplined—could be called out at a moment's notice. The officers were creoles, many of whom would opt for independence. The troops often were employees and dependents of the officers, especially in the rural regions. Thus, the crown had supplied a critical ingredient for a successful independence movement. However, some militia units remained royalist during the wars for independence; and when these forces clashed with patriots the battles were often brutal and pitiless.

Free Trade

Apart from the expulsion of the Jesuits in 1767, the most famous Bourbon reform was the freedom of trade decree of 1778. Actually, a policy of limited free trade had been instituted for Cuba in 1765, and further developed over the following decade. Now in 1778 this commercial liberalization was greatly expanded. The new decree permitted 13 ports in Spain to trade directly with all of the important ports in the Spanish American colonies except Veracruz, Mexico, and La Guaira, Venezuela, which were included in 1789. The Spanish American ports authorized to participate in the transatlantic trade were also generally permitted to trade among themselves. Thus, the colonial trade monopoly held by the Cádiz merchants was ended. By reducing some tariffs and, in general, facilitating commerce within the empire, the 1778 decree allowed Spanish and colonial merchants to compete with the vast and lucrative contraband network that crisscrossed the colonies. The result was quite dramatic. During the period from 1782 through 1796 (when war with Great Britain led the crown to introduce trade with neutral countries), the average annual value of trade between Spain and the Spanish American colonies increased by 400 percent.[3] This meant far greater revenue for the royal coffers. Additionally, expanding commercial opportunities and breaking the monopoly of the

Cádiz merchants contributed toward the creation of a new group of colonial merchants, many of whom were creoles of relatively limited means.
They were dependent on the open system in which they could participate
with less capital than had been previously required.

When the Spaniards spoke of free trade, they were not advocating Adam
Smith's *laissez-faire* economics. They introduced certain economic reforms
in order to strengthen, not weaken, the mercantilist system. At the same
moment that trade was liberalized, the crown expanded the powerful state-
run tobacco monopoly, the tobacco *estanco*, which controlled the manufacture and distribution of tobacco products. *Estancos* had been established in
Cuba, Peru, and Mexico prior to the introduction of freedom of trade, and
others were added in 1778. The monopoly successfully produced revenue
for the royal treasury. Tobacco growing was not monopolized, although
prices were administratively fixed, and in Mexico, and almost certainly
elsewhere, the *estanco* extended credit to tobacco growers, especially to
cover labor costs. It was also an important source of employment. In 1790
the Mexico monopoly was the largest manufacturing enterprise in the
Americas, employing approximately 17,000 people in its total operations.
And there was another important benefit: The Mexican *estanco* held prices
of tobacco products to moderate levels as a means of making contraband
less attractive. Nonetheless, some people were hurt by the monopoly. For
instance, in Mexico City in 1765 there were about 543 privately owned
tobacco shops. By 1775 far fewer existed, and all of them were controlled
by the *estanco*.[4] Thus an important outlet for private entrepreneurial en-
deavor had been eliminated, and this effect was multiplied throughout the
colonies.

In fact, many people suffered from the liberalized trade reforms, most of
all the affluent and influential merchants who depended on the restrictive Cádiz trade monopoly for their livelihoods. During the independence
movements the powerful merchant communities split, and not always according to a predictable pattern. Although, understandably, the great majority of peninsular merchants were royalist, many creole merchants were
also royalist. A more liberal trading system simply did not favor all creole
merchants. Similarly, freer trade did not favor all creole manufacturers. In
many regions manufacturing, especially in textiles, was overcome by the
newly arrived and cheaper European goods (although in some places the
decline in colonial manufacturing resulted from local competition from
new colonial establishments that were both small and flexible). While
many colonial manufacturers supported independence, some may have
done so precisely because they opposed liberalized trade reforms. Thus, the

Bourbon economic reforms of the colonial economy did not produce a uniform political reaction, and people within a single area of the economy frequently took opposing political positions during the era of independence.

The economic reforms of the late colonial period made it patently clear to many influential colonists that they needed to design their own economies. Once the independence movements presented them with the opportunity to formulate their own political economies, that is exactly what they did.

The Chileans, for instance, issued a free trade decree shortly after the establishment of the first national junta in September, 1810. Although the trade decree of February 1811 greatly expanded trading possibilities, certain items still could not be imported at all; and others might be excluded in the future in order to promote the country's industry. Particular items of war were permitted tariff-free entrance into the country for a year and a half. The article dealing with war items also mentioned that, under the same conditions, implements and machines for the manufacture or weaving of hemp, linen, cotton, and wool could be introduced. It is unlikely that all members of the junta considered the production of hemp, linen, cotton, and woolen goods limited strictly or even primarily to military defense. The month before the decree was announced a leading government official, José Santiago Portales, presented the junta with an analysis of the economic, cultural, and political situation of Chile, observing that since free trade in itself would leave Chile at an international disadvantage, its manufacturing and agricultural base should be developed. He counseled that manufactures competitive with European products should be emphasized, singling out the production of linen. In fact, the free-trade decree did give special attention to linen production.

The point is that the Chileans wanted to trade with whomever they desired while protecting and promoting their own industrial and agricultural base. This was true of other Spanish Americans as well. For instance, the province of Buenos Aires, Argentina proclaimed its first general tariff in January 1822. Although it established a basic rate of 15 percent ad valorem on overseas imports, a number of necessary items, such as agricultural tools and mining machinery, were subject to only a 5 percent tariff. Foreign products that competed with domestic commodities—such as sugar, coffee, cocoa, tea, and foodstuffs—were subject to a 20 percent tariff, while goods imported from other provinces of the Argentine confederation generally were subject to only a 4 percent ad valorem rate. Thus, like the Chilean decree of 1811 this tariff incorporated protection within the broad concept of free trade. The 1822 tariff protected the wine and brandy industries of the provinces of Mendoza and San Juan and the sugar industry of Tucumán. This meant that the consumers of Buenos Aires were required to support Argentine provincial industry by paying more for wine and brandy. Both the Chilean and Argentine trade decrees sought to protect specific industries from foreign competition, something that the liberal trade regulations of the late colonial period did not always do.

Clearly the colonists needed free trade less than a political economy attentive to their national requirements; and this is precisely what independence produced. Economics did not cause the initial break with Spain, but the obvious need for an economic policy of their own design motivated many Spanish Americans to move toward independence once the opportunity was thrust upon them.

The Intendancy System

Even prior to the Bourbon reforms, the Spanish monarchs took steps to rationalize the imperial administration and to centralize control; thus it created the Viceroyalty of New Granada in 1717. During the era of the reforms the crown followed this initiative with the creation of the Viceroyalty of the Río de la Plata in 1776. The configuration of the Viceroyalty of Río de la Plata (much of which would later become Argentina) would be extremely consequential, since Upper Peru, which contained the great silver-producing region of Potosí, was separated from the jurisdiction of Peru and placed within the new viceroyalty, whose capital was in Buenos Aires. This arrangement became the source of prodigious commercial activity between Buenos Aires and Upper Peru, while causing commercial dislocation and fiscal problems for the venerable Viceroyalty of Peru that would require decades to overcome.

In a further attempt to enhance defense and revenue collection in the colonies, the Bourbons established the intendancy system, which was first introduced in Cuba during the 1760s and later in the rest of the colonies, with the exception of the Viceroyalty of New Granada. The intendants, who were usually but not always peninsulars, replaced the provincial governors, but enjoyed far greater powers than their predecessors. In their provinces, they were given control over justice, general governmental administration, finance, and defense. They were subordinate to the viceroy, but, in certain respects (such as financial matters), they enjoyed some independence from him. In fact, some viceroys came to oppose the intendant system vigorously.

Overall, the intendants had a notable impact on life in the late colonial period. In many regions, they restored economies and won approval from the residents. For a long time the town councils (the *cabildos* or *ayuntamientos*) in most provinces had been lethargic and unproductive. Often the position of councilman, which was for sale, remained vacant for years because no one cared to purchase a position on mostly moribund town councils, even when the asking price was set remarkably low. Intendants, however, were given direct political control over the town councils (as well as control of the intendancies at large), and some injected economic life into municipalities and energized town councils. At the same time, precisely because they interfered so directly in the affairs of the councils they sometimes antagonized influential local residents, many of whom were creoles.

In many places, then, the intendants did a great deal of good; in others, however, they were rendered ineffectual by jealous central authorities. Perhaps their most enduring contribution was to alienate sectors of the creole population, who would shortly decide about whether to strike out for independence.

Church Reforms

For centuries the Church had met little resistance in its efforts to acquire vast economic wealth and to exert influence at all levels of colonial life. The Bourbon reformers, especially the Count of Campomanes and the Count of Floridablanca, considered the Church to be a clear obstacle in their plan to invigorate both royal absolutism and the colonial economy. Thus just at the time that the crown was strengthening the military *fuero*—an indication of where it chose to place its trust—it was curtailing the Church *fuero*. Yet, with the exception of one significant instance, the reformers' efforts to limit ecclesiastic political power in the colonies were largely undermined after the death of Charles III. The sole exception was the crown's determination to destroy the political and economic power of the Jesuits. They were expelled from Spain and the empire in 1767, and their extensive economic assets were disposed of on behalf of the royal treasury. Many of the great estates of the Jesuits were sold to prominent merchants, who now broadened their elite status. Several of the Jesuits in exile became prominent promoters of complete independence for the colonies. The most famous among them was Juan Pablo Viscardo, who published his *Letter to Spanish Americans* during the last decade of the eighteenth century. This bitter denunciation of three centuries of Spanish rule concluded by urging the Spanish Americans to revolt and establish their independence. While the exiled Jesuits do not seem to have seriously influenced the independence movement, they must have caused some colonists to question the sanctity of the imperial system.

The secular hierarchy (those who did not belong to the religious orders) were not greatly disturbed by the crown's attack on the Jesuits, with whom they felt themselves to be in competition anyway. Yet there were members of both the regular and secular clergy who became advocates for independence in the late colonial period. For instance, young Bernardo O'Higgins, already a convinced separatist, came into contact with two Spanish American clerics in Spain who favored independence at the beginning of the nineteenth century. One was Juan Pablo Fretes, Argentine by birth, but later canon of the Cathedral of Santiago and president of Chile's first national congress. Probably O'Higgins was merely confirmed in his own views, but it must be assumed that other creoles who were undecided were pushed a bit in the direction of independence by the attitudes of clerics like Fretes.

An economic program initiated at the end of the colonial period did encourage many clergymen to favor independence. In 1782, to finance its international wars, Spain created its first central bank, the Banco de San Carlos, which issued interest-bearing notes called *vales reales*. When this modern method of disciplined state financing proved insufficient to meet the crown's needs, it resorted to its traditional method of confiscation. In 1804 the crown expropriated all land and capital belonging to the pious works and chantries (endowments for saying masses in behalf of someone's soul) in Spanish America; the confiscated wealth would be used to back the value of the *vales reales*. Throughout the colonial period the affluent, as well as some who were less wealthy, had traditionally left a legacy, and often a substantial one, for the creation of a pious work or a chantry. The chantries and especially the pious works came to possess great sums of money, which the Church made a practice of loaning at the standard 5 percent interest. Primarily through this source of capital, which was continually being renewed by new legacies, the Church became the leading credit institution in the colonies. Generally, parish priests throughout the colonies depended directly on the chantries as a supplement for their income.

Limiting the Church's banking activities antagonized laymen and clergymen alike. The crown's action in 1804 meant calling in loans that were essential to many regional economies. Thus, in some places, like parts of Mexico, the very existence of a functioning economy was threatened. By 1809, when the program was terminated, between 10 and 12 million pesos had been collected by the *Caja de Consolidación* from Mexico alone. There were regions in the colonies where the crown's efforts never really got under way, and therefore few people were harmed. Although the elite were more likely to be able to reduce the impact of the *Consolidación* by arranging favorable terms, some powerful members of both the commercial and agricultural sectors were estranged from the colonial system.

In colonies such as Mexico where the crown's efforts extracted the greatest amount of capital, as well as in regions where results were modest, the lower secular clergy, the parish priests, were prominent among those who suffered the deepest economic dislocations. By 1810 many parish priests had become determined advocates of independence, or they proved to be easy converts once the movements got under way.

Yet some clergymen would have become advocates of independence even without any reforms. Clergymen like Miguel Hidalgo of Mexico were caught up in the momentum of the Enlightenment, and they were reading the most modern and provocative works. Surely, they would have eventually questioned the validity and efficacy of the colonial system.

The Creole-Peninsular Controversy

The controversy between creoles and peninsulars for public office has long been considered one of the chief causes of the independence movement. Although there was no legal distinction between creoles and peninsulars seeking public office, European-born Spaniards clearly were given preference for the highest decision-making posts. With independence won, nationalist writers often seized upon this example of prejudice in colonial life to justify the actions of the creoles. In the 1820s a Chilean newspaper actually attributed the struggle for independence to the preferential treatment given to peninsulars in the selection of public officials.

There can be no doubt that such a controversy existed and that it encouraged some creoles toward independence. In some colonies creoles achieved all but the very highest positions—including that of intendant, a post that generally was unavailable to them—but in other colonies peninsulars dominated the bureaucracy. Thus at the moment when the first national junta was created in Santiago, Chile, in September 1810, the interim governor and captain general was a creole (although a titled aristocrat); so too were the bishop-elect of Santiago, two judges of the royal *audiencia* (the supreme court), the superintendent of the royal mint, the administrator of the customs house, and the *asesor* (the chief government counsel in the colony). By the end of the colonial period the upper bureaucracy in Chile was staffed mostly by creoles. On the other hand, toward the end of

the colonial period the upper bureaucracy in Mexico was largely peninsular. Contrary to the situation in Chile, in Mexico the superintendent of
the mint, the administrator of the customs house, and the chief counsel of
the realm were all peninsulars. Viceroys throughout Spanish America were
overwhelmingly peninsular.

Just as the creoles were flexing their economic muscles, the crown instituted a less equitable policy for the selection of public officials. Whatever
the situation had been before (and there is no certainty as to what it was
exactly), it is clear that during the final phase of empire there was no fundamental social difference between peninsulars and creoles in the colonies.
Peninsulars belonged to whatever social group they could enter by way of
their personal credentials, even if these were acquired through advantageous familial ties. By the last decades of the eighteenth century creoles
competed with and often superseded peninsulars, even in economic areas
such as trade, where the Europeans previously had been dominant. Creoles
often shared political power with peninsulars at the local level of government. However, many peninsulars married creoles, and by the last decade
of the century their sons were replacing them on the town councils—and
the sons were usually born in the colonies. Many among these and other
successful creoles resented the introduction of a domineering local official,
the intendant, who was usually (as already mentioned) a peninsular. Many
creoles also resented the crown policy of not appointing creoles to the very
highest posts.

Creole disenchantment was provoked in particular by Minister of the
Indies José de Gálvez, who had a striking preference for European bureaucrats. For instance, around 1769 the most important *audiencia* in Mexico
was comprised of 6 creole superior judges out of a possible 7. There were
also 2 lesser creole judges, and these lesser judges generally ascended to
superior positions. A decade later there were only 4 creole superior judges
and no creole lesser judges. Still later only 3 creoles sat among the 11 members of the upper court. Altogether, between 1751 and 1808, the crown
made 266 appointments to Spanish American *audiencias,* with creoles re-
ceiving 62 (23.7 percent) and peninsulars 200 appointments (76.3 percent).[5] Gálvez's policy clearly was working as well as undoubtedly antago-
nizing innumerable creoles—Spanish Americans who in ever-increasing
numbers reached the top of the social and economic ladder in the colonies.

During the last decades of the eighteenth century many creoles were
successful, confident, and assertive. The crown's preference, inspired in part
by Minister Gálvez, for Europeans in certain critical posts and the creation of the intendancy system headed by peninsulars must be considered

as factors that alienated creoles from the imperial system and helped prepare a climate of opinion that would be hospitable to independence once
the opportunity arrived.

The Reforms: An Appraisal

The Bourbon reforms were a composite—in some instances, a rational
and assertive approach to imperial reorganization, but in others, more
nearly a reaction to events and circumstances of the moment, such as European war and naval blockades. The results were equally mixed. International trade clearly increased, as did royal revenues. Some colonial regions
benefited greatly, while others saw traditional markets removed by administrative action, or home markets were overrun by European-manufactured
goods. Fiscal reform increased certain revenues, but often added an insidious burden that incited revolt. Not that it was a simple matter to reorganize
the empire, provide for its defense, and raise necessary revenues. Witness
the efforts of Great Britain in attempting to manage its North American
colonies.

The area in which Spain most concentrated its economic reforms was
mining. In addition to scientific expeditions and improved technical education, the crown supported silver production, its single greatest source of
colonial revenue, through several subsidies, such as lower prices for mercury and gunpowder, and lower taxes. The result was a success; silver production increased and brought with it royal revenues. But the crown had
provided support for an inefficient sector of the economy by transferring
capital through subsidies that might have been applied elsewhere—for instance, in infrastructure or agriculture (which was fundamental to the
economy but was technologically backward), areas that did not benefit proportionately but might have been more important to long-term economic
development. (Our present state of knowledge, however, permits only this
limited speculation.)

In any case, the economic success of the Bourbons was extremely un-
even and fragile. Many geographical regions and sectors of the economy
were hurt by the reforms, though others did well—at least until the 1790s,
when in some places there appears to have been a generalized leveling off
of productivity. In some instances, increased production had nothing to do
with the reforms but were responses to wartime events that interrupted the
flow of European commodities to the colonies. In some rural regions of
Mexico, increased population growth led to a lowering of real wages; while

in Buenos Aires, inflation produced the same result.[6] And it is likely that these were not isolated occurrences.

By the end of the eighteenth century the Spanish crown had created many aggrieved parties. Not all would support independence, but there were enough who did to cause the destruction of the vast Spanish American empire.

3

The Late Colonial Revolts and Protests

Spanish America in the eighteenth century was a place of protest and revolt. Generally, protest involved limited Indian revolts in response to the burdens of tribute, forced labor quotas, or the *reparto* or *repartimiento de mercancías*—the device used by the crown to require the Indian communities to purchase goods supplied by *corregidores,* the administrators of Indian affairs at the local level. The *reparto* system caused Indians to produce items such as coarse textiles to pay for the things they were forced to buy, which ranged from European-manufactured commodities to mules. Prices for these goods were set by the *corregidores,* rather than by the marketplace. Frequently, this invidious process placed the Indians in debt, which was often paid off through their labor. Indians sometimes revolted against these abuses. Whites, mestizos, free people of color, and slaves also rose in protest, but for other reasons. Depending on their central character, we may categorize these late colonial protests and revolts as political, social, or civil.

The Political Revolts

The few political revolts were unsuccessful, though they were intellectually inspired and radical in purpose. For instance, in 1780 Chile witnessed the conspiracy of the *Tres Antonios,* a stillborn revolt carrying the deepest political meaning. Two Frenchmen living in Chile, Antonio Gramusset and Antonio Berney, enlisted the aid of one of Chile's most prominent citizens, José Antonio de Rojas, in a plan to establish a republican government based on an inclusive electoral process. Social classes were to be eliminated and slavery abolished, according to a plan that actually anticipated nineteenth-century socialism. An ambitious program of agrarian reform was included in their plans, along with a broad policy of free trade with the world at large. Nearly a decade before the French Revolution, the three

Antonios conjured up one of the most democratic conspiracies in Spanish American history until the middle of the nineteenth century. Unfortunately for those involved, this poorly supported plan was discovered by the authorities in early 1781. The conspirators were punished and the Chilean public never even learned of the planned revolt.

A similar revolutionary conspiracy occurred in Caracas, Venezuela, in 1797. Two creoles, José María de España and Manuel Gual, organized an uprising in favor of a classless society, but it was quickly defeated and some of the conspirators were apprehended. Gual escaped, but España was hanged and quartered, with his head and limbs placed on display as a public warning.

The Great Social Rebellion

The great social rebellion of late colonial Spanish America had its origins in the scores of local uprisings and revolts by Indians in response to specific grievances such as the *reparto*. During the decade of the 1770s, more than 60 such revolts occurred in the Andes alone, and there were many in Mexico. But these uprisings rarely moved beyond their place of origin, and the leaders did not attempt to rearrange the social structure.

The most famous Andean uprising was the revolt, or as it is usually referred to, the rebellion of Túpac Amaru II, which began in 1780 and conveyed serious social overtones. José Gabriel Condorcanqui Noguera was an educated mestizo muleteer (an *arriero*), a moderately affluent owner of land and some 350 mules. He was a hereditary ruler, or *curaca* (sometimes spelled *kuraka*), of Tinta, a position that made him responsible for collecting the annual tribute owed by the Indians in his charge and for supervising their forced work schedules. The real authority over the Indians at the provincial level in the Andes was the *corregidor.* No one exploited anyone during the colonial period as much as the *corregidores* exploited the Indians, often working hand in hand with the local *curacas,* who themselves were usually Indians. José Gabriel was a *curaca* who developed a social consciousness, deeply troubled by the outrageous exploitation that he witnessed. He was radicalized by the system of forced labor and forced sale of goods to the Indians, coupled with recent increases in taxes. Sometime during the 1770s he took the name Túpac Amaru II, suggesting his supposedly direct lineage from the great Inca monarch of the same name.

Early in November 1780, Túpac Amaru, with a few followers, seized the notorious *corregidor* of the province of Tinta, Peru, and forced him to sign over arms, ammunition, and money. The *corregidor* was then ordered to issue a demand that all residents of the province appear at the town of Tungasuca within 24 hours. Thousands of people showed up, and in their presence the *corregidor* was executed by hanging. Túpac Amaru insisted that he was carrying out a royal order that called for the execution and suppressed the *alcabala* (sales tax), the *derechos de aduanas* (customs duties), and the *mita* (enforced Indian labor). The thousands who were assembled there actually thought they were witnessing the fulfillment of a royal order. Túpac Amaru gathered an army of Indians and castes and began marching through the countryside, destroying the detested *obrajes* (textile factories, but often merely sweatshops) and the houses of the *corregidores,* who were quick to flee.

News of the rebellion spread rapidly throughout the Andean regions, and a wave of Indian and Indian-caste uprisings followed. A full-blown war, aimed especially at Europeans, was now being waged throughout an area of thousands of square miles. Indians and castes fought on both sides. Fundamentally, the rebellion of Túpac Amaru was an Indian uprising, yet mestizos and even whites were among its prominent leaders. At the end of December 1780, Túpac Amaru had an army of more than 40,000 soldiers outside the gates of Cuzco, but he withdrew his forces without attacking, leaving to the realm of speculation whether he had the capacity to take the ancient capital. Before the rebellion ended—in 1783 in most places—tens of thousands of people had lost their lives. Túpac Amaru II was captured in the spring of 1781. Atrocities had been committed on both sides, and now there would be additional ones. Túpac Amaru, his wife, and younger son were forced to witness the public executions of his older son and an uncle. Their tongues were cut out, and then they were hanged. His wife was then executed. Then Túpac Amaru's tongue was cut out. Four horses were attached to his limbs, but they were unable to dismember him. Finally his head was cut off, and he was quartered. His head was sent to Tinta and his limbs elsewhere, to be placed on public display as an admonition. Even before the execution of Túpac Amaru, the viceroy of Peru created a *Junta Extraordinaria* (a Special Junta) to look into the causes of the rebellion. It concluded that the *reparto* system was the central Indian complaint and the cause of the rebellion. It therefore abolished *reparto;* the *mita* was continued, however. Eventually, the *corregidor* system itself was abolished and replaced by one of intendants. A special *audiencia* was established at Cuzco for the purpose of hearing Indian grievances.

The rebellion of Túpac Amaru II instructed the crown in the urgent need to reform the administration of Indian life. And reforms were in fact taken, but they were designed not so much to enhance the Indians' life as to prevent future uprisings and guarantee a steady source of cheap labor for colonists and crown alike. The rebellion conveyed other lessons. It demonstrated loudly and clearly that masses of Indians would fight, and they would do so bitterly and effectively. Túpac Amaru's relatives continued a second phase of the rebellion for a while after his death, and brought its virulence home to colonists in many regions throughout the Andes.

It is difficult to gauge the impact of the rebellion on the future independence movement. With its vast destruction of life and property, and with its clear racial overtones, surely the rebellion must have convinced some creoles that a war with Spain might unleash a massive Indian uprising that would tarnish the potential benefits of independence; and it may have retarded independence in Peru and Upper Peru (later Bolivia), where nationhood virtually had to be forced upon the colonists. Túpac Amaru's rebellion also cannot be considered a precursor of the independence movement because Indians and castes fought on both sides, some with the crown and some against it. Indians usually took the side supported by their local priest or *curaca,* and their choice was not always directly related to the degree of exploitation they had experienced. Indians often fought with the occupying forces, regardless of who they were, and this would occur during the wars of independence.

The Civil Protests

The colonial uprisings with the most lasting consequences were the civil protests, some of which escalated into open revolt. They occurred throughout the colonial period and continued right up to the time of independence. They were an inseparable part of the colonial system, and were founded in traditional Spanish political theory. The independence movements themselves were the direct result of the logic and method of the protests. The following examples demonstrate how widespread and socially accepted these civil protests had become by the late colonial period.

One of the consequences of the Bourbon reforms was a series of protests in both rural and urban areas. The urban protests were more threatening to the imperial fabric, and the first important one occurred in Quito (later the capital of Ecuador) in 1765. As a matter of reform, the viceroy of New Granada took steps to increase revenues from the *aguardiente* (sugarcane brandy) monopoly and the sales tax by transferring their administration from private tax-farmers to officials of the royal treasury. The first to react were the city's elite, who were essentially concerned with the changes in the *aguardiente* monopoly. The *estanco de aguardiente* had long offended the urban elite, and now its reorganization also provoked the *hacendados* (large landowners) who grew sugarcane and usually produced *aguardiente*. The *hacendados* spearheaded the opposition. Also opposed to the reforms, however, were the small storekeepers who sold the cane brandy. Significantly, so too were the local monasteries, where *aguardiente* was also distilled. The Church supported the opposition for an additional reason: its various branches owned haciendas and mortgages on cane-producing property.[1]

The opposition called for the convening of a *cabildo abierto,* an open meeting of the town council, to formulate a petition demanding a redress for their grievances. In so doing they called upon traditional Spanish political theory in stating that they represented the community at large and the public good. The petition of the *cabildo abierto* was supported by another one from a senior judge of the *audiencia* of Quito. Both petitions argued that royal legislation must address local conditions in order to be valid and enforceable. These appeals were founded in traditional Spanish political theory, which stated that when accurately informed the king would rule justly. Inherent in these appeals, that is, was an argument against taxation without representation. The petitions, however, left the viceroy, located in Bogotá, unimpressed.

While these elite protests went forward, the general population grew deeply concerned with the inequities arising from a more efficient collection of the sales tax and its application to items of popular consumption that had not been taxed previously. As efforts of redress failed, the popular "classes" joined with the elite in a protest that expanded into an open revolt, the "Rebellion of the Barrios." The riots began in May 1765, and the rebellion did not end finally until September of the following year, when the city was occupied by royal troops. Throughout this struggle the rebels professed loyalty to the king.

Two aspects of the "Rebellion of the Barrios" are significant to an understanding of the period of Spanish American independence. First, when grievances crossed socioeconomic lines, a broadly based rebellion might occur, and the participation of the masses might lead to actions not sought by the elite leadership. The Quito rebellion started on the night of May 22, 1765. The call to action was the ringing of parish bells in three barrios, where most residents were either Indians or mestizos. A small force sent by the *audiencia* to confront the rioters had little effect. The rioters broke into the tax office and destroyed its contents, including the sales-tax records. Within hours local officials had granted a general pardon to the several thousand rioters, and the uprising was essentially over. Although it ignited in the popular barrios, members of the middle and upper segments of society had also taken part.

A second riot occurred in late June. It was more violent and deadly than the first. Perhaps as many as several hundred rioters lost their lives. This riot, however, was not aimed at administrative reforms; it targeted peninsulars and the government itself. By the end of June the civil government had lost control of the city to armed rebels. The *audiencia* agreed to rebel demands and expelled all peninsulars who were not married and not residents of the city, while granting a general amnesty to the rioters. Throughout, the rioters professed loyalty to the king. On September 1, 1766, a military expedition entered the city and restored royal authority. On February 14, 1767, the *aguardiente* monopoly was reestablished without incident.

Although the Quito rebellion united various sectors of the local society and was directed by members of the elite, more important was the political argument developed by the leadership, which anticipated later debates about representation. In its own way, the *cabildo abierto* was representative of the city's general population. The elite were certainly represented in the *cabildo abierto,* and so were the Indians, indirectly, by the *protector de indios.* The remainder of the population, the lower socioeconomic sectors, were represented, in theory at least, by the leader of the opposition, Francisco de Borja, who had recently replaced his father-in-law, a leading producer of sugarcane, on the town council. Borja framed his arguments during the crisis on behalf of the "*común*", and the "*bien común*". Here is our first example of the elite's belief in virtual rather than actual representation. Actual representation through direct election by the general population would have made no sense to the elite. The view that the elite would govern equitably on behalf of society at large, providing virtual representation, was rooted in traditional Spanish political theory and practice, and would play a central role in shaping the political theories and realities of the new Spanish American nations.

It is not clear whether the Quito rebellion helped to generate the independence movements. What is certain is that Spanish political theory incorporated within it a justification for revolt. And as in the case of Quito, there was a willingness to resort to it. Both theory and practice were well known in the empire.

Northwest of Mexico City lies the mountainous city of Guanajuato, capital of a province famous for silver production. During the 1760s Guanajuato suffered severe revolts. In 1766, about 6,000 people stormed the royal treasury in protest against plans for a militia, new taxes on wheat, flour, meat, and wood, and against the inferior products marketed by the newly created tobacco monopoly. In their rage they shouted, "Long live the King! Death to bad government!" Once again, as in other civil protests in Spanish America, the people were carefully loyal to the king. As a result of the protest, plans for the militia were abandoned, and no one was imprisoned or otherwise punished. A more threatening protest occurred the following year because of the expulsion of the Jesuits. For three days mobs controlled the streets of Guanajuato, and when the protest spread beyond Guanajuato, it was considered a full-fledged revolt by the authorities. The royal representative in Mexico, *visitador* José de Gálvez, soon to be named Minister of the Indies, had 9 of the rebels hanged and 31 imprisoned for life, while another 148 were given prison sentences of six to ten years.[2]

Another royal *visitador* (inspector), Juan Francisco Gutiérrez de Piñeres, provoked popular resistance in New Granada by his actions on behalf of the Bourbon rationalization of the colonial system. He also raised existing taxes, applied new ones, and reorganized the administration of the tobacco and *aguardiente* monopolies. In 1781 a riot against the taxes and the resulting higher prices broke out in Socorro, near Bogotá. Several thousand people prepared to march on the capital of the viceroyalty to protest taxes and monopolies. They took the name *comuneros,* self-consciously declaring their kinship to the famous Spanish municipal rebellion of the 1520s. In June royal officials signed an agreement with the *comuneros,* ordering that new taxes and monopolies be abolished and that creoles be given additional positions in the government. The viceroy and the *visitador,* who had not participated in the agreement, denounced it.

Although the *comunero* movement was largely a creole venture, it also had mestizo and Indian participation. At this juncture, however, a smaller rebellion, led by an Indian inspired by the Túpac Amaru rebellion, developed among the indigenous population. It scared colonial officials and undermined creole support for the *comuneros.* An army soon put down the revolts of both the *comuneros* and the Indians.

The revolts of the barrios in Quito, the uprisings in Guanajuato, and the revolt of the *comuneros* in New Granada all posed serious challenges to colonial authorities. Yet there were other civil protests that were much less spectacular but more ominous. One of these occurred in the town of Concepción, Chile, in 1794. Residents of the province of Concepción, Chile's south, objected to the extension of a special tax established to compensate for Chile's negative trade balance with Peru. The town council of Concepción held a *cabildo abierto* and addressed a letter to the captain general of Chile, arguing that the *audiencia's* desire to extend this special tax was unfair and should be terminated. In this argument of no taxation without representation, the southerners observed that, according to law, special taxes were not to be imposed without a hearing from the municipal attorneys. What is more, they argued, far from helping to balance the trade deficit, the tax actually aided in destroying southern trade while increasing Santiago's trade.

The economic aspects of this civil protest properly belong to a study of the economic origins of Spanish American federalism. What is important here is that the southerners were protesting against what they considered to be the invidious actions of the central region, the Santiago-Valparaíso axis. Concepción pointed out that only the town council of Santiago and the commercial community of that capital had been consulted about establishing the tax, and the southerners well understood that the interests of the capital's town council and commercial community were different from those of Concepción.

This last argument was more than simply a matter of the existence of a disturbing tax; it questioned the legitimacy of the institutions that established taxes. Although Concepción's position was not narrowly justified by law, it was valid according to the traditional interpretation of the rights of municipalities. It appeared to the residents of the southern capital—as, at the same time, it appeared to colonists throughout the colonies—that imperial law and colonial custom were not being followed because of the insistence of the imperial administration and that, consequently, the colonists were being placed at a serious disadvantage.

If the Concepción community thought it could solve its tax problem by writing to the captain general of Chile, it was in for a shock. In September 1795, the *audiencia* rejected the Concepción appeal with a severe reprimand, ordering the intendant of Concepción to prevent the southerners from convening a *cabildo abierto* without express license from the *audiencia* or the captain general.

Two fundamental rights of municipalities were thus weakened. One was the right of no taxation without representation. According to tradition, the municipalities had a right to a hearing before taxes were established by the central authorities; but the actions of the *audiencia* were effectively denying this right. Also weaker now was the right of the town councils to convene the *cabildo abierto* and to direct appeals to higher authorities. The *audiencia* had affronted a great Spanish American tradition. Just a decade and a half before the start of the Chilean independence movement, the *audiencia's* actions must have impressed some people as very provocative indeed.

The fact remains, however, that none of the ideas mentioned here, none of the features of the colonial system that might have or properly should have caused independence, and none of the late revolts and protests did actually cause independence. If Napoleon's actions of 1807 and 1808 had not occurred, the Bourbon reforms might have accomplished their goals and independence movements might not have got under way for quite some time. In fact, even the colonial revolts and protests might have worked on behalf of an enduring empire by generating a flexibility and safety-valve effect that neither the crown nor the colonists had envisioned.

The Actual Cause of Independence

An independence movement occurred in the Caribbean even before Napoleon invaded the Iberian peninsula. It took place in the French colony of Saint-Domingue, situated on the western portion of the island of Hispaniola. When the insurrection began in 1791, Saint-Domingue was the most prosperous sugar-producing colony in the world. By the time the insurrection ended in 1804, with the establishment of independence as the country of Haiti, the sugar economy was ruined, and a long period—not yet ended—of severe poverty and underdevelopment would ensue. In this period, Saint-Domingue experienced a full-fledged revolution. The white planter class was eliminated by either death or self-imposed exile, and their plantations were destroyed.

The immediate political antecedent of the Saint-Domingue revolution was the French Revolution, which began in 1789. As in France, there was a great deal of talk about liberty and the "Rights of Man" in Saint-Domingue. In May 1791 the French National Assembly gave free men of color born to free parents the right to vote for colonial and provincial assemblies. The whites in Saint-Domingue did not recognize the validity of the French decree, and the colonial governor did not enforce it. While whites and free people of color moved toward open warfare against each other, the island's slaves struck out on their own behalf. The revolution began in August 1791 in the North Province, with an insurrection carefully planned by a group of slave leaders who had met on Sundays. Once under way, the insurrection spread rapidly and within days between a thousand and fifteen hundred slaves were ravaging plantations, killing the white planters and their families, and destroying not only cane fields but sugar mills and anything else they encountered. In a few more days several thousand slaves were in violent revolt, and within one month hundreds of sugar and coffee plantations in the North Province had been completely destroyed, while as many as 15,000 slaves had fled their plantations. Bands of rebellious slaves not only killed white planters, they killed many slaves who hesitated to join them.

The man who brought coherence and effective leadership to the spreading insurrection was Toussaint Louverture. Toussaint was a former slave who had been free for more than a decade. Even so, he remained on a plantation where he was the coachman for the plantation manager. During the first years of the insurrection, he ably led a band of five to six hundred troops. When Spain and Great Britain went to war against France in 1793, both countries sent armies to Saint-Domingue. (By the time the British withdrew in 1798 they had suffered the death of more than 13,500 troops to yellow fever or battle.) Toussaint fought alongside the Spanish in the hope of establishing a full emancipation in Saint-Domingue. When this goal proved to be illusory, Toussaint switched sides and fought with republican France. By now he led an army of several thousand soldiers and was the dominant figure in the North. The insurrection had spread also to the West and the South, but in these regions the racial issue was much less clear. In the North it had been blacks against whites, but in the West and South, mulattoes, free blacks, and whites competed in shifting alliances for control of the volatile situation. By early 1801 Toussaint was in control of Saint-Domingue, and as a result of having sent an army of ten thousand troops into neighboring Spanish Santo Domingo he was in control of that colony, too.

In early 1801, Toussaint Louverture was one of the most powerful people in Latin America and perhaps in the Western Hemisphere. To institutionalize his power in Saint-Domingue, he called a constituent assembly to write a constitution, which was promulgated in July. It abolished slavery and elevated Toussaint to the position of governor-for-life. All legislation would originate with the governor and be sanctioned by an assembly. Saint-Domingue would remain within the French empire, but France was not allowed any authority over its affairs.

Toussaint had a keen sense of power and power politics, and he well understood the central nature of Saint-Domingue's economy. To bring the economy back into production and to provide an export crop, Toussaint was determined to revive the plantation system, and this he did in two provocative ways. First, he made it impossible for the great mass of former slaves to acquire enough property to support themselves. Thus they had to work on the plantations in order to survive. Furthermore, the plantation workers were not permitted to change either plantations or their occupations. Second, he ensured the place of plantations in the economy by leasing many plantations to generals and other officers of the Haitian army, by encouraging the return of white planters, and by supporting the various economic needs of the mulatto elite in the South and West. Toussaint understood the economic needs of Saint-Domingue, but the central issue during the 10 years of insurrection had been emancipation and, in effect, he had now debased the revolution's most glorious achievement. It was not long before new revolts were ignited.

But Toussaint faced a greater problem. Napoleon Bonaparte was determined to reestablish French authority in Saint-Domingue. While planning an invasion of the island, Napoleon sought the support of the United States and Great Britain, and in fact, the temporary peace established by the Treaty of Amiens in 1802 between France and Britain provided just the opportunity he needed. An armed expedition of twenty thousand troops under the command of Napoleon's brother-in-law, General Victor–Emmanuel Leclerc, began to land in Saint-Domingue in February 1802. Within months Toussaint's position became untenable, and he began to negotiate with the French. At an arranged meeting with a French general, he was arrested and shipped off to France, where he soon died in a prison cell of what was probably tuberculosis.

The demise of Toussaint, however, did not signal a French triumph. Leclerc had mounted an extensive campaign to disarm the blacks, and this resulted in widespread rebellion against the French. Even before Toussaint's imprisonment, a virulent epidemic of yellow fever had severely thinned the French ranks. In his weakened position, Leclerc responded to the spreading rebellion with a campaign of extermination that was marked by official atrocities.

By the fall of 1803 Saint-Domingue was wracked by a massive insurgency. In October all of the black and mulatto generals who had been allied with the French defected, and Jean-Jacques Dessalines, who had been an officer under Toussaint, gained command of the combined black and mulatto army. In November, Leclerc, like thousands of soldiers, succumbed to yellow fever, and even with the influx of fresh troops, the French could not maintain their position. When war against Britain was renewed, Napoleon could not sustain any additional effort to conquer the former colony, and in November 1803 the French finally were defeated. In the course of just 2 years, more than 50,000 French soldiers had lost their lives. On

January 1, 1804, Dessalines declared the independence of Haiti, the first colony south of the United States to achieve this status.[3]

However, both independence and emancipation were greatly tarnished during the succeeding decades. Dessalines installed himself as an emperor, with the title of Jacques I. Two years later, in 1806, he was murdered. Haiti was then divided into two political units, with the North controlled by Henri Christophe, a black who styled himself King Henry I, and the South led by Alexander Pétion, a mulatto who would play a key role in the independence of Spanish America through his aid to Simón Bolívar.

Napoleon contributed unwittingly not only to the independence of Haiti, but to the independence of much of Spanish America. In 1796 Spain joined France in an alliance against Great Britain, which resulted in a series of military disasters for Spain. British fleets interrupted trade between Spain and its colonies and defeated a Spanish fleet off Cape St. Vincent in Europe in 1797. The British captured Trinidad, whose loss Spain recognized in the peace of 1802. Furthermore, Santo Domingo was ceded to the French. Charles IV of Spain was inept and dull-witted, the opposite of his distinguished father, Charles III, but the blame for these calamities was generally laid at the feet of his chief minister, Manuel de Godoy.

Godoy became the great scandal of Charles IV's reign. He arrived at court as a young royal guard, and soon caught Queen María's eye. It is not certain that he became the queen's lover, but he spent inordinate amounts of time with her in private, and, in any event, the relationship was generally believed to be true in Spain and throughout the courts of Europe. By the time Godoy was twenty-five, in 1792, he was a duke and the king's chief minister. He was temporarily deprived of his office in 1798, but by the following year he had regained his dominant position in the government. All this led only to further catastrophes. When France went to war with Britain in 1803, it pressured Spain to do likewise. Spain refused, signing a treaty with France that permitted Spain to remain neutral at the cost of a monthly tribute of 6 million gold francs. The British in turn renewed their attacks on Spanish ships carrying bullion from the American colonies. For its part, Spain declared war on Britain in 1804. A year later the Spanish fleet was destroyed by Nelson at Trafalgar. The stage had been set for Napoleon's entrance into Spain.

One of the reasons Napoleon's plan to isolate Britain commercially from the rest of Europe did not function effectively was that Britain had enjoyed a special protective relationship with Portugal for centuries, and now continued to dock ships at Lisbon. To plug the gap Napoleon, with Spanish support, sent an army of 28,000 men under Marshal Andoche Junot through the peninsula to Portugal in 1807. The Portuguese royal court—including the mad queen María I; her son, Prince Regent João, who ruled in her place; and thousands of nobles—boarded ships for Brazil. As a result, that colony's independence movement was postponed for a decade and a half because it now became the seat of the Portuguese empire.

In return for Spain's support of the French invasion of Portugal, Godoy was promised control of several southern Portuguese regions. Instead, Napoleon occupied a portion of northern Spain. Charles IV moved his court out of Madrid to Aranjuez, in an attempt to put some distance between him and the French armies. For many years, Charles's son Ferdinand, the Prince of Austurias, had chafed under Godoy's dominance and had attempted to maneuver himself into a position of power. Now he conspired against his father. On March 17, 1808, a mob at Aranjuez attacked Godoy's residence, sending him into hiding. The king at once dismissed Godoy, but the rioters clamored for more. Two days later, on the nineteenth, the king abdicated and Prince Ferdinand became King Ferdinand VII. On the twenty-fourth, Ferdinand, clearly the most popular person in Spain, entered Madrid. Napoleon refused to recognize either Charles or Ferdinand as king of Spain. He managed to induce both to meet with him at Bayonne, where he pressured Charles to renounce his rights to the throne in his favor. Then he pressured Ferdinand to renounce in favor of his father.

The throne now belonged to Napoleon. Early in May he placed his brother, Joseph Bonaparte, who had been king of Naples, on the Spanish throne. Even before final arrangements were announced at Bayonne, Spanish civilians were engaging French troops in Madrid. It was a bloody confrontation on that day of May 2, 1808, the day that marked the beginning of the Spanish war of independence. Juntas came into existence in many parts of Spain to organize the war effort and to govern in the absence of the lawful monarch, Ferdinand VII, *el deseado,* the desired one, who would be detained in France by Napoleon for the next 6 years. In September 1808, the many juntas joined together and established a central junta in Seville, often referred to as the *suprema.* It attempted to win the support of the Spanish American colonies, which it generally achieved. In 1810, however, the French took Seville, and the *suprema* was forced to flee. It reached Cádiz, where it was replaced by a Council of Regency, which began to rule in the name of Ferdinand VII. The Regency called for the convening of a *Cortes* (a legislative body), to which the colonies were invited to send delegates.

The colonies did not belong to Spain but to the crown of Castile, whose monarch had been deposed. Government now reverted to the "people," as represented by town councils and the juntas they elected. As these juntas sprang up in Spain to govern in the name of Ferdinand, so too did they appear in the colonies, and with perfect logic. Between 1810 and 1814, when Ferdinand regained the throne and proclaimed the reestablishment of royal absolutism, several colonies had grown decidedly accustomed to governing themselves and were manifestly pleased with their greater autonomy. With the restoration of Ferdinand, they were ready to fight for their official independence.

In this way the Spanish American independence movements began. Without the events in the Iberian peninsula, there is every reason to believe that the empire would have survived longer. The Spanish American reaction to the Iberian events will be discussed in Chapter 4. Before doing so, however, one other aspect of the colonial system needs to be considered—the professional nature of the bureaucracy.

The Disruption of the Bureaucracy

One of the most important reforms undertaken by the Bourbon kings was the professionalization of the royal bureaucracy. This effort began prior to the great thrust of reform under Charles III. By the late eighteenth century the empire was administered by professional bureaucrats who had started their careers at lower level positions and worked their way up through a standard career track. The crown sometimes showed favoritism and made appointments outside the normal rhythm of career advancement, but those thus favored were normally professional bureaucrats. In every colony the royal administration was conducted by professional bureaucrats, exemplified by such men as Juan Martínez de Rozas and José Santiago Portales in Chile and Fernando José Mangino in Mexico.

When the wars of independence began, the bureaucracy proved remarkably durable. Except in some war zones, the bureaucracy continued to function effectively even as independent governments emerged. Some peninsular bureaucrats fled early in the conflict, especially once creole patriots in some areas began to vent their rage against any peninsulars in sight. Still, many peninsulars—bureaucrats among them—remained. Once independent governments were in power and the colonial regime had ended, the professional bureaucracy sometimes faced insurmountable challenges. One such challenge was the antagonism toward remaining peninsulars, sometimes even those who swore allegiance to the new regimes. One of the most blatant examples occurred in Mexico, where a series of efforts were taken between 1827 and 1834 to expel peninsulars, and where in 1827 the national congress legislated that until Spain recognized Mexican independence, which did not occur until 1836, no peninsulars could be employed by the government.

But there was a far more comprehensive and enduring threat to the professional bureaucracy during the early years of independence. In some of the newly emergent countries, politicians dismantled the institutions of colonial bureaucracy and replaced them with an organizational structure seemingly more suitable to an independent nation. Simultaneously, professional bureaucrats were replaced by political appointees. In countries where governments changed with some frequency, so did the bureaucracy, sometimes resulting in the loss of efficient government.

Simón Bolívar. Based on an anonymous portrait painted in Quito or Lima, late 1822 or early 1823. The portrait is part of the Maury A. Bromsen Collection, Boston. Reproduced with permission from the Maury A. Bromsen Collection.

José de San Martín.

Bernardo O'Higgins.

Antonio José de Sucre.

4

The First Phase
of the Independence Movements

The Spanish colonies in America refused to recognize the authority of Joseph Bonaparte; instead, they continued to function more or less as they always had, but now in the name of the deposed King Ferdinand VII. The imperial bureaucracy was essentially intact, and calm prevailed on the surface at least. But the Spanish crown had been disgraced, and Spain itself was in turmoil. During the 2 years following Bonaparte's accession, there were several ominous signs of the future independence movements.

On June 8, 1808, Mexico's official newspaper, the *Gazeta de México*, informed the public that the king of Spain had abdicated in favor of his son, who became Ferdinand VII. On July 16, the *Gazeta* announced the calamitous news that Ferdinand had renounced in favor of his father, who then turned the throne over to Napoleon. On July 15 and 16, the *cabildo* of Mexico City discussed the proposition that Viceroy Iturrigaray govern Mexico in the king's absence. The proposal was presented to the viceroy on July 19, but during the presentation the *cabildo* also asked the viceroy to convoke a consultative junta of leading citizens, to be followed by an assembly of representatives of the cities. The *cabildo*'s actions struck some as provocative, and, in fact, the request was adamantly opposed by the powerful *audiencia*. Yet nothing could have been more "conservative" than for power to devolve temporarily during the absence of the king to the viceroy, in conjunction with the representatives of the town councils. Four days later, on July 23, the viceroy called for a junta of the city's leading citizens to meet to discuss the Spanish crisis. The news that Joseph Bonaparte had been placed on the throne of Spain, and the announcement that a patriotic war of reconquest had erupted, appeared in the *Gazeta* on July 29.

By September, Mexico City was a place of animated political activity. Iturrigaray asked the *audiencia* for permission to invite representatives to the junta from other cities in the viceroyalty. The *audiencia* maintained its opposition to the proposal, asserting that such an enlarged junta would all too closely resemble the French Estates General of 1789. Further complicating the situation, Iturrigaray now offered to resign in favor of retired Field Marshal Pedro Garibay. At the same moment, a peninsular *hacendado,* Gabriel de Yermo, was planning a preemptive *coup d'état,* with the support of the *audiencia,* the archbishop, and other peninsulars (referred to derisively by the creoles as *gachupines*). The *coup* occurred early in the morning on September 16. The viceroy was detained, then shipped back to Spain, and Garibay was appointed viceroy by the *audiencia.* He was succeeded in July 1809 by the archbishop, who, in turn, was replaced by the *audiencia* in May 1810. Finally, in August, Viceroy Francisco Javier Venegas, sent by the Regency in Spain, arrived in Mexico.[1]

The events of 1808 and 1809 in Mexico City were an affront to many creoles, but they suggested clearly how easily a viceroy could be removed from office. The capstone of the colonial system was neither inviolable nor permanent; but while this may have offered a lesson to creoles in other parts of Spanish America, the Viceroyalty of Mexico continued to be governed by peninsulars until 1821. That is, roughly 15,000 peninsulars, including military and clergy, continued to control a viceroyalty of more than 6 million people, and at a time when other colonies had moved toward independence.

Even before the Mexican events a viceroy in Spanish America had been ousted by popular will. This occurred in the Viceroyalty of the Río de la Plata. In 1806 a British force, under the command of Admiral Home Popham and General William Carr Beresford, invaded the viceroyalty and captured Buenos Aires. Popham and Beresford had acted on their own, although they understood that the British government desired to promote the independence of Spanish America, since Spain was an ally of Napoleon. The British governed Buenos Aires temperately, but many *porteños* (residents of the port) left the city and joined a militia that was being formed by Santiago de Liniers, a French naval officer serving in the Spanish regular army. Viceroy Sobremonte (the Marquis de Sobremonte), who had fled the city, was also gathering an army; but before he could get it under way, Liniers and his volunteer *porteños* took the capital and forced the British to sail away. The British had been able to hold Buenos Aires only 6 weeks.

Later that year a much larger British force, under the command of General John Whitelock, invaded and captured Montevideo. Viceroy Sobremonte again fled, but the town council of Buenos Aires now deposed the viceroy and gave his military responsibilities to Liniers. During the summer of 1807 Whitelock crossed the Plate estuary and tried to take Buenos Aires, which was fast becoming a focal point of patriotic zeal in the colonies. Liniers and his *porteño* troops were waiting for him, and they drove the British off. The empire was overjoyed with the *porteños,* and Charles IV proclaimed Liniers interim viceroy. It was a popular choice.

That some Spanish American colonists could both defeat the forces of a major foreign power and depose a viceroy were lessons that could hardly have been lost upon the others. And, moreover, these lessons occurred just as Napoleon's machinations were set to humiliate the Spanish monarchy and cut the colonies adrift.

The First Revolts

A year after Joseph Bonaparte was placed on the Spanish throne, 4 revolts jarred the colonies. The first one centered on the famous University of Chuquisaca in Upper Peru. In May 1809, a junta representing the university and local governing agencies was formed in imitation of the Spanish example to rule in the name of the dethroned king. Chuquisaca now became one of the more radical political centers in the Atlantic world, filled with animated talk of progressive social reform. In July the town council of La Paz, also located in Upper Peru, declared itself the governing authority in its region. In a matter of months, both Chuquisaca and La Paz had refused to recognize the authority of the Seville junta. Both revolts were put down by viceregal forces, and the leaders were executed. In August a group of creoles forced the town council of Quito to establish a junta in the name of Ferdinand. This revolt also had to be quelled by viceregal forces. Shortly, a similar revolt took place in Bogotá, but it too failed. In December 1809, creoles plotted at Valladolid, Mexico, to overthrow the viceregal administration and convene a congress of delegates from the leading urban centers to govern in the name of the dethroned king. The plot was uncovered before it was put into effect, and several of the conspirators were punished. Not all of them were caught, however; and with regard to causes, goals, and conspirators, there is a direct link between this plot and the famous Hidalgo revolt that occurred the following year.

The revolts and plots of 1809 failed, but they must have been very inspiring to creoles who already were questioning the legality of the Seville junta and anticipating the formation of their own popular institutions.

The 1810 Revolts

There were 5 major revolts in the Spanish colonies during 1810, and all of them failed except the one at Buenos Aires. Nevertheless, they eventually led to the independence of most of the colonies.

Venezuela

In April 1810, news began reaching the colonies that the patriotic war effort in Spain had failed, that Seville had fallen, and the *suprema* had fled to Cádiz, where it was replaced by a Council of Regency in preparation for convening a national parliament, a *Cortes*. Many colonists, creoles, and peninsulars now thought it was time to establish their own juntas to carry on in the name of the dethroned king. In April the town council of Caracas forced the creation of a junta to govern in Ferdinand's name and invited other town councils to do the same. The Caracas junta refused to recognize the Council of Regency in Cádiz, and soon proclaimed its independence from the patriot Spanish government. In turn, the Regency ordered a blockade of the Venezuelan coast and sent troops from Cuba to enforce its supremacy. To ensure its independence, the Caracas government turned to outside help, sending a delegation to England, which was headed by Simón Bolívar.

Bolívar, the preeminent figure of Spanish American independence, was born in Caracas on July 24, 1783, to one of the wealthiest families in Venezuela. His father, Don Juan Vicente Bolívar, was a militia colonel in Aragua, the owner of productive copper mines in the Aroa sierra, and the proprietor of valuable haciendas. Simón was born into the pinnacle of *mantuano* society, the white elite of Caracas, who derived their name from the elegant lace shawl the women wore to church. Nevertheless, there were early hardships. Simón's father died when the boy was only 3, and his mother died about 6 years later.

During these early years, Simón came under the influence of two extraordinary tutors. The first one mentioned by Bolívar was Andrés Bello, only 3 years older than his student, who went on to become a leading intellectual in Chile and the first rector of the University of Chile. The second, and the more influential on Bolívar, was Simón Rodríguez, an enigmatic individual devoted to the ideas of the European Enlightenment, especially those of Jean-Jacques Rousseau. It was from this tutor that Bolívar developed a lifelong interest in Rousseau. Bolívar later wrote of Rodríguez, "I have travelled the road you have shown me. . . . You have moulded my heart for liberty and justice—for the great and the beautiful."[2] Rodríguez became involved in the 1797 Caracas uprising and was imprisoned. Because of a lack of evidence he was soon released, and he left Venezuela. But this was not the end of his relationship with Bolívar.

In the same year, 1797, Bolívar, at age 14, joined the militia of Aragua, which had been organized by his father, and he received a commission as ensign. He spent a year in the militia, and the following year, at age 16, set out to seek his own fortune in Spain. After stops in Mexico and Havana, he arrived in Spain in the spring of 1799. He soon became enamored of María Teresa Rodríguez del Toro, a young lady whose father had been born in Caracas. He proposed marriage when he was only 17, but due to his youth, he agreed to a postponement. In 1801 he visited France, but he soon returned to Spain to marry María Teresa in May 1802. Bolívar and his bride traveled to Venezuela, where they soon took up residence on a family hacienda at San Mateo, and where he spent—he later recalled—the happiest months of his life. But it was to be a short interlude. In January 1803, his young bride died. Simón Bolívar never remarried.

With the death of his wife, Bolívar returned to Europe, first to Spain and then to France, where he resided in Paris. Bolívar had been impressed with the glories of republican France and with Napoleon's role in bringing about its success. Now, however, Napoleon had turned the republic into a hereditary empire, and he had himself crowned on December 2, 1804. Bolívar declined an invitation from the Spanish ambassador to attend the coronation at the Cathedral of Notre Dame, finding the whole affair sordid. "He became emperor," Bolívar observed, "and from that day I regarded him as a hypocritical tyrant."[3]

It was in Paris that Bolívar again came into contact with his tutor Simón Rodríguez, and a productive relationship followed. The two traveled together in France and then to Italy. While in Rome they visited the Monte Sacro, and it was there that Bolívar supposedly vowed to liberate his homeland. In any event, decades later he wrote to Rodríguez, "Do you remember how we went up the Monte Sacro to pledge on its holy soil the liberty of our country? Surely you have not forgotten this day of immortal glory." From Italy Bolívar returned to France, and from there he traveled to the United States, visiting Boston, New York, Philadelphia, and Charleston. He arrived in Venezuela in February 1807.

During the next few years he lived the life of an extremely wealthy aristocrat, attending to his estates and other investments, but all the while speaking his mind about independence. After Napoleon usurped the Spanish throne, Bolívar involved himself in various conspiracies. When the

Caracas junta was formed, Bolívar offered his services and was granted the rank of lieutenant colonel in the militia. It appears to have been his own idea that he be sent to England in search of aid, and since he offered to finance the trip himself, his request was granted.

A commission of three envoys sailed for Britain in June 1810. One of the envoys, and the commission's secretary, was Andrés Bello, who would remain in Britain for several years, where he was a forceful and articulate advocate of Spanish American independence. In dealing with the British government, Bolívar faced the same disheartening barriers that would also greet diplomats from other colonies for at least a decade. Britain was primarily concerned with the defeat of Napoleon, and now valued patriot Spain as an ally in this struggle. In the Peninsular War, a large British army, under the command of the future Duke of Wellington, was fighting the French in Spain. Thus Bolívar was not recognized as a visiting diplomat, and his mission to secure British support was a failure—that is, a failure for Venezuela but not for Great Britain. In fear that Britain would support the rebels, the Council of Regency in Cádiz sought to buy off the British by permitting them to trade directly with the colonies for the duration of the war to restore Ferdinand. After Napoleon was defeated and Ferdinand back on the throne, Britain maintained its alliance with Spain. It was impelled by its expanding industrial development to trade with the colonies, but it was not yet willing to disrupt relations with Spain by encouraging an independence movement.

Bolívar's instructions permitted him to see the old Venezuelan revolutionary Francisco Miranda, now living in London after a remarkable career. Bolívar was very much impressed with Miranda, and went so far as to arrange for him to return to Venezuela. Bolívar envisioned Miranda as the person to lead the independence movement at home.

If Simón Bolívar was the most important figure in Spanish American independence, Francisco Miranda was the most fascinating and colorful.[4] With good reason, he is usually called the precursor of Spanish American independence.

Miranda was born in Caracas in 1750, the son of a wealthy merchant who had emigrated from the Canary Islands. In 1772 the young Miranda traveled to Spain, where he purchased a commission of captain in a Spanish infantry company. He was quickly thrust into battle against the Moors in northern Africa. When Spain joined France in an alliance in support of the American Revolution, Miranda was sent to the West Indies, where he became aide-de-camp to General Juan de Cagigal, governor of Cuba. In this capacity, Miranda fought in the battles that led to the capture of Pensacola, in West Florida, and Providence, in the Bahamas, during the American Revolution. General Cagigal raised him to the rank of colonel. Because of his conduct in carrying out a mission in Jamaica for Cagigal, a royal commission in 1783 stripped him of his commission, fined him heavily, and banished him for 10 years. The harsh sentence was later reversed, but the harm was done.

In any event, Miranda fled to the United States, where he visited the main eastern ports. He even spent some time at Yale University, sitting in on classes and meeting with President Stiles. It was during this trip that he may have met Thomas Paine; it is certain that he met Alexander Hamilton and Henry Knox, with whom he spoke about the independence of Spanish America. In 1785 he returned to Europe, where he traveled for several years. By 1789 he was in London, where the following year he presented Prime Minister William Pitt with a plan for the liberation of Spanish America. It came to nothing.

Miranda now became involved in the French Revolution. A French plan to attack the Spanish colonies proposed to install Miranda as governor of Santo Domingo. The plan was not put into effect, but when France declared war against Austria in 1792, Miranda was given the command of a French division fighting in the Austrian Netherlands. Within a month he was made brigadier general, and he soon captured Antwerp. He had now fought in both the French and American revolutions, and with similar success. But he soon became involved in a French defeat and was called before a revolutionary tribunal. Acquitted of wrongdoing, Miranda took up a quiet residence near Paris, but in 1793 he was imprisoned. He was freed in early 1795, but by the end of the year he was back in prison. He was soon free again, remaining near Paris until 1798, when he returned to London. Again he proposed independence to Pitt, and he wrote to others, including Alexander Hamilton. In 1805 he sailed for the United States.

It was in the United States that Miranda's plans first found willing support, but not in the manner that he would have wished. In Washington he met with President Jefferson and Secretary of State Madison, but to no avail. In New York City, however, Miranda arranged for an armed ship, the *Leander,* to be outfitted with 200 men and munitions, and in February 1807, with Miranda in command, it set out for Spanish America. This was hardly the beginning of the revolution that Miranda had envisioned for so long; rather, it was merely a filibustering expedition, and as it turned out, a sad one at that.

Miranda's attack on the northern coast of South America provoked no local support, and it ended as a dismal failure. Miranda fled to the British

West Indies. From this sanctuary he continued to promote his plans for independence. Now the possibility of British support was greatly increased because Britain was at war with Spain, now allied with France. Miranda therefore sailed for Britain to pursue this opportunity. One of those who became interested in Miranda's plans was Sir Arthur Wellesley, a soldier of high regard. Wellesley was ordered to plan an expeditionary force of 10,000 troops, and by June 1808 he had gathered thousands of soldiers and a fleet at Cork, on the Irish coast. But it was at precisely this moment that Napoleon's intervention in Spain came crashing down on Miranda's plans. In July Britain announced a peace with Spain, and Wellesley and his troops soon sailed for the Iberian peninsula in support of patriot Spain. Many years later, Wellesley, long since the Duke of Wellington, remembered that when he informed Miranda of the change in Britain's plans the latter responded: "what grieves me is that there never was such an opportunity thrown away." There is no way to know for certain, but it may have been one of Miranda's most accurate statements.

Miranda spent the next two years in London, actively promoting the independence of Spanish America and sending messages and plans of government to various Spanish American town councils. He became the center of a group of intellectuals and reformers who favored independence, such as Jeremy Bentham, William Wilberforce, and the educator Joseph Lancaster, who devised the method of reciprocal education whereby students taught other students, which became very popular in early nineteenth-century Spanish America, and was especially important to Simón Bolívar. It was probably at this time that Miranda established a secret Masonic lodge, which attracted many men interested in Spanish American independence, especially several future leaders of that independence, such as Bello, Bolívar, Bernardo O'Higgins, and José de San Martín. The Masons were devoted to the Enlightenment. Some members undoubtedly were republicans, and certainly Miranda's London lodge favored independence for Spanish America.

Bolívar and Miranda arrived in Venezuela a few days apart at the end of 1810, to find the captaincy general in intense political ferment. Miranda, at 54, and in his uniform of a French revolutionary general, was an imposing figure. Quickly elected to a congress called to discuss the compelling issues facing the colony, he soon became the dominant figure in Caracas. A Patriotic Society for the promotion of agriculture and commerce had been formed recently, and Miranda became its president. Through the Society he strongly promoted independence. Miranda also founded a secret Masonic lodge modeled after his London lodge. With Miranda and Bolívar in it, the lodge quickly seized the initiative and took control of the independence movement in Caracas. The congress that convened in Caracas held effective control over only a part of Venezuela; nevertheless, on July 5, 1811, it declared the independence of republican Venezuela. Venezuela thus became the first Spanish American colony to declare independence.

But the First Republic, the *Patria Boba* (or "foolish nation"), endured only one year. Within days after declaring independence, the western city of Valencia revolted against the new regime. Miranda was given command of the patriot army, but he agreed to accept only on the condition that Bolívar not be included in the campaign. The two had come into conflict over the treatment of Spaniards. Bolívar wanted them expelled, while Miranda, whose father was a Spaniard, was more tolerant. However, Bolívar went along as aide-de-camp to the Marqués de Toro and distinguished himself in the battles that defeated Valencia. The city capitulated to Miranda in August.

During the following months a federal constitution was drawn up under Miranda's influence, and we shall speak of it later. Valencia was chosen as the capital for the new republic, and a congress convened there in mid-March 1812. But disaster struck ten days later, when in the afternoon of March 26 a devastating earthquake hit Caracas and many other towns and cities. In Caracas alone perhaps as many as 10,000 perished. As soon as the quake struck, Bolívar ran out of his house and worked for hours in the rubble trying to save lives. Thousands were left homeless and without food. The clergy and the faithful immediately blamed the catastrophe on the patriot revolt against Spain. This moment marked the beginning of the end for the First Republic.

Early in March, a naval captain from the Canary Islands, Domingo Monteverde, left the town of Coro in western Venezuela at the head of a force of 230 soldiers to begin the reconquest of republican Venezuela on behalf of the Spanish Regency. His rapid successes brought him many recruits, and soon he had a thousand troops. With this royalist counterinsurgency under way, the congress appointed Miranda commander in chief of the Venezuelan army and granted him full dictatorial powers over the state.

Miranda raised an army to defend the republic and gave Bolívar the important task of defending Puerto Cabello, the republic's most strategic port. This assignment placed Bolívar outside the main theater of action, and he took it as a slight from Miranda. Monteverde worked his way toward Valencia, which Miranda defended. Miranda had the superior force, but he was determined not to risk the republic in a battle with Monteverde. He chose to evacuate Valencia. In the plains to the south of Miranda's army, royalist troops were having continued success, and, in the process, burning republican villages, beheading republican soldiers, and murdering civilians. It was a war of atrocities, and its example would not be lost on either side. With Miranda stalled and royalist successes continuing, Bolívar's defense of Puerto Cabello became essential.

Puerto Cabello was important not only as a port, but because its main fort contained much of the republic's reserve of arms and ammunition. It also held many political prisoners from among the republic's social and economic elite. Bolívar was concerned about their ability to subvert the guards, but he did not remove them from the fort. By June 30, 1812, several of the political prisoners had successfully bribed some officers of the fort to revolt against the republic. The royal flag was raised, and the fort's guns fired on the port. With royalist troops attacking the port and the fort firing on it, Bolívar could not defend it. He appealed to Miranda for help: "If Your Excellency does not attack at once from the rear, the city is lost. Meanwhile I shall hold it as long as I can." On July 6 Bolívar fled by ship to the port of La Guaira. The following week he sent his report of the events to Miranda, concluding: "As for me, I have done my duty, and although the city of Puerto Cabello has been lost, I am blameless and have saved my honor."[5] In fact, it is fair to conclude that either Miranda or Bolívar could have averted the loss of the port—Miranda by attacking, Bolívar by removing the political prisoners from the fort.

With the military situation bleak, but with an army of 5,000 well-armed troops, Miranda chose to surrender to the royalists. On July 25 he signed the pact of San Mateo, which left Monteverde in control of Venezuela. The First Republic no longer existed. Miranda arrived at La Guaira a few days later, destined for Europe with a large amount of cash and gold from the public treasury. Bolívar and several other officers were infuriated by the capitulation and Miranda's flight, and they were determined to stop his departure. Miranda was detained and turned over to the royalists. He was imprisoned first in Venezuela, then in Puerto Rico, and finally in Spain, where he died in a prison in 1816. Bolívar escaped to Curaçao and then made his way to Cartagena, in New Granada.

New Granada

The collapse of the Seville junta had shocked many creoles and peninsulars into action in other regions, and the news of the first successes in Caracas steeled their nerve. The first New Granadan city to create its own junta to rule in the name of Ferdinand was Cartagena, in May 1810. Others followed suit until, in July 1810, the town council of the viceregal capital, Santa Fe de Bogotá, did likewise, and in the process removed the viceroy. The Bogotá junta called a congress to govern New Granada; but even more so than in neighboring Venezuela, geographical divisions and cultural and economic differences undermined the chances for consensus and a central government.

New Granada occupied the northwestern corner of Spanish America, stretching to Peru in the south, to the isthmus in the north, and to the captaincy general of Venezuela in the northeast. The northern Andes were divided into three ranges by the Cauca and Magdalena rivers. New Granada's terrain was extremely varied, passing from dense jungles to snow-covered mountains. East were the *llanos*, the savannas, or plains, that were sparsely settled cattle ranges. To travel from the Caribbean port of Cartagena to the viceregal capital of Santa Fe de Bogotá took 5 or 6 weeks, and to travel from there to Quito to the southwest took 8 to 10 weeks. Both trips required navigating difficult rivers and negotiating formidable mountain ranges.[6]

Not surprisingly, some critical regions remained indifferent to the coming congress; others were overtly royalist, that is, nonseparatist. Cartagena, which started the process, declared its own independence from Spain in 1811. By the time Bolívar and other Venezuelan refugees arrived in 1812, separatist New Granada was comprised of two main governments. A congress of delegates from several provinces met in Bogotá in late 1810 to fashion a government for New Granada. However, the province of Cundinamarca, whose capital was Bogotá, was greatly aware of its importance and desired a strong central government. It was led by one of the precursors of Spanish American independence, Antonio Nariño. Other provinces wanted greater local autonomy and sought to distance themselves politically from Bogotá. They formed a Confederation of New Granada, with its capital at Tunja. Its first president was Camilo Torres.

Bolívar was not yet 30 when he arrived in the former Viceroyalty of New Granada. It was here in December, 1812, that he made his first important public policy statement (known as the Cartagena Manifesto) which informed his future thought and action. Significantly, he strongly advocated the creation of a professional army to prosecute the wars for independence rather than the traditional and commonly informal militia. In fact, Bolívar would achieve the great success of independence for northern South America at the head of a professional military. The Confederation appointed him an officer in its army, and he began to clear the upper Magdalena River of royalists. In short order, he was appointed to the rank of brigadier. While fighting royalists and preparing defenses against an invasion from royalist Venezuela, Bolívar planned a return to his homeland. With permission from the Confederation, he began working his way eastward in February 1813. Soon he took a small army into the Venezuelan mountains and began to fight his way toward Caracas. Monteverde had set 2 lines of defense against an invasion from New Granada, each with about 2,000 soldiers. Bolívar, with a force of some 600 men, pierced the royalist western line and captured the provincial capital of Mérida on May 23, 1813.

Now back in Venezuela, Bolívar heard firsthand of atrocities committed by the royalist troops. On June 8, 1813, he announced a war of extermination: "Our hatred knows no bounds, and this is a war to the death." Bolívar drew an uncompromisingly harsh line that recalls Robespierre and the French Reign of Terror and perhaps reflects his French experience. The proclamation reached far beyond the royalist army; all Spaniards who did not join the patriot army or otherwise directly support the patriot civilian population would "face certain death, even if you are merely indifferent." Bolívar quickly gave orders that put into effect his official terror. Both sides were now committed to this extreme warfare.

By early August 1813, Bolívar's forces had expanded to number over 2,000 and he had occupied the strategic city of Valencia, which opened the road to Caracas. The *campaña admirable* (admirable campaign) had ended in triumph. Contrary to the threat of the war to the death, Bolívar now offered a generous amnesty. On August 6 he entered Caracas as a conquering hero. To Camilo Torres he wrote, "Here your Excellency has the fulfillment of my promise to liberate my country." This was part bravado, even if it was understandable in the moment of his great success. He had traveled a long and difficult distance, and he had won 6 battles in 3 months; but in fact he now controlled only a portion of Venezuela. Furthermore, much of eastern Venezuela was in the control of patriots who felt little allegiance to Bolívar.

Bolívar formed an interim government, establishing himself as dictator. Thus came into being Venezuela's Second Republic. A congress that was convened to write a constitution proclaimed Bolívar *El Libertador,* and from that moment on he would be known as the Liberator. The First Republic was federalist in structure; the Second was centralist, with Bolívar enjoying more or less dictatorial powers. The east was under the control of General Santiago Mariño, who, still in his early twenties, had declared himself dictator of the east. Serving under him was the charismatic Manuel Piar, son of a Spanish father from the Canary Islands and a mulatto mother from Curaçao. The plains to the south of Caracas, the *llanos,* were under the control of José Tomás Boves, a Spaniard who rose to personalist power in the plains by attracting the support of bands of *llaneros* (cowboys), most of whom were of African descent. He and his *llaneros* were Monteverde's main military support. To make matters worse for Bolívar, Monteverde was being resupplied from Cuba and Puerto Rico.

For the Second Republic to endure it was essential that Bolívar win the allegiance of Mariño, but his supplications failed to impress the dictator of the east. In the face of this failure, and with Monteverde growing stronger, Bolívar struck out against those he could reach. On September 21, 1813, the Liberator had 60 peninsular and creole prisoners executed. It was in this vulnerable position that the republic had to confront its deadliest foe, the hordes of *llaneros* marching on Caracas. Their leader, Boves, was one of the first *caudillos* (provincial chieftains) of the independence period. A man of military prowess and charisma, he was somewhat of a social democrat, elevating people of color to positions in his army and civil government to a degree that was unprecedented in Spanish America. Understanding the nature and needs of his followers, Boves was also a person who tolerated the savage plundering that followed his victories. Such savagery occurred, however, in a state of war in which brutality existed on all sides, and in a region where large amounts of property had to be confiscated to support the logistical needs of an army. Nevertheless, Boves's *llaneros* did indeed become the Legion of Hell, and with justification they carried as their standard a black flag emblazoned with a death's-head. Boves had formed his army into a capable infantry and a superior cavalry, which usually compensated for his limited artillery.

While republican Venezuela was still divided into two political entities, with Mariño dictator in the east and Bolívar dictator in the west, Boves pressed on toward Caracas. In early February 1814, Boves won an important battle at La Puerta. No matter how Bolívar appealed to Mariño to attack Boves's rear, he refused. A second royalist force was led by Manuel Cagigal, who replaced Monteverde after Monteverde's jaw was shattered in a battle in October. The fate of the republic seemed precarious once again. And once again, Bolívar lashed out where he could. He offered to exchange 800 royalist prisoners held in republican prisons for 1 patriot. The offer was denied, and a rumor supposedly circulated that an attempt would be made to free the prisoners. Bolívar had all 800 executed.

Bolívar decided to make a stand against Boves at his hacienda of San Mateo, where he had spent the final few months of his married life. Intense fighting was waged off and on from the end of February to the end of

March 1814. Now, however, Mariño finally came to the aid of the republic, and Boves turned to seek him out. Bolívar withdrew to Valencia, and on May 28, 1814, on the plains of Carabobo he fought and defeated a royalist army, but it was not Boves's army, which he knew he would still have to face to save the republic.

On June 15, with a force of about 3,000 troops, Bolívar confronted Boves with an equal force near the town of La Puerta. Boves sent his infantry into the patriot's center and his superior cavalry against both flanks. In only two and a half hours, the *llaneros* thoroughly vanquished the patriots. Bolívar managed to escape to Caracas. Boves took Valencia and then pressed on toward Caracas. An advance force defeated Bolívar's troops outside the capital on July 6. The following day, Bolívar evacuated the capital. Thousands of people fled, some to the west and Valencia, and many with the Liberator to the east and to sanctuary in Mariño's domain. On horseback, muleback, and on foot, men, women, and children undertook a 20-day march to Barcelona. While Caracas was being plundered and many of its inhabitants murdered, those with Bolívar suffered hunger, fear, and sometimes death.

Boves sent an army under the command of Francisco Morales in pursuit of the fleeing patriots. A few days after entering Barcelona, Bolívar had to face Morales and his larger army. At Agagua the patriots were routed, with nearly 4,000 men killed during the bloody encounter. Bolívar and Mariño boarded ship and escaped to Cartagena. The Second Republic was essentially dead, but some patriots continued to fight; in fact, Boves was killed in a battle in early December. By the beginning of 1815, Venezuela was again a royal colony.

By the time Bolívar reached New Granada, the situation there had deteriorated noticeably. The patriot leader Nariño had been captured and sent to Spain. Bolívar was well received in Cartagena, and he soon sailed up the Magdalena to Tunja, to seek the support of the Confederation's congress. With the congress's approval, Bolívar set out to conquer Bogotá and thereby bring the province of Cundinamarca into the Confederation. This he accomplished with little difficulty in December, and was rewarded with the title of Captain General of New Granada. The seat of government was moved from Tunja to Bogotá, but a revolt against the new government developed in Cartagena. In January 1815, Bolívar set out from the capital to subdue the strategic port, but it was too well fortified for him to defeat it.

Now two other developments hampered efforts to create a unified New Granada. The first occurred in February 1814, when Napoleon's fall from power permitted the return of Ferdinand VII to the throne of Spain.

Ferdinand proclaimed the restoration of royal absolutism, meaning in theory that the Spanish Americans could no longer legitimately claim to rule in his name. If they now chose to do so, they would be in open revolt. The second development was Spain's decision to send a major military expedition to South America to enforce Ferdinand's rule. It sailed from Cádiz in February 1815, with more than 10,000 well-equipped and experienced troops, comprising infantry, cavalry, and artillery. It took 18 warships and 42 transports to convey the expedition. In command was the distinguished General Pablo Morillo. Morillo entered Caracas in May, where he declared an amnesty, but nonetheless confiscated the property of anyone who had supported the patriot cause. On May 8, 1815, Bolívar sailed on a British warship for self-imposed exile on the island of Jamaica.

As soon as Morillo established his authority in Venezuela, he turned to New Granada. He sailed with an army from Puerto Cabello on July 12, and soon arrived at Santa Marta, on the coast of New Granada. He quickly sent two columns to clear the banks of the Magdalena. On December 6, 1815, Morillo entered Bogotá, and New Granada as well as Venezuela were Spanish colonies once more.

Buenos Aires

The Buenos Aires movement for independence can be understood only within the context of its geographic relationship to the rest of the Viceroyalty of the Río de la Plata. The port of Buenos Aires was situated on the Plate River, which connected with the Paraná River, the primary commercial route to the far north and Paraguay. Along the way, the Plate and Paraná rivers gave Buenos Aires access to the products of the Littoral provinces, which were blessed with great expanses of grass-rich pampas. In return for the products of the north, Buenos Aires exchanged domestic and imported goods (a subject to be further explored in a later discussion about Argentine federalism). Also to the north lay Upper Peru, which later became Bolivia, where vast amounts of silver were produced. Upper Peru was central to the economy of Buenos Aires. To the west of the port were the Interior provinces, backing up to the high and rugged Andes. These provinces generally yielded products that did not compete with those of the port and its province, which consisted mainly of pampas. To the south was Patagonia, barren, arid, and largely controlled by nomadic Indians.

Buenos Aires was a commercial and bureaucratic center that desired freedom of choice and action in matters of trade. In the four or so years since the British first invaded Buenos Aires, many consequential changes had occurred there. To defend the port, a militia of 8,000 soldiers was raised, meaning that roughly one-third of the port's adult male population was militarized. Many of these militiamen came from the lower socioeconomic segments of the city; some were free men of color, and some were slaves. In November 1808, Santiago de Liniers, the popular hero of the recapture and defense of Buenos Aires, opened the port to British goods. The customs revenues from this trade vastly improved the port's finances and, among other things, made it possible to pay the salaries of the militia, which had been in arrears for several months. This in turn produced two beneficial results. The payments to the militiamen amounted to a state-induced transfer of income to the general population, which kept thousands of people solvent during financially insecure times, and simultaneously maintained their political support for Liniers. In August 1809, a new viceroy sent by the Seville junta arrived from Spain to replace Liniers. The viceroy, Balthasar de Cisneros, nullified Liniers' policies of free trade, with the result that government revenues declined and the militiamen's salaries could not be paid. Facing much opposition, Cisneros arranged a compromise that permitted the importation of British goods, but he had alienated many influential people, including the militia itself. Cisneros went further, and attempted to reduce the size and strength of the militia.[7]

It was in this circumstance that news arrived in Buenos Aires during the second week of May 1810, reporting that the Seville junta had fallen. Many local leaders advocated the convocation of a *cabildo abierto* to deal with the situation, and Cisneros agreed in the belief that he would be elected its president. However, the open town council concluded that with the fall of the Seville junta, the viceregal administration no longer held authority. Cisneros was deposed and deported, and on May 25 a junta was proclaimed to govern in the name of Ferdinand. In Argentine history, this was the Revolution of May 1810.

The competing commercial port of Montevideo, located across the Plate estuary, traditionally took positions that opposed those of Buenos Aires for economic reasons. Now war broke out between the two rivals, ending in 1814 when Montevideo was captured by the *porteños*. The colony of Paraguay, with its capital of Asunción, was also traditionally fearful of Buenos Aires, and also refused to follow the *porteño* lead (as will be shown shortly).

Upper Peru was even more important to Buenos Aires than Montevideo and Asunción. Asunción meant trade, and Montevideo controlled the entrance to the Plate estuary, but Upper Peru meant silver and a major market for Argentine products and transshipped European goods. The long, arduous trade route from Buenos Aires to Potosí, in Upper Peru, was the most lucrative in the port's commercial repertoire. As already mentioned, Upper Peru had been a part of the Viceroyalty of Peru until 1776, when the crown integrated it into the new Viceroyalty of the Río de la Plata. With the events of independence unfolding in Buenos Aires, royalists in Upper Peru severed ties with the Viceroyalty of the Río de la Plata and returned the colony to its traditional place in the Viceroyalty of Peru. This was a threat of enormous proportion to the interests of Buenos Aires, and in 1810 an Argentine army began a war against royalist forces in Upper Peru. By early 1811 the Argentines had ended royalist control there, but patriot support for the conquering Argentines quickly waned, and in July they were defeated in battle by royalist troops who reestablished Spanish control. Royalist forces then marched into northern Argentina, where they were defeated in early 1813 by an army led by Manuel Belgrano. This defensive action a success, Belgrano led the Argentines north into Upper Peru on a second war of conquest, but by the end of the year they were decisively defeated.

A year after the junta was established in Buenos Aires, it was clear that only a minor portion of the former Viceroyalty of the Río de la Plata had fallen under the suzerainty of Buenos Aires. Buenos Aires itself was doing relatively well under the new system; but many provincial towns suffered, especially those that were accustomed to trading with Upper Peru, whose market was now closed to them by the royalists. These provincial trading centers on the route to Upper Peru were now in fundamental conflict with the port of Buenos Aires over matters of commercial policy. This commercial conflict would soon manifest itself in a political conflict that would delay the creation of a unified country until midcentury.

In 1811 political power in Buenos Aires was transferred to an executive triumvirate, an experiment that lasted three years. The triumvirate was strongly centralist in its dealings with the provinces, and it was driven by its forceful secretary, Bernardino Rivadavia, who proposed many far-reaching and provocative reforms, including the creation of a maritime insurance company, new meat-salting plants, and a scheme to colonize the interior with Europeans. The triumvirate's centralist program alienated the provinces, but its interest in creating a constitutional monarchy undermined its political control at the very center of its power, Buenos Aires.

By early 1812 there was much political agitation in the port, led especially by José de San Martín, Carlos de Alvear, and Bernardo Monteagudo. San Martín was born in the Río de la Plata in 1778, and was sent as a boy to Spain for his education as a soldier. He worked his way up the ranks to the position of lieutenant colonel, but aware of the events in his homeland he deserted the Spanish army and fled to England. In London he was inducted into Francisco Miranda's secret Masonic lodge. Certainly, it was there that thoughts about the independence of his homeland were nurtured. He arrived at Buenos Aires in January 1812. With Alvear and Monteagudo, he created the *Sociedad Patriótica,* the Patriotic Society, devoted to independence and to a policy that was more attentive to the needs of the other provinces. It took the *Sociedad Patriótica* until October to bring down the triumvirate.

A new triumvirate was more willing to acknowledge the economic and political needs of the interior provinces than its predecessor had been, and it was openly committed to independence. In 1813 a congress was convened with delegates from other provinces, and began to legislate in the name of the United Provinces of the Río de la Plata. In 1814 the triumvirate was superseded by a single executive with the title of supreme director. With independence movements failing all around them, the *porteños* understood that to consolidate their position they must enlist the support of other provinces. In late 1815 another congress was convened, this time at Tucumán rather than Buenos Aires. The deputies considered many and somewhat conflicting paths to follow. Finally, in July 1816, they declared unequivocal independence from Spain. A new supreme director, Juan Martín Pueyrredón, a man of commanding administrative talent, was elected, and he governed for three years.

In the meantime, events were not going well in Montevideo, capital of the region called the Banda Oriental, the eastern shore of the River Uruguay. The movement for independence in the Banda Oriental was led by José Gervasio Artigas. Artigas had been born to a wealthy landowning family. As a youth he received a formal education, but he seems to have been more influenced by summers on his father's *estancias* (ranches), where he learned the skills of the *gauchos* (cowboys). Before becoming an officer in the royal army, he had been a merchant in cattle hides, and a smuggler of cattle.

When the royal governor of Montevideo declared war on the Buenos Aires junta in early February 1811, Artigas at once deserted the Spanish army and crossed the river to Buenos Aires. By this time Artigas had acquired a reputation for being a capable creole army officer, and the Buenos Aires junta gave him the rank of lieutenant colonel. He was placed in charge of 150 men, and ordered to stir rebellion in Montevideo. Attracting a large army, especially of *gauchos,* in the Banda Oriental, Artigas marched on Montevideo. Buenos Aires sent an army in support of him, and Montevideo was besieged, but the port was able to withstand the siege because of its access to the sea. In September 1811, however, the Portuguese invaded from Brazil and forced Buenos Aires to accept a truce. Artigas and several thousand followers, soldiers and civilians, departed the Banda Oriental for the Argentine province of Entre Ríos. In 1812 the Portuguese withdrew from the Banda Oriental, and Buenos Aires reestablished the siege of Montevideo, but again the port's outlet to the sea prevented its capture. To resolve the problem, Buenos Aires created its own small navy under the command of William Brown, a deserter from the British navy. Brown defeated Montevideo's navy, and in June 1814 the port fell to the Buenos Aires forces.

Artigas and his army had not taken part in the final siege, but once Montevideo capitulated he insisted on being given control of the city. At first Buenos Aires refused, but Artigas, the *Jefe de los Orientales* (Chief of the Easterners), was the most popular and powerful person in the Banda Oriental, and he challenged the Buenos Aires troops. Buenos Aires agreed to Artigas's demands, and the leader of the *gauchos* entered Montevideo. Artigas had great popular support, especially from the lower socioeconomic sectors. He declared the Banda Oriental a sovereign state, the *Estado Oriental* (Eastern State), abolished slavery, and set out plans to redistribute land to the rural population. Artigas established a federalist confederation, the *Liga Federal* (Federal League), including the Argentine Littoral provinces, and Córdoba. In 1816, however, the Brazilians attacked the Banda Oriental, and the following year took Montevideo. The Banda Oriental was annexed by Brazil, and Artigas went into exile in Paraguay.

Chile

By the time news of the French intervention in Spain reached Chile, the captain general had alienated so many people that the *audiencia* feared outright rebellion. Consequently, the *audiencia* requested that the captain general resign, which he did on July 16, 1810. The position devolved by law upon Brigadier Mateo de Toro Zambrano, *Conde de la Conquista*. Born in Santiago and well over 80 years old, Toro Zambrano was one of Chile's most prominent landowners. His promotion to the rank of brigadier only the year before was undoubtedly inspired by a desire to secure his allegiance. He seemed an excellent choice for captain general. Not only was he the highest ranking military official in Chile, he was a Chilean held in great esteem by his fellows. However, the tense political situation proved to be more than he could handle.

Less than two months after he became captain general, the situation had deteriorated to such a point that Toro Zambrano feared open warfare. To avoid a destructive internal struggle, he called for a *cabildo abierto* to meet on September 18. Several hundred people attended and voted for the creation of a national junta. The junta was licensed as a provisional body, to function only until a national assembly could convene.

The Spanish American juntas of 1810 were not particularly radical bodies; nor did they represent the triumph of the creole over the peninsular. The Chilean junta perhaps was the least radical of all of them. The *cabildo abierto* elected Toro Zambrano as president of the junta. For vice president, José Antonio Martínez, bishop-elect of Santiago, was selected. The body of the junta was supposed to comprise three *vocales* (voting members). First *vocal* was Fernando Márquez de la Plata, born in Spain to a distinguished family and a leading government official in his own right. Juan Martínez de Rozas was elected second *vocal;* he was a bureaucrat married to the daughter of southern Chile's wealthiest merchant. For third *vocal,* the *cabildo abierto* chose Ignacio de la Carrera, a prominent landowner from Santiago. No plans were made for additional members, but sentiment among the leading citizens favored the election of two more *vocales.* Consequently, over 400 people voted a second time during the same *cabildo abierto* and elected Francisco Javier Reina and Juan Enrique Rosales. Reina was a peninsular colonel of artillery and a fervent supporter of the old regime, while Rosales was elected to represent the powerful Larraín family (to which he belonged by marriage), whose enormous size and influence permitted it to be a political grouping in itself called the *ochocientos*—the eight hundred.

Pains were taken to assure both the Spanish Council of Regency and Ferdinand that a very respectable movement was under way. Only the views of Rozas—who had been elected, in part at least, to ensure the loyalty of Concepción—were suspect. It is true that several leading Chileans considered the establishment of the junta more than just an unusual event; they perceived in it a strong indication that independence could be a reality in the near future. But the overwhelming majority of the active citizenry saw in the junta either a means of preserving the empire intact, under pressure for reform, or a means of achieving reform without destroying the empire. These distinctly different points of view, however, amounted to the same thing for the moment—loyalty to the crown. It was only during the years immediately after 1810 that a potent and popular sentiment developed in support of independence; and only after independence was declared was it common to refer to the meeting of the *cabildo abierto* on September 18, 1810, as the first patriotic step. Chile began to govern itself in 1810, and, for the privilege, fought a war with the royalist government

of Peru in 1813. It was during these three years that many Chileans culti-
vated an enthusiastic preference for self-government.

On December 15 the junta called for the meeting of a national congress. The convocation decree stated that representatives of the entire realm
would meet in Santiago to decide upon the system that best suited its "regi-
men, security and prosperity during the absence of the king." It met the
following year and elected a new junta, one whose powers were pointedly
subject to congressional control. However, in September 1811, the 25-year-
old José Miguel Carrera seized control of the congress. Born in Santiago in
1786, he had only arrived back home from a study trip to Spain at the end
of July. Carrera's father, Ignacio de la Carrera, was descended from the early
conquistadors and was a member of one of the colony's most aristocratic
families; his brothers were military officers in control of key forces. Perhaps
the most important factor contributing to his success, however, was that by
the end of August there was no other dynamic personality in Santiago to
lead Chile out of the calm that had fallen over the colony.

But at once other juntas sprang up to represent local interests. The most
important was the one established in Concepción. However, while the
provinces and the capital were in the process of provoking a final confrontation, the Carrera-inspired congress proceeded to produce a commend-
able record and become the center of progressive activity in Chile. As the
Carreras gained greater power in the capital, southern Chile prepared for
war. At this juncture an invasion force sent by the viceroy of Peru landed
in the south, and both provinces joined in the fight to preserve the Chilean
homeland.

The Peruvian army arrived in Chile in March 1813. On April 6, a small
advance force met patriot troops led by Bernardo O'Higgins at Linares and
were defeated. During the next months, further small victories contributed
to O'Higgins's reputation and he became a popular military hero. On November 6, O'Higgins was appointed general in chief of the Army of Restoration. His appointment called for immediate action.

Bernardo O'Higgins was the Chilean who would lead his country to
independence and become one of the great names of Spanish American
independence, prominent in the second tier just below Bolívar and San
Martín, and alongside men like Francisco de Paula Santander and Antonio
José de Sucre. O'Higgins had experienced a somewhat tormented youth.
He was born in 1778, in the southern Chilean town of Chillán and bap-
tized five years later—not an unusual occurrence when a child was born
out of wedlock. His father was Ambrosio O'Higgins, colonel of His
Majesty's Royal Armies and a bachelor, while his mother was a leading lady

of Chillán, whose name was withheld from the record of baptism to protect her reputation. Ambrosio O'Higgins was one of many Irishmen who
served the Spanish government in the military. Bitter against English policy
in Ireland and discriminated against as Catholics in the British military,
they served the Spanish king. In 1788 Ambrosio became President of
Chile, the title Chileans gave to their governor and captain general. In
1796 he was granted the title of Marquis of Vallenar and Osorno, and
he was appointed viceroy of Peru. At no time during his lifetime did
Ambrosio legally recognize his son, but he did supply funds to the young
Isabel Riquelme, who he knew was the child's mother, so that mother and
son could be comfortable. On the other hand, Ambrosio received reports
of his son's development, and he took steps to influence his maturation. In
1790 Ambrosio arranged for the 12-year-old Bernardo Riquelme to pursue
his studies in Lima. At the *colegio* (secondary school) of San Carlos, where
he studied for 4 years, Bernardo developed boyhood friends who would
later play significant roles in the Peruvian independence movement and
make Peru an hospitable place of exile for him.

In 1794 Ambrosio made arrangements for Bernardo to continue his
studies in Europe. After a brief stay in Spain, he traveled to England where
he spent the next few years. It was there that he met Francisco Miranda
and became a member of his Masonic lodge; and in England he met others
who later became influential leaders of Spanish American independence.
But the English period was not a happy one for him. Ambrosio did not
send sufficient funds, and Bernardo existed in a state of constant penury.
More distressing, perhaps, his letters to his father were never answered. At
age 21 Bernardo returned to Spain, which turned out to be an eventful trip
indeed when his ship was captured by the English. Bernardo passed himself off as an Englishman and served as interpreter; nevertheless, the English "robbed me of everything I had, although little, leaving me only with
what I had on," he informed his father when he arrived in Cádiz.[8] His
sadness reached deep. To his father he wrote: "I have abandoned all hopes
of seeing my father, mother and my country. . . . Goodbye, beloved father,
until the heavens grant me the pleasure of embracing you; until then I will
not be content, nor happy. I send Your Excellency the heart of a son who
so much esteems and desires to see you." Still there was no communication
and no further funds. It was the emotional nadir of his young life. In 1801
the viceroy died and the news reached Bernardo in Spain, along with the
mention of an inheritance for him. He sailed for Chile in April 1802.

Once in Chile Bernardo took up the life of a southern landowner and
cattle raiser. He convinced the royal authorities to permit him to operate

the Hacienda Canteras, which his father had bequeathed him pending the termination of official proceedings to evaluate the viceroy's administration. The hacienda prospered, and he soon had a home in the town of Chillán, where he became a member of the town council. It was sometime during the early 1800s that Bernardo began to call himself O'Higgins, although his petition to the crown to permit this name change was not approved. When news of the creation of the junta in Santiago in September 1810 reached him, O'Higgins referred to it as a "revolution." This was an interesting choice of term, and it was not casual. In 1811 he wrote that the liberty of Chile was the "essential object of my thought and that which occupied the primary anxiety of my spirit, since in the year 1798 General Miranda inspired me." In early 1811, O'Higgins became lieutenant colonel of his local Second Regiment of Cavalry.

When the viceroy's army landed in southern Chile in 1813, the Chilean soldiers were poorly organized and dispirited. As general in chief, O'Higgins did what he could to raise the army's capabilities, but funds were desperately short and his efforts were not markedly successful. Then at the end of January 1814, a new army from Peru arrived in southern Chile, led by the Spanish general Gabino Gaínza. By the end of March both the royalists and patriots were marching toward Santiago along parallel lines, often only a few miles apart. A truce was arranged, but it endured only a few months; yet this period of truce was one of great political turmoil among the Chilean patriots.

In June the viceroy decided to send a new expeditionary force under the command of the Spanish general Mariano Osorio. O'Higgins chose to make his stand at the town of Rancagua, situated on the road between Talca and Santiago. O'Higgins reached Rancagua on September 20 and immediately began to construct its defenses. Ammunition was in short supply, and he knew he could not stage a lengthy defense. He hoped for reinforcements and additional supplies, but now politics compounded his difficult situation. A new junta in Santiago was under the control of José Miguel Carrera, and when O'Higgins recognized this junta he had to accept Carrera as the general in chief of the Chilean army, as well as accept being general of only one division, the Southern Vanguard. Carrera sent two divisions to Rancagua under the command of his brothers Juan José and Luis Carrera. However, these two new divisions took up positions to the north of Rancagua, rather than reinforcing O'Higgins in the town. Carrera had obviously chosen not to place his brothers' forces under O'Higgins's command. On September 30 Carrera left Santiago to take charge of the entire operation.

On October 1 the battle began. With the royalists ready to attack, Juan José Carrera entered the town with the members of his cavalry who had not deserted. Fortunately, this Carrera brother placed himself under O'Higgins's command. The battle was intense, with many casualties. O'Higgins had approximately 1,700 troops, while the royalists had several thousand regular and militia troops. Osorio cut off the flow of water to the main plaza, the center of the patriot defense. O'Higgins anxiously awaited the arrival of José Miguel Carrera and his division, but they were routed by the royalists and fled. By midday the patriots had been fighting for about 30 hours. They were without water to drink and to cool their cannons, which were beginning to explode, and soon a part of the ammunition supply exploded. By 3 in the afternoon the battle was nearly over, and O'Higgins formed a column of about 500 mounted horsemen to charge through the enemy. Most of them survived the charge and gained safety, but as they did so the royalists took the plaza, seeking revenge on the remaining patriots.

It was an enormous and consequential military defeat. Of his 1,700 men, O'Higgins lost about 600 dead, 300 wounded, and another 400 taken prisoner. The road to Santiago was now undefended, and in a matter of days Osorio entered the capital and put an end to the *Patria Vieja* ("The Old Fatherland"). Between October 1814 and February 1817 Chile was once more a royal colony. By the evening of October 4, 1814, a long line of patriots stretched toward the Andean town of Los Andes and the route to Mendoza, Argentina. More than 3,000 men, women, and children attempted the dangerous trip. They had too little food and shelter, and too few pack animals. The Chilean soldiers proved themselves extremely helpful to the suffering émigrés, and when news of the disaster reached Mendoza, the governor of the province of Cuyo, José de San Martín, began sending supplies and pack animals back across the Andes to help the Chileans.

Mexico

No event of the Spanish American independence movement has captured the fancy of later generations more than Miguel Hidalgo's ringing of the bell in his parish church at Dolores on September 16, 1810—calling hundreds, then thousands (and scores of thousands) of Indians and castes to fight behind the standard of the Virgin of Guadalupe and in the name of Ferdinand VII for a government that would treat them more equitably.

Father Miguel Hidalgo y Costilla was a creole well known in the Church for his liberal views; he had even been investigated by the Inquisition.

Hidalgo had been associated with a group of enlightened creoles who conspired at Querétaro, in the silver-mining region northwest of Mexico City, in an attempt to oust peninsulars from the viceregal government. Multiple uprisings were planned, but authorities learned of the conspiracy before it could be consummated and many conspirators were arrested. With little time to spare, Hidalgo made his famous *grito de Dolores,* his call at Dolores that started the revolt. Probably he did not speak to the Indians at length about independence or protecting the homeland against possible invasion—themes that motivated him and his fellow conspirators, since the Indians were not much concerned about such matters. But Indians had their own grievances, and these were brought into sharper focus by agricultural crises and the rising cost of corn during the last decades of the colonial period.

While Indians throughout the colonies shared many characteristics, those of the Bajío, the rich agricultural, mining, and manufacturing region northwest of Mexico City, were distinguished by the level of their integration into the general economy. Whereas Indians to the south of Mexico City generally lived and worked within Indian-controlled communities and enjoyed fairly secure social and economic lives, except in times of dearth, those north of the capital more often lived and worked on agricultural estates, or if they lived in Indian-controlled villages, they had to work all or part of the time on the estates. This was a direct result of what, in some respects, was a favorable circumstance: a large increase in population during the eighteenth century, indicating a healthy birth-to-death ratio (as well as in-migration). At the same time the Indian population was expanding in the Bajío, so too was commercial agriculture. Indian communities could not enlarge their landholdings to support the rising population, and estate owners required laborers. Furthermore, with an expanded labor supply, estate owners no longer needed to offer favorable terms to their laborers, and their compensation indeed deteriorated during the last decades of the eighteenth century. Famines in 1785 and 1786 were devastating in the Bajío. A period of dearth struck some areas of the Bajío, including Dolores, again in 1789 and 1790. The price of corn increased from 10 to 40 *reales* per *fanega* (about 1. 5 bushels). And this calamity was followed by another period of dearth in 1809 and 1810. Falling wages, rising prices, and lack of security combined to render revolt a not unlikely choice.

Agricultural workers were not the only ones afflicted by economic problems. Rising wool costs and imports of cheaper textiles from Europe, including those from the Catalan region of Spain (a result of freedom of trade), greatly disrupted Bajío textile production and caused widespread unemployment. The third leg of the economy, silver mining, also suffered depression. Many mines were closed and thousands of workers were unemployed. The Hidalgo revolt began in the agricultural region around Dolores, and Indians, mestizos, and people of color from Querétaro and Guanajuato and other towns and agricultural areas within the Bajío soon joined the Hidalgo uprising.

This uprising was massive, but it was only a regional movement. Indians in areas outside the Bajío generally were not attracted to it. Those who lived in Indian communities in the central highlands south of the Bajío tended to follow the wishes of their traditional leaders, and most of them remained loyal to the crown. Indians north of the Bajío, who generally were estate dependents much like those of the Bajío, also tended to remain loyal to the estate owners and to the crown. These landlords in the north had worked with leading merchants to import corn from the Bajío during the famines of 1785–1786 and 1809–1810. As a result, Indians north of the Bajío, especially in San Luis Potosí, not only were opposed to the Hidalgo uprising, they fought against it.[9]

At first, Hidalgo was joined by some leading creoles, but soon the bitterness and savageness he had loosed upon the Mexican countryside frightened away many. The violence even frightened Hidalgo, who had not imagined that a race war would develop from his more limited plans. When the insurgency began, Hidalgo had with him less than a thousand men. A week later, his army counted 25,000 soldiers, and soon it would have three times that number. Tens of thousands of Indians and castes left fields and mines, joined Hidalgo's army, and satisfied a rage that had been building over the decades. Not only were many people killed, but the damage to property was widespread—haciendas were destroyed, and many mines without workers filled with water. This destruction would challenge Mexico's best economic intentions for decades to come.

Hidalgo won his most notorious victory soon after the revolt began. Within a few days, the mining city of Guanajuato began to prepare itself for a massive attack. Guanajuato held more than 60,000 inhabitants and was one of the largest cities in the Western Hemisphere. Unfortunately, it was situated in a narrow canyon, which made it extremely difficult to defend. The intendant of Guanajuato, Juan Antonio Riaño, chose not to attempt to defend the city, but rather to make a stand in the public granary, the *Alhóndiga,* which was constructed along the lines of a fortress. Inside the granary, Riaño gathered the royal treasury, government documents, all of the city's peninsulars, and some creoles. Riaño estimated that he had enough supplies to last three or four months. But the decision to defend only the granary appeared to some members of the general population that they were being sacrificed to the insurgents.

The battle for Guanajuato began on September 28, with thousands of Hidalgo's followers attacking the granary. Most, if not all, of the city's lower socioeconomic sectors joined the insurgents. The doors of the granary were set ablaze, and within a short time thousands of Indians and castes charged inside. Riaño was killed as the assault began. Within 5 hours the battle was over. About 300 peninsulars, creole civilians, and militia were killed, while the insurgents suffered about 2,000 dead. The insurgents then sacked the city and the neighboring mines. After two days of destruction, Hidalgo attempted to control what was now a mob, but he could not do so, even by threatening death. Soon the destruction ended, its energy spent.

Five weeks after the revolt began, Hidalgo led some 80,000 mostly ill-trained troops toward Mexico City. Poised just outside the capital, Hidalgo made the decision to withdraw without attempting to capture it. It is almost certain that he could have taken the city, and equally certain that his followers would have dissolved into a rampaging and uncontrollable mob. Hidalgo also knew that a royal army was approaching, and that a celebrating mob would be no match for disciplined troops. The retreating Hidalgo was decisively defeated by royalist forces on January 17, 1811, but he managed to escape. Two days later Hidalgo's officers deposed him, but because of his appeal among the masses he was left a figurehead.

On March 21 he was captured by the royalists. To avoid any unnecessary popular agitation on his behalf, Hidalgo and several other leaders of the revolt were transported for trial to the northern province of Chihuahua. They were tried, convicted, and executed. Hidalgo's more important followers were executed by firing squad, ignominiously shot in the back. On July 30, 1811, Hidalgo, now a defrocked priest, was permitted to face his executioners in consideration of his priestly past, and was shot in the chest.[10]

The Hidalgo revolt was taken over by another parish priest, the mestizo José María Morelos, a man of greater military and administrative ability. Morelos was less of an intellectual than Hidalgo and, fortunately for the revolution he headed, emphatically more pragmatic. He gave his followers a more specific program than Hidalgo had done, emphasizing social and racial equality, complete independence from Spain, and the perpetuation of the Catholic religion. Morelos attracted intellectuals to the fold, and in 1813 he convened a congress at Chilpancingo, where independence was declared and a draft constitution prepared. The constitution was promulgated the following year, at Apatzingán. Morelos continued the war started at Dolores until 1815, when he too was captured and executed. This appeared to be the end of the Mexican independence movement. During the next few years patriot guerrilla forces continued to operate in many regions, but the colony as a whole was governed by the traditional viceregal administration as it slowly recovered from the economic dislocations of the war.

By the end of 1816 all of the independence movements in Spanish America had been effectively stifled, except those in Buenos Aires and Paraguay (to be discussed in Chapter 5). The powerful and strategic colony of Peru had not even taken the first steps toward independence, nor had the Central American colonies or Cuba and Puerto Rico. Not many people would have thought that the independence movement would get under way again in 1817, this time successfully.

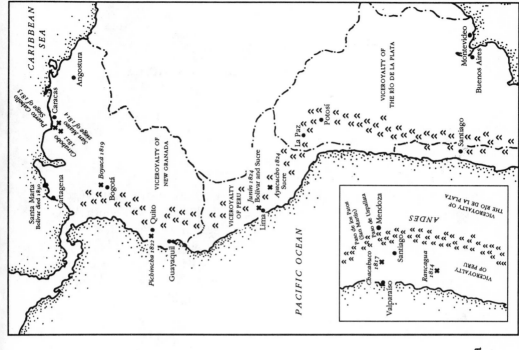

MILITARY CAMPAIGNS
IN THE WARS OF INDEPENDENCE

Above: Hidalgo's Campaigns of 1810–11
Opposite: Key Battles in the Campaigns of Spanish America

5

The Second Phase
of the Independence Movements

Two men loom largest and nearly overwhelm all others during the successful phase of the independence movements. Both operated in South America—Simón Bolívar in the north and José de San Martín in the south—
and both reignited the movements in 1817. Ferdinand VII was back on the
throne of Spain, so no one could properly speak of independence in his
name. Now it was all or nothing; now the king of Spain could ostracize
rebels and send troops; now it would be full-fledged independence movements.

San Martín, O'Higgins, and the Liberation of Chile

As we have seen, José de San Martín arrived in the Viceroyalty of the
Río de la Plata (Argentina) in 1812, in time to take part in the independence movement. In addition to his public and private political activities,
he became involved in organizing Buenos Aires's military forces. The militia
army formed in 1806 to fight the British was disbanded and replaced by a
disciplined regular army, and San Martín helped to shape it. By 1814, however, San Martín had come to believe that the permanent independence of
the Río de la Plata could not be achieved without the liberation of the rest
of the continent. Central to such a goal was the liberation of the powerful
and prestigious Viceroyalty of Peru.

Two possible attack routes were available to an Argentine army determined to liberate Peru. The more obvious route, and the one most logical
militarily, passed through Upper Peru and into Peru itself. However, as we
know, an Argentine army under Manuel Belgrano had been defeated already in an attempt to gain control of Upper Peru, thus leaving the land
that would become Bolivia as a formidable barrier to Peru's liberation. The
less obvious route lay across the southern Andes, and would require liber-

ating Chile before proceeding north to Peru. Thus, using the pretext of poor health, San Martín left his position in the army in 1814, and became governor of the Andean province of Cuyo, the point from which he could plan the liberation of Peru.

This situation met the needs of the many Chilean refugees, including Bernardo O'Higgins, who had fled across the Andes in 1814 after the defeat at Rancagua. They had spent three years in Argentina planning and thinking about the liberation of their homeland. Now, with the support of the central government in Buenos Aires, San Martín organized a combined Army of the Andes that included Chileans. O'Higgins, who was given the rank of brigadier in the Argentine army, was excited by the prospects for liberating his homeland. In July 1816 he wrote to a friend in Buenos Aires to send him any available French books on military tactics, the more modern the better; in fact, any books on the art of war would be welcome, so long as they were relatively recent. In early January 1817, San Martín mobilized his Army of the Andes, a force of some 5,000 troops, nearly half of whom were former slaves, liberated on the condition that they serve a stipulated period in the military. During the wars for independence, slaves were freed under similar conditions by both patriots and royalists throughout Spanish America. Practical as well as ideological reasons justified the policy, but the result was the undermining of slavery in many regions of Spanish America.

With this army San Martín was about to achieve one of the most spectacular feats in the history of military logistics. Except for Francisco Miranda, no other Spanish American general was as well trained and experienced at warfare as José de San Martín, and none more brilliantly prepared for battle. San Martín's Army of the Andes was mobilized on January 9, 1817, and on the thirteenth a force of 80 soldiers and 20 cavalrymen, under the command of Lieutenant Colonel Ramón Freire—a future president of Chile—headed over one of the southern passes. Its destination was southern Chile, and its purpose was to create a guerrilla diversion. On the eighteenth, a large division under the command of Colonel Juan Gregorio de las Heras, who had led an Argentine auxiliary force in Chile during the campaigns of 1813–14, headed toward the famous Uspallata Pass; and on the twentieth another division headed for a third pass. The main body of the army comprised two additional divisions, with one commanded by O'Higgins. O'Higgins took his division toward the *Garganta de los Patos*— the Ravine of the Ducks—on the twenty-first, with the remaining troops following their arranged routes within days. On the twenty-fourth, San Martín began the ascent with his aides and bodyguard.

The royalists in Chile did not expect an entire army to cross the Andes—even during the southern summer—and cut through the Chilean flank, the central region leading to Santiago. The obstacles were believed to be too great. It was more than merely a daring feat to move an army of thousands over passes higher than the St. Bernard Pass in the Alps. The steep and rocky inclines, the rarefied atmosphere, and the cold all took their toll. Furthermore, the expedition posed a severe challenge to San Martín's logistical skill. Food, ammunition, weapons, and artillery—all had to be carried over mountains and across ravines. History has recorded appreciatively the magnitude of this extraordinary achievement.

Thus the royalists in Chile were taken by surprise. They met the invaders on the plains of Chacabuco, northeast of the capital, and the Army of the Andes easily defeated the Spanish force. San Martín reported that the enemy lost 450 dead, and 600 taken prisoner, while his forces lost fewer than 100.[1] The patriots quickly took Santiago.

Subsequent events in Santiago are crucial to understanding the nature of the first Chilean government and of Bernardo O'Higgins's later fall from power. As soon as the royalists fled Santiago, the town council moved to elect an interim governor. On February 15 an assembly of notables named San Martín governor of Chile, granting him unlimited powers, but he refused the position. On the following day the assembly again elected San Martín, and again he refused. Then, at the same session O'Higgins was elected as interim supreme director; he was the choice of both San Martín and the government that had sponsored the liberation of Chile. That O'Higgins would become supreme director had been decided long before in Buenos Aires; San Martín's instructions were specific on the matter, and O'Higgins himself knew of this decision before crossing the Andes.

It was natural for the Chileans to express their gratitude to San Martín, the man responsible for their dramatic liberation. And it was natural for the Argentines to want O'Higgins as head of the new government. Chile, after all, represented merely the first stage in the Argentine plan for the liberation of the entire South American continent; and it was in the Argentines' interest to enable San Martín to proceed to Peru after placing in the new directorship a Chilean dedicated to the overall plan. On all accounts, O'Higgins was a likely choice. He was the ranking Chilean in the combined army, a close personal friend of San Martín, and a leading Chilean patriot. O'Higgins represented the continental plan to the Argentines and nationhood to the Chileans. Yet he became the supreme director because of a military feat, not through winning the support of a reasonably large proportion of the active citizenry. In the early excitement of victory, slightly more than 200 government officials and residents of Santiago elected him to the post as their second choice.

Once independence was declared officially in 1818 and the element of nationalism had become a factor, and especially after San Martín departed for Peru in 1820, O'Higgins began to remind Chileans more of their Argentine benefactor than of their own national identity. And this was the catalyst that stirred the resentment of various segments of the population toward his specific governmental actions and contributed to his overthrow in 1823.

Although the Chileans had won a great victory at Chacabuco, their independence was not yet secure. In March, 1818, they were routed by royalist forces only a short distance from Santiago. However, in April, at the battle of Maipo, dangerously close to the capital, the Chileans defeated the royalists in one of the bloodiest battles of the entire independence period. There would be further confrontations with royalists in the South for years to come, but with the victory at Maipo, the independence of the new nation was achieved. One final point, however, must be considered.

Miranda's secret London lodge had its offshoot in Chile, and a view of the Chilean branch during the O'Higgins years provides a means of gauging the power of these lodges in other new states. The Chilean branch was called the *Logia lautarina* (named for the rebellious Araucanian chieftain, Lautaro), and the impetus for its founding was furnished by San Martín, who was determined to create a branch of the Buenos Aires lodge. At bottom, it was a secret organization dedicated to the liberation of Spanish America. According to its statutes, any brother who revealed its existence would be punished by death. A brother who became a government official could make no important decision without first consulting the lodge. Since no official lodge records exist, it is impossible to say precisely who belonged; nor is it possible to know what it actually accomplished. It is certain that San Martín and O'Higgins were members and that between February 1817 and August 1820, when the *Expedición Libertadora* (Liberating Expedition) sailed to Peru, the lodge was the power that governed Chile. Once San Martín and his expedition finally left Chile for Peru, the lodge no longer could justify its existence. And in fact, in terms of its influence, it ceased to exist at that moment.

It is unlikely that the Spanish American lodges in other regions reached the power and influence of those in Argentina, Chile, and Peru. This was partly because Bolívar was quite flamboyant, something of a one-man institution of government in himself. Yet there were lodges in the Bolivarian lands, and they often wielded considerable influence. Thus the independence movement in general had its revolutionary cadres, which were responsible for the consummation of independence in at least several of the new states.

Peru

In August 1820 San Martín's *Expedición Libertadora,* comprising several thousand Chileans and Argentines, sailed to Peru on a Chilean fleet of ships commanded by one of the most colorful and controversial figures of the entire period of Spanish American independence, Lord Thomas Cochrane. Many British citizens distinguished themselves in the independence movements, but none more dramatically than Cochrane. By 1821 San Martín had captured the port of Pisco, south of Lima, and Cochrane was blockading Callao, Lima's port. But there was no general uprising in support of the forces of liberation, as San Martín had calculated would occur.[2] Finally, San Martín moved his army to a position north of Lima, and again he expected the Peruvians to share his enthusiasm for liberation and rise up against Spanish rule. While his officers—particularly some who were not under his direct supervision, like Cochrane—grew restless through the lack of resolution and action, San Martín entered into fruitless negotiations with Viceroy Joaquín de la Pezuela, with both men apparently determined to avoid a decisive military confrontation. Eventually, though, San Martín chose to march toward Lima, and as he approached the city the royalist army deposed Pezuela and selected a new viceroy. Pezuela was overthrown for a variety of reasons, but especially because he failed to meet the challenge presented by the invading expeditionary forces under San Martín. He was replaced by the Spanish general José de la Serena.

La Serena's prospects were not good. Lima was on the verge of starvation. The coastal haciendas had suffered physical damage and the loss of slaves impressed into the armies of both the royalists and the patriots. In the capital a loaf of bread had reached the extraordinary price of one peso (equal to a U.S. dollar). In early July, La Serena arranged with San Martín to provide Lima with an emergency provision of wheat, but the Spaniard knew that the supply would not last long. Furthermore, the city was isolated from productive regions in the interior, and La Serena had no hope of opening supply lines. To compound matters, an epidemic that seems to have been cholera inflicted heavy losses on both the royalists and patriots, but more so on the royalists, perhaps because they were already in a weakened state. By June the royalist army in Lima was losing 20 soldiers a day to the epidemic.[3] La Serena decided to withdraw from Lima, which he could no longer defend, and seek refuge in the highlands, where he might rebuild his forces. On July 10, 1821, the army of the *Expedición Libertadora* entered Lima, finally triumphant.

The independence of Peru was quickly proclaimed, and San Martín was named chief of state, with the title of *Protector.* But the new government did not control all of Peru; a powerful royalist army still roamed the nearby countryside and controlled the highlands. Both royalist and patriot armies varied in size, usually from a few thousand to five or six thousand troops, and according to the season, the levels of desertion, and their ability to find conscripts and attract volunteers, especially slaves.

San Martín did not easily make the transition from soldier to statesman. He was beset by a multitude of vexing problems. Lima and the surrounding area he controlled were impoverished, and it was difficult to find adequate food supplies. Furthermore, the viceroyalty was on the verge of financial collapse. And in addition to the many perplexing daily problems of domestic government, there was the burdensome issue of how to continue the momentum of the independence movement itself. By now Bolívar was having great success in northern South America, and in 1822 he invited San Martín to the port of Guayaquil in Ecuador to discuss the liberation of royalist Peru.

The two preeminent generals of the wars of independence met in July. It is not clear what was said at the meeting, but it is certain that there were political differences between the two. San Martín inclined toward monarchy, and Bolívar now favored autocratic republicanism. Furthermore, Bolívar had momentum on his side, while San Martín had clearly lost his. The Argentine was also troubled by the problems that his government in Lima was facing. Assaulted by tuberculosis, his addiction to opium (which was the standard nineteenth-century medical treatment for the pain of diseases like TB), and his inability to find the economic resources to further the pacification of Peru, San Martín chose to withdraw from Lima and permit Bolívar to lead the independence movement in the rest of the viceroyalty. San Martín returned to Lima from the meeting with Bolívar to find that his most influential minister, Bernardo Monteagudo, had been expelled from office, a popularly acclaimed event. San Martín did not attempt to reestablish his own authority; instead he sailed for Chile and then went on to Argentina. Shortly thereafter, he left for permanent self-imposed exile in Europe. Bolívar was now free to continue the independence movement in Peru.

Bolívar in the North

The same year that San Martín took his Army of the Andes into Chile—1817—Simón Bolívar began the long process of organizing a liberation movement in the North. When we last saw Bolívar, in 1815, he was on the way to his self-imposed exile in Jamaica. In early December of that year, he made plans to return to Cartagena to resume his command and help the city in its determined resistance against the royalists. He departed Jamaica on December 18, but while evading the Spanish blockade at sea he received news that Cartagena had fallen to the royalists. He chose to sail for the free republic of Haiti, and landed there on December 27. On January 1, 1816, Bolívar arrived at Port au Prince, where on the following day he was warmly greeted by the president of Haiti, Alexander Pétion. During the following days, Bolívar told Pétion of his plan to liberate Venezuela, and the Haitian agreed to support the plan on condition that Bolívar emancipate the slaves in any colonies that he might liberate.

It is never pleasant to consider the imperfect side of a great hero, one who accomplished so much good, but indeed Simón Bolívar was a deeply flawed person. Nowhere is this more apparent than in his changing attitude toward people of color. During the many years that the Liberator participated in the struggle for independence, his political ideals evolved. So too did his racial views. In fact, he did not always live up to his promise to Pétion. When he did, it was for military purposes not humanitarian principle. Furthermore, when he did liberate slaves for his military advantage, the liberation was contingent upon service; and even this generosity applied only to male slaves. Notwithstanding his 1816 pledge to Pétion and the liberation of specific numbers of male slaves to serve in the patriot armies (rather than a general emancipation), in 1820 he could ask: "Is it not proper that the slaves should acquire their right on the battlefield and that their dangerous numbers should be lessened by a process both just and effective?" Bolívar was clearly determined to place slaves in the line of fire and to keep their numbers under control as a matter of what he considered fairness to whites. "In Venezuela we have seen the free population die and the slave survive . . . unless we employ slaves . . . they will outlive us again."[4] Yet, the following year he urged the emancipation of all Colombian children born to slaves then and in the future. By 1826 this very complicated man was advocating the complete abolition of slavery.

With a small fleet and about 250 soldiers, Bolívar set sail for Venezuela on March 31, 1816. Even with the need to evade Spanish warships off Puerto Rico, the voyage should have taken 10 days, but because of Bolívar's personal needs it took 32 days.

The Liberator of Spanish America made several blunders during his career. Some were military—tactical errors on the battlefield, for example, or strategic errors such as concentrating on capturing Caracas rather than the more important hinterland. Others were personal, especially his many love affairs. Bolívar never remarried, but he seems never to have been without a woman, whether encamped for battle, on long marches, or in the great capitals of his conquests. Such behavior was not unusual for a general during the early nineteenth century in the Americas or in Europe. In fact, women routinely followed their husbands or lovers through their military service, and when we speak of the hardships suffered by the soldiers in marching through swamps and over practically impassable mountain ranges, we rarely mention the women who also marched and died, since the official documents are silent or extremely elliptical about these matters. Likewise, there is rarely reference to the traveling brothels that routinely accompanied armies. Bolívar, at any rate, took few pains to conceal his many affairs, sometimes with married women of aristocratic standing. Apparently, he antagonized some members of the elite whose political support would have been helpful, but more importantly, he sometimes placed military operations in jeopardy so that he could pursue his personal life. Thus during the voyage to Venezuela, Bolívar took time to pursue an onboard affair with Josefina Machado, which greatly lengthened the time required to travel from Haiti to Venezuela and unnecessarily exposed his expedition to risk.

Bolívar's small fleet reached the island of Margarita, just off the Venezuelan coast, in early May. His initial contact with the royalists proved successful and he captured 2 Spanish warships. The Liberator planned to gain control of the great Orinoco River, which led to the vast plains of Venezuela. The interior was rich in cattle, horses, and other consumable and salable products, and it was the home of the *llaneros*. On May 26 Bolívar sailed for the mainland, but after a successful landing he altered his plan and focused on Caracas. In early July 1816 he landed at Ocumare, situated between La Guaira and Puerto Cabello. The royalists easily defeated the invaders, and during hours of great confusion Bolívar left some of his officers in Ocumare in the mistaken belief that the port had fallen to the royalists. The officers felt betrayed, but they escaped to the interior.

This was perhaps the most controversial moment in the Liberator's career. Apparently, Bolívar was not in complete control of the invasion because of the time he was spending with a woman. General Carlos Soublette, who was part of the invasion, wrote: "Into these events came love. . . . Marc Antony, unmindful of the danger in which he found himself, lost valuable time at Cleopatra's side."[5] For whatever reason, the invasion was a patriot disaster, and the Liberator fled once more to Haiti.

Pétion again came to Bolívar's aid, and on December 21, 1816, Bolívar set sail for Venezuela. He was confident, and correctly so, as it turned out. "This time," he declared, "we shall deliver the final blow." This time he maintained his course: to control the Orinoco and the great hinterland, and then to take the capital. For Bolívar the earlier expedition from Haiti had been a disaster; however, some of the soldiers he left behind had continued to fight and with considerable success. Those in the east fought their way into the interior, while those Bolívar deserted at Ocumare selected the Scotsman Gregor MacGregor to lead them south and into the high plains. Working their way from the coast to the plains, these patriots fought successfully against small royalist forces and, in the process, attracted recruits. In a month MacGregor's division had reached the plains province of Barcelona, and there he was met by other patriot forces. In September MacGregor defeated the royalist forces and captured the capital of the province, Barcelona. Now he was joined by another patriot division commanded by General Manuel Piar, who had worked his way west. Three days after occupying Barcelona, the patriots, under Piar's command, marched a few miles to the plains of Juncal and there routed a larger royalist army. Of some 3,000 royalist troops, only about 300 escaped. The patriots had won a great victory, and the course of the war for independence was changing.

Hearing of this success, Bolívar proceeded to Barcelona. There he learned that guerrilla bands in the West under the command of José Antonio Páez were also defeating the royalists. Now Bolívar began one of his most important contributions to the liberation of Spanish America—the practice of military diplomacy. There were many patriot forces and as many leaders, some of whom were generals in control of large land areas, resources, and men. Bolívar began to give them orders, to cajole them, to mollify them, to appeal to them, and finally to lead them.

The liberation of Venezuela finally gained significant momentum, with

Piar and MacGregor combining their divisions and marching to the Orinoco, intending to capture the large southeastern province of Guayana. When Piar reached the strategic port city of Angostura, he discovered that its heavy fortifications could not be breached. Astonishingly, Bolívar again deviated from his plan. With a small division of poorly equipped and poorly trained troops, he left Barcelona and marched toward Caracas, where he was quickly defeated by the royalists—causing him to return to the original plan. In early April Bolívar joined forces with Piar at Angostura; and in practicing his military diplomacy, he confirmed Piar as commanding general of the army of Venezuela, while he himself would be *el jefe supremo*—the supreme chief. Piar soon met a royalist force of some 1,500 men, and thoroughly defeated it, taking few casualties and killing about 500 royalists. After the victory he ordered the execution of 160 prisoners. By mid-July Angostura could no longer suffer the patriot siege, and the city was abandoned. Bolívar entered Angostura at once, and he now controlled the Orinoco and access to the plains.

The prospects for liberation had altered radically, but this was only the beginning since there were still fundamental internal problems to confront. Word came to Bolívar that Piar was planning to revolt. Bolívar sent orders for Piar to appear at headquarters, but Piar fled to the east. He was captured, tried by military tribunal, and executed by firing squad. Bolívar's authority was now greatly enhanced.

During succeeding months, Bolívar solidified his command over potentially disruptive patriot factions. He won the allegiance of General Santiago Mariño, who controlled a large area in the east. And perhaps more importantly, he won the allegiance of the leader of the *llaneros,* General José Antonio Páez. With control of the western plains and the support of the *llaneros,* who were a lethal (as well as plundering) cavalry, Bolívar could defeat the royalists in Venezuela and proceed on to New Granada. The *llanero* leader, about 30 years old, was a talented tactician who used his cavalry with consummate skill. At the beginning of the wars for independence Páez could neither read nor write. He would later become president of Venezuela.

Altogether, Bolívar was the titular head of a combined army of approximately 4,000 men. In early 1818 he decided to leave Angostura and march west to join Páez and his soldiers. In February Bolívar offered to terminate his war to the death, and although the Spanish general Pablo Morillo did not reply to the offer, Bolívar suspended the practice of executing prisoners. On March 25, 1818, Morillo defeated Bolívar, with both sides suffering heavy casualties. Bolívar managed to escape, however, and continue to fight the royalists for the next month and a half, suffering further defeats. Finally, in May he retreated to Angostura to regroup.

A profound change now occurred in the patriot army. Bolívar had several foreign officers on his staff, and they had suggested that he form a foreign legion. This he decided to do at a propitious moment. The Napoleonic Wars were over, and tens of thousands of soldiers had returned home in Europe to find that few jobs were available. About 4,000 European soldiers sailed to the Orinoco and formed the patriots' foreign legion. The most famous part of this force became the British Legion, comprised of about 500 troops. Bolívar grouped the foreigners by national origin, but he also created mixed regiments of European and American troops. In the process, there were innumerable, and sometimes insufferable, difficulties. The foreigners came to the Orinoco with splendid uniforms that were poorly suited to the tropics. Few of them could speak Spanish, and they tended to be spectacular drinkers. Finally, because the patriots could not pay them, the foreigners were expected to survive through looting, and this was particularly humiliating to the British troops. Nevertheless, in a year's time a powerful patriot fighting force had been assembled and trained.

In March 1818, the young Daniel Florencio O'Leary arrived at Angostura as a junior cavalry officer; he would rise to the rank of general, aide-de-camp, and later diplomat. O'Leary met Bolívar shortly after his arrival, and wrote what remains perhaps the most famous description of Bolívar, who was 35 years old at the time. O'Leary later said of his description "many years after that period, he [Bolívar] changed so little in his physical appearance and in his moral character that it differs little from the person who received me kindly in 1818."[6] O'Leary went on to say:

> Bolívar had a high, rather narrow forehead that was seamed with
> wrinkles from his early years—a sign of the thinker. His eyebrows
> were heavy and well shaped, his eyes black, bright, and piercing.
> On his long, perfectly shaped nose there was a small wen that
> annoyed him greatly until it disappeared in 1820, leaving an
> almost imperceptible scar. His cheekbones were prominent, his
> cheeks sunken from the time that I met him in 1818; his mouth
> was ugly, his lips rather thick; the distance between his nose and
> mouth was notable. His teeth were white, uniform, and beautiful,
> and he took the greatest care of them. His ears were large but well
> placed. His hair was black, curly, and of fine texture; he wore it
> long between 1818 and 1821, when it began to turn grey, after
> which he wore it short. He had side-whiskers and a mustache, both
> rather blond, and he shaved them off for the first time in Potosí in

1825. He was five feet six inches tall. His chest was narrow, his figure slender, his legs particularly thin. His skin was swarthy and rather coarse. His hands and feet were small and well shaped—a woman might have envied them. His expression, when he was in good humor, was pleasant, but it became terrible when he was aroused. The change was unbelievable.[7]

Bolívar was fastidious about his person. Whenever circumstances permitted, he bathed several times a day, even when on his many long marches, and he splashed enormous amounts of cologne about his body. He required little sleep, and at every opportunity—and there were many as his victories accumulated and he entered city after city in triumph—he attended balls and danced hour after hour. Bolívar also loved his horses and was an excellent rider; and probably because he rode so many thousands of miles and sat a saddle so well, the *llaneros* referred to him, apparently with affection, as *Culo de Hierro*—Iron Ass.

Bolívar was also a tireless letter writer. O'Leary remembered that he would dictate letters and other correspondence to as many as three secretaries, "for he never left a letter unanswered, no matter how humble the person who wrote to him might be." O'Leary "never heard him make a mistake or get confused on resuming the interrupted sentence." He was inundated by official and personal petitions. "Swinging himself in a hammock, or walking up and down, usually with long steps—for his restless nature precluded repose—with his arms crossed or with his left hand grasping the collar of his coat and the forefinger of his right hand on his upper lip, he would listen to his secretary reading official correspondence and the innumerable petitions and personal letters addressed to him. As the secretary read, he would dictate his decisions regarding the petitions, and, as a rule, these decisions were irrevocable."[8]

The year 1819 began favorably for Bolívar and the patriots. In February the Congress of Angostura convened and created the Republic of Colombia, including the liberated regions of Venezuela and New Granada. The congress elected Bolívar as the new country's first president, with Francisco Antonio Zea, from New Granada, named vice president. Bolívar refused the presidency, observing that he could not direct the affairs of the new state while acting in his military capacity. The congress resolved the problem by authorizing the vice president to govern in the president's absence. Bolívar now enjoyed a status hardly imaginable just a few years earlier. He was president of a country and the general and commander in chief of its military, which now comprised large numbers of disciplined foreign troops. A few days after becoming president, Bolívar set out to meet the army of the plains, taking with him a battalion of 300 Englishmen under the command of Major John Mackintosh.

While Bolívar was at Angostura, which today is Ciudad Bolívar, General Pablo Morillo assembled an army of some 7,000 troops at the entrance to the plains. There Páez elevated guerrilla warfare, which had been "invented" (at least in the annals of European warfare) by the Spanish during the war against the French usurpation, to the level of an art form. With his cavalry he lured royalist forces into swamplands where many perished, and he burned the savannas, depriving the royalists of forage for their horses and cattle. By the time Bolívar reached Páez, General Morillo realized that his chances of defeating the patriots in the plains were slim. With his combined force, Bolívar went on the attack, and on April 2 Páez led a force of 150 of his best cavalry on a reconnaissance of the terrain the royalists occupied. When Morillo saw them, he thought the entire patriot army was marching toward him, and he countered with his cavalry and some of his infantry. Páez withdrew, drawing Morillo farther from his main force. When the moment was right, Páez wheeled about and attacked the advancing royalists, who retreated as best they could. The *llaneros* suffered few casualties, but the royalists lost more than 400 dead.

During the following weeks, *llanero* cavalry units harassed the royalists continuously. It was then that word arrived from Casanare, the far eastern plains province of New Granada, that patriot forces under the command of Francisco de Paula Santander, later president of Colombia, had won several victories over a royalist division. Bolívar now decided to invade New Granada. The rainy season was approaching and soon the *llanos* would turn into swamps and marshes. While Morillo faced the changing seasons by setting up winter quarters, Bolívar chose to march west to Casanare.

On May 26, 1819, Simón Bolívar marched toward New Granada and initiated a campaign that in half a dozen years would liberate a vast area and result in the creation of 5 new nations. O'Leary, then aide-de-camp to General Anzoátegui, remembered that Bolívar was "at the height of his physical and mental powers." He "arose at daybreak and visited the various units, encouraging them as he went. Accompanied by his staff, he followed the army, dismounting at midday to bathe whenever it was possible. After lunching like the others on meat alone, he dictated his orders and dispatched his correspondence while swinging in his hammock."[9] Bolívar set out for New Granada with an army consisting of 4 infantry battalions comprising some 1,300 men, and 3 cavalry squadrons totaling another 800 men.

It was a difficult march to the plains of Casanare, but on June 4 the patriots crossed the Arauca River and entered the province. The rains were flooding the plains. O'Leary recalled that "it was necessary to construct cowhide boats, both to prevent the ordnance supplies from getting wet and to transport those soldiers who did not know how to swim." The water became so deep that the "troops marched for a week with water up to their waists, having to camp in the open at places not covered by the water."[10] Nevertheless, on June 11 Bolívar's troops reached Santander's headquarters.

This was a young man's army. The soldiers were young, and the officers were young. Bolívar was one of the oldest generals. His second in command and chief of staff, General Carlos Soublette, was 29. General José Antonio Anzoátegui, commander of the rear guard, was also 29 or perhaps 30. He "hated Santander with his heart and soul," his aide-de-camp O'Leary recorded, "but out of respect for General Bolívar he concealed this profound dislike as far as he was able."[11] One of the youngest generals was Francisco de Paula Santander, then 27. He would become one of the Liberator's most effective political enemies.

It was good that the patriot army was young, because Bolívar's plan of attack was extremely demanding, as well as militarily unsound. First he sent Páez with a force of *llaneros* toward Cúcuta to cut the royalists' communications with Venezuela and divert enemy troops from the patriots' main force in New Granada. This made good military sense, but next he took his main force toward the Andes, which were considered impassable at that time of the year. Morillo had concentrated his defense of New Granada at Bogotá and Cartagena, and with good logic. To reach the Andes, Bolívar's troops had to wade through what Santander described as "more like a small sea than solid ground."[12] The ascent of the Andes took a great toll on the invading patriots. Cold and thin air caused weakness and illness. Torrential rains washed out paths, making it impossible for some of the unshod plains horses to climb without falling. Only a few of the horses, as well as only a few beef cattle, survived the 5-day march. Carcasses of dead animals littered the patriots' path making the ascent even more difficult. There was both death and desertion, but the army survived. On June 27 the advance guard encountered a royalist force and dispersed it, renewing the patriots' spirit. Bolívar gave the army a few days' rest, then continued his march.

We have been speaking of military chance, of military genius, and of military hardship. But again there is an underside that is rarely heard, for historians can only guess how many women accompanied the soldiers and how many of them succumbed to the cold, the rain, the falls, the dysentery. On July 2 the patriots moved out along a road seemingly so impassable that the royalists chose not to defend it. The cold air was fatal to many soldiers, O'Leary remembered, "most of whom were almost naked." His "attention was drawn to a group of soldiers who had stopped near the place where I had sat down, overwhelmed by fatigue." A soldier informed him "that the wife of a soldier of the Rifles Battalion was in labor." The next morning he "saw the same woman with the newborn baby in her arms, and apparently in the best of health, marching along behind the battalion, having already walked two leagues over one of the worst paths of that rugged terrain."[13] We can only wonder how many more women followed and survived—or did not survive the bitter ordeal. The following night, we are told, many soldiers "perished as a result of their sufferings and privations."

After an encounter with the royalists in which the patriots narrowly escaped defeat, Bolívar attacked the royalist force with the intent of placing himself between it and Bogotá. At 2 o'clock in the afternoon of August 7, 1819, Bolívar's advance guard attacked the royalists as they crossed the bridge of Boyacá. Simultaneously, Santander's division took the heights overlooking the royalist main force. The first fighting broke out as skirmishes between light horsemen, as O'Leary characterized them.[14] The royalists withdrew from the bridge. Santander was ordered to attack the bridge, and Anzoátegui the royalists' right wing and center. Anzoátegui and his lancers soon encircled the right flank of the Spanish infantry and captured their artillery. The royalist cavalry fled, but "was cut to pieces," resulting in the royalist infantry's surrender. Two thousand patriots had defeated 3,000 royalists at the Battle of Boyacá, taking 1,600 prisoners and a large amount of war matériel. The battle lasted 2 hours, and the patriots lost only 13 dead. Furthermore, the road to the capital of New Granada, Bogotá, was now open.

On August 10, 1819, Simón Bolívar entered Bogotá in triumph, having liberated the capital and much of New Granada in less than three months from the time he began his march toward the plains of Casanare. Once in Bogotá, Bolívar created a provisional government, and ordered the confiscation of the property of all peninsulars who had supported the crown and all creoles who had fled in the face of the patriot march toward Bogotá. As a means of building his army, Bolívar offered to free all male slaves who agreed to serve for two years in the patriot army.

One of Bolívar's most consequential acts was the appointment of General Francisco de Paula Santander as vice president of the department of New Granada. Santander was a complex figure. Born near Cúcuta, on the border between New Granada and Venezuela, he went to high school in Bogotá, and remained in the capital to study law. In fact, Bolívar referred to him as "the Man of Law." It was he who organized the new government and gave it stability. Because Bolívar wanted to pursue the liberation of those parts of New Granada still under royalist control, he soon departed Bogotá, leaving Santander, at age 27, as the acting chief executive. Santander was very talented, and cruel.

At the conclusion of the Battle of Boyacá, Bolívar was notably generous toward the men he had defeated. To build his army, he invited all of the creole soldiers who had fought with the royalists to join the republican army at equal rank, and those who chose otherwise were pardoned and sent home. The European royalists he treated as prisoners of war. There was one exception to his generosity. Francisco Vinoni, who had gone over to the royalists at Puerto Cabello and contributed to Bolívar's failure to defend the port during the First Republic, came to his attention as a prisoner of war. Bolívar had him hanged. Otherwise, the infamous war of extinction, the war to the death, had ended so far as the Liberator was concerned. Santander apparently had his own thoughts on the matter. Many of the officers of Colonel José María Barreiro, who had commanded the royalists at Boyacá, were imprisoned, as were several prominent peninsulars. Bolívar had offered an exchange of prisoners to the viceroy, who had fled to Cartagena, but no reply was received; and when Bolívar left Bogotá, Santander had Colonel Barreiro and 38 other royalists taken to the main square and executed. Barreiro was ordered to kneel, and he was shot in the back; then, the others were executed in similar fashion. Afterward, Vice President Santander took part in a parade and a ball that celebrated the executions.

Bolívar departed Bogotá toward the end of September to continue the liberation of New Granada. At the end of October, however, he received disconcerting news of factional disputes in Angostura, which caused him to leave at once for Venezuela. On December 11, he arrived at Angostura to warm greetings. He had fought for the unification of Venezuela and New Granada, and he was deeply gratified that on December 17 the constitution for the Republic of Colombia was ratified. Years later O'Leary remarked that this was a memorable date for two reasons: "it was the birthday of the great republic and the anniversary of the death of its founder."[15] Bolívar died 11 years later to the day.

The Republic of Colombia was divided into 3 departments: Venezuela, Quito, and Cundinamarca, with capitals in Caracas, Quito, and Bogotá. (Generations of historians have referred to the new country of Colombia as Gran Colombia, although that term will not be used in this book.) A new city with the name Bolívar was to be built as the republic's capital.

The Congress of Angostura elected Bolívar president of the republic; Dr. Juan Germán Roscio vice president of Venezuela; and Santander vice president of Cundinamarca. (Quito was not yet liberated.) Bolívar appointed Francisco Antonio Zea as the republic's special commissioner abroad, assigned the task of seeking both a loan and foreign recognition. Zea was told to consolidate debts contracted by previous agents of the governments that now comprised Colombia. Then, on the evening of December 24, 1819, Bolívar left Angostura for Bogotá. His plan was to attack the royalist strongholds on the northern coast of Cundinamarca, that is, the former New Granada.

At this juncture, events in Spain again resounded forcefully in the New World and threatened the very existence of the empire. For some time, Ferdinand VII had been gathering an immense military expedition at Cádiz, at times reaching more than 20,000 troops, with which he planned to reestablish his authority in the former colonies. The arrival of an army of such magnitude might well have turned the tide against the new nations. Spanish America at the end of 1819 was still only partly independent; many large and strategic areas remained royalist. Further, the other European powers were not yet prepared to support the colonists directly. Kings were not anxious to see one of their peers humiliated and stripped of valuable territories by his subjects. This was an era defined by the conservative objectives of the Congress of Vienna and the Holy Alliance. Even the United States was not prepared to jeopardize its interests, especially the diplomatic acquisition of Florida from Spain. Thus, not many people who saw the troops at Cádiz would have wagered against Ferdinand at the end of 1819.

On the first day of January 1820, a regiment of troops at Cádiz rebelled and proclaimed the restoration of the defunct Liberal constitution of 1812. Troops that had been at Cádiz for several years had become demoralized, and secret lodges, often with liberal political inclinations, had sprung up within the army to promote insurrection against the king. The revolt, led by Colonel Rafael Riego, found fertile ground throughout Spain, and other units joined the movement. With the defection of the Madrid forces, Ferdinand realized that a concerted fight against the movement now might lead to his fall from power. Therefore, in March 1820 Ferdinand seized the moment and placed himself at the head of the liberal movement by proclaiming the restoration of the 1812 constitution and calling for the convocation of the *Cortes.* A newly liberal Spain, however, did not satisfy the Spanish American patriots. The independence movements continued, but now without the threat of a large military invasion from Europe.

The changes in Spain did produce an immediately tangible benefit for Bolívar and the patriot forces. General Pablo Morillo was instructed to negotiate with the rebels, and on November 25, 1820, a 6-month truce was arranged between the royalists and patriots, which applied to all areas of the Republic of Colombia. On the same day the truce was signed, the two generals signed a treaty for the regularization of future warfare, which required that all soldiers captured in battle be treated as prisoners of war until exchanges could be arranged. This treaty officially ended the war of extermination.

After the treaties were signed, General Morillo successfully sought a meeting with his adversary. On the morning of November 27, the two met at the desolate village of Santa Ana, which lay midway between the royalist and patriot camps in the western Venezuelan interior. General Morillo rode out to meet Bolívar accompanied by 50 of his leading officers and a squadron of hussars, but when O'Leary told him that Bolívar would arrive with only 10 or 12 officers, Morillo sent the hussars back to camp. The patriots approached and Morillo, in his much decorated dress uniform, asked which one was Bolívar. When Bolívar was pointed out, Morillo exclaimed, "What, that little man with the blue coat and the campaign cap, riding a mule?" At that, "the little man was at his side, and they both leaped to the ground and embraced each other warmly and cordially." Morillo gave a "simple banquet in honor of his illustrious guest." That night, according to O'Leary, the two generals slept in the same room.[16]

Bolívar knew that the truce with the royalists would not result in a permanent peace based upon Spanish recognition of the Republic of Colombia, but he viewed it as a much-needed opportunity to organize the new republic and strengthen his army. In fact, the peace lasted only 5 rather than the arranged 6 months; yet it greatly aided the patriot cause. General Morillo, an excellent commander, retired to Spain and was replaced by General Miguel de la Torre, who was not his equal. It was now time for Bolívar to proceed with his long-standing plan to liberate Caracas and the remaining royalist areas of Venezuela.

Once again, the patriots fought an important battle on the plains of Carabobo, south of Valencia, which controlled the road to Caracas. General La Torre intended to block Bolívar's march to the capital, and he commanded a force of about 5,000 troops. The Colombians arrived with an army of New Granadans, Venezuelans, and a foreign legion that in June 1821 totaled some 6,500 men. La Torre expected an attack on his center or his left wing. Bolívar obligingly sent 2 divisions at the royalist center as a diversion. As they moved on the royalists, Bolívar sent Páez and his *llanero* cavalry around the royalist right wing to attack from the rear, and the royalist reserve divisions now had to fight as the advance force. Meanwhile, La Torre's center held and even gained ground. A patriot battalion withdrew under the royalist fire, and the British Legion filled the gap, taking heavy losses, including the loss of 17 officers in 15 minutes. In the end, 2 royalist regiments were destroyed and another surrendered. Most of the remaining royalists fled, but Bolívar had 2 divisions in reserve that he sent in pursuit. The Battle of Carabobo lasted only an hour and a half, and ended in complete victory for the Colombians. The road to Caracas was open, and Bolívar soon entered the capital in triumph. He remained only briefly, setting out for western Venezuela, and soon to Cúcuta. At this juncture, we should turn our attention to the future Ecuador and to Peru.

Bolívar had two great political goals. One was the formation of a "*union*" of the liberated nations of Spanish America to guarantee independence. We shall speak of this later, but here it can be observed that this goal was never achieved. The other goal was the creation of the country of Colombia. At this the Liberator succeeded, but only in the short run, since his glorious achievement would soon tear apart. But for now it was real and remarkable, except that Quito had not yet been liberated and Guayaquil, although patriot, leaned toward unity with Peru rather than with Colombia.

For the task of unifying Guayaquil with Colombia and liberating Quito, Bolívar chose one of the most talented and tragic figures of the independence period, General Antonio José de Sucre, born in Venezuela in 1793. A few months before Sucre was appointed to command the Colombian Army of the South, O'Leary saw him for the first time and asked Bolívar "who the poor horseman approaching us was." The Liberator replied: "Strange as it may seem, he is not well known, nor does anyone suspect his capabilities. I am determined to bring him out of obscurity, for I am convinced that some day he will rival me." In fact, Sucre would win the two most decisive battles of the wars of independence.

Ecuador's two important cities were in entirely different circumstances in 1821. The port of Guayaquil had declared itself independent, but had not joined the Republic of Colombia, and Quito was under royalist control. Sucre first made an alliance with Guayaquil and then marched to the highlands, where he met the royalists in battle on the plains just outside Quito on May 24, 1822. The royalists expected Sucre to attack from the south, but Sucre had climbed the heights of the volcano of Pichincha before dawn on the twenty-fourth. When the royalists became aware of Sucre's location, they charged the Colombians but were defeated. The Battle of Pichincha left the capital undefended, and Sucre entered it and established republican control. Bolívar arrived at Quito on June 16, and the intermediate goal of a Republic of Colombia was now realized. This was Bolívar's greatest political triumph, and he celebrated it intensely, even voraciously. It was in this state of triumph and exhilaration that the Liberator invited San Martín to meet him at Guayaquil, and this pivotal meeting took place shortly thereafter (as we have seen).

It was in Quito that Simón Bolívar met Manuela Sáenz, the great love of his mature years. No other woman kept his attention so long, although he continued his many short-lived liaisons. Actually, Manuela's full name was Manuela Sáenz de Thorne, the wife of Dr. James Thorne, an English physician. Her family had placed her in a convent at age 17, but she eloped with a young military officer, who soon deserted her. The Englishman loved her dearly and married her when she was 20 and he 40, but she was indifferent to his affection. Bolívar was struck by her beauty, and over the succeeding years their tempestuous affair would be regarded as a scandal. Nevertheless, the relationship brought incomparable comfort to the Liberator as he experienced a slow, and soon agonizing, physical decline before dying of tuberculosis in 1830. In his letters he addressed her as "My adored"; "My enchanting Manuela"; "My love"; "My beautiful and good Manuela."[17] In 1825 she was his "*Manuela the beautiful*" (Bolívar's emphasis). But during the years of their affair they were often separated. In 1825 he wrote to her: "I think of you and your fate every moment. Yes, I adore you, more today than ever."[18] Bolívar's romance reveals itself more fully in his language: "*Cada momento estoy pensando en tí y en el destino que te ha tocado. . . . Sí te idolatro hoy más que nunca jamás*". They were both volatile, and that apparently brought them close. When she planned a trip to London, he responded, "Why don't you answer me clearly about your terrible trip to London???!!!" She had been writing to him in riddles, and it was more than he could take. "Tell the truth, and do not go anywhere: *I love you unwaveringly*" ("*yo lo quiero resueltamente*") (Bolívar's emphasis).[19] Manuela shared his emotions, his love of riding, apparently his barracks language, and his bed. All told, they seem to have had insatiable appetites for their shared interests. She would become his secretary and be entrusted with a part of his archives. She also saved his life.

In 1829, an assassination attempt was made on Bolívar in Bogotá the evening of September 25. The Liberator, staying at the government palace there, was not well, and he sent for Manuela. The streets were damp, so— according to a letter she wrote to O'Leary in 1850 describing the events of that evening—Manuela put on high boots over her shoes, boots that

Bolívar would soon wear during his flight through the streets of the capital. When Manuela arrived at the palace, Bolívar was taking a bath. He asked her to read to him. Soon he got into his bed and fell into a deep sleep. About midnight, Manuela heard the barking of two of the Liberator's dogs, and then what appeared to be an attack on the sentries. She awoke Bolívar and he grabbed his sword and a pistol and tried to open the door. She stopped him and got him to dress. She remembered he had mentioned to her that the window of his bedroom was suitable for an escape, and she reminded him of this. When the street was clear of people, she let him jump; then she opened the door and admitted the conspirators. Seeing the open window, they shouted that Bolívar had fled, but she insisted he had gone to the conference room. Then why was the window open? She replied that she had opened it to find out what all the noise was about. Enough of the conspirators believed her to begin a time-consuming search through the building, but realizing their failure, they soon fled. Meanwhile, the Liberator had met one of his servants, and the two hid in the water under a bridge. After some hours, Bolívar sent the servant to find out which barracks had remained loyal. When the servant returned, Bolívar made his way to a loyal barracks, where he received a uniform and a horse. He then went to the main plaza where he met Manuela. When they returned to the palace, he told her that "you are the liberator of the Liberator"—"*tú eres la libertadora del Libertador.*"[20]

Once San Martín had departed, the Peruvians attempted to govern themselves and continue their own independence movement. They did not seem anxious for the arrival of Bolívar. However, within a year the situation had deteriorated to the point of chaos. In February 1823 the Peruvian congress abolished the governing junta and replaced it with a president, José de la Riva Agüero. Riva Agüero held office only four months, but during that time he asked Bolívar to send a Colombian army in support of Peruvian independence. The Liberator sent an army of 4,000 Colombians under the command of Sucre. What Sucre found was an impoverished country fractured by political divisions. Contrary to the royalist army, which had restored itself in the highlands and was unified, the Peruvian military was actually a collection of armies, comprised of separate Peruvian, Chilean, Argentine, or Colombian troops. With independent Peru on the verge of collapse, General José Canterac marched his royalist army toward Lima. Sucre understood that he could not defend Lima successfully, and on June 17, 1823, he withdrew his troops to the port of Callao. Canterac entered Lima the following day, while a mass migration of perhaps 10,000 Peruvians fled the city. Within a month Canterac recognized that no army could defend Lima, and he withdrew. In Callao the patriot congress deposed Riva Agüero and replaced him with the Marqués de Torre Tagle. Riva Agüero refused to recognize his removal from office, and with a group of congressional supporters he moved his government to Trujillo, north of Lima.

As independent Peru was disintegrating, renewed appeals went out to Bolívar to bring order to the disarray. Recognizing that his presence was necessary, Bolívar arrived in Lima on September 1, 1823, and was appointed military dictator and commander of all the armies of independent Peru. By the end of the year Bolívar understood well that he would have to take the fight to the royalists. Perhaps because his illness had weakened him, he was not optimistic about Peru's future. To Sucre he wrote, "Providence only with her omnipotent finger can create order out of this chaos." At the end of December he sailed to the little village of Pativilca, 30 miles north of Lima, and while still on board, he collapsed and had to be carried ashore. He lay gravely ill for a week with a high fever, but then it lessened and soon broke. This almost certainly was the Liberator's first full-fledged attack of tuberculosis. He hardly looked like the man who had been leading armies of independence for 12 years. To Santander he wrote, "You would not recognize me, for I am very spent and very old." It took two months for him to regain enough strength to continue his plans to defend the independence of Peru.

Just now events in the Iberian peninsula again threatened the independence of Spanish America. In 1823 the Holy Alliance decided to deal with Spanish liberalism through military intervention. Great Britain did not support the venture, but neither did it forcibly oppose it. A massive French army invaded Spain, and this time it was not repulsed by the Spaniards; in December 1823 royal absolutism was established once more. A liberal movement in Portugal was also overturned, and royal absolutism was proclaimed there, too. As a result, Britain and the United States were concerned that the independence movement in the New World would be thwarted and the region's lucrative new markets closed to international trade. Britain encouraged the United States to join in a combined declaration against European intervention in the New World. In the process, Britain issued the strategically important Polignac Memorandum, which quite effectively protected the new nations. Before a joint statement could be worked out, President James Monroe made his famous declaration of December 1823, warning against foreign intervention in the New World, which later came to be known as the Monroe Doctrine. Spanish Americans understood well that it was not Monroe's message that protected them, but the British navy. The United States navy could not have stopped a large-scale European invasion of Spanish America, but the British navy was capable of doing so; and thus, the independence movement was permitted to proceed.

Bolívar waited until well into 1824 before confronting the main royalist forces in Peru. During the early months of 1824, independent Peru suffered another major blow. In early February 1824, Argentine and Chilean troops in Callao revolted to force payment of back wages and to gain permission to return to their homelands. A few days later, Callao's Spanish prisoners were released and the royal flag raised. Lima was quickly occupied by royalist forces, and the Colombian ambassador to Peru visited the Liberator at Pativilca to inform him of the events. Bolívar, his head bound in a kerchief and his body wasted by disease, seemed to the ambassador to be a dying man. "What will you do, my General?" the Colombian asked. "Triumph," responded the little man. "In three months I shall have an army for the attack. I shall climb the Cordilleras and defeat the Spanish." And he did.

In March 1824 Bolívar established his headquarters in the northern city of Trujillo, and began to lay the groundwork for his military campaign. Independent Peru had been reduced to one province, Trujillo, while the royalists controlled the rest of Peru. With the restoration of absolutism in Spain, Viceroy La Serena nullified all acts passed under the Spanish constitution and reestablished the colonial system. Bolívar's chances for success were exceedingly limited.

Nevertheless, the Liberator gradually regained his strength and infused his plans with a contagious energy. O'Leary recalled that he supervised the making of "a large quantity of uniforms, leather belts, arms, and ammunition." Bolívar "himself taught people how to make horseshoes and nails and how to mix the various kinds of iron."[21] In late April, Bolívar moved his headquarters to the interior. There he enlarged and trained his army, and, very crucially, gathered supplies. He stored supplies of food strategically in the mountain ranges, the *cordilleras,* which the army would have to ascend and where it would have to fight. At the last moment reinforcements arrived from Colombia, and on June 15 he mobilized his army into 3 divisions and sent them by different routes into the mountains. Within a month the 3 divisions had crossed the *cordilleras* and met at Pasco. On August 2 Bolívar had an army of 6,000 Colombians and 3,000 Peruvians in the sierras.

At 5 o'clock in the afternoon of August 6, 1824, the patriot and royalist armies clashed on the plains of Junín. It was a fierce encounter of swords and lances, of infantry and cavalry. In an hour and a half the battle was decided. The royalists were routed, and General Canterac fled in haste. The royalists lost 400 men and the patriots 120. It was an important and an unusual battle. Not a single shot was fired. O'Leary reported: "The terrible silence was broken only by the piercing call of bugles, the clash of swords and lances, the galloping and stamping of horses, the curses of the vanquished, and the moans of the wounded."[22]

During the next two months further reinforcements arrived from Colombia, but rain made it impossible to continue the campaign. Bolívar reappointed Sucre as commander in chief of the army, and then with a small force marched for the coast. Lima and Callao were still in royalist hands, but by the beginning of December 1824 the Liberator had taken control of Lima. Everywhere he went he reestablished republican government.

On November 1, 1824, Sucre learned that Viceroy La Serena was marching toward him with a force of nearly 10,000 soldiers. La Serena had intended to surround Sucre, but Sucre retreated on a march of 30 days. La Serena pursued, tiring his troops. When the royalists and patriots faced each other, ready for battle on the morning of December 9, there was a serious imbalance in their forces. The royalists had 10,000 soldiers and the patriots less than 6,000. Both armies were drawn for battle on the small plain of Ayacucho, more than 10,000 feet high in the Andes, and the royalists and patriots were ready to fight a battle to decide the political fate of Spanish America. As the moment for battle approached, a touching and revealing event took place. There were friends and relatives on the opposing sides, and before battle they broke ranks and greeted each other, saying to each other what we can only imagine.

Sucre placed the Colombian division on his right wing; the left wing was taken by the Peruvians; and he took the center with his cavalry. In addition to his troops and superior artillery on the plain, La Serena controlled the hills. His right wing attacked the Peruvians, pushing them back. Sucre used his reserves and sent forward his right wing and his cavalry. La Serena countered with his center, but it was too late. The Colombians moved forward, breaking the enemy and capturing the royalist artillery. Then charging up the hills, the Colombians captured the viceroy. General Canterac quickly approached Sucre and offered an unconditional surrender of all of the royalist soldiers in Peru. The royalists then surrendered control of Peru. This was the most decisive battle during the entire period of independence. The wars were now virtually over. When informed of the glorious victory, Bolívar, who was President of Colombia and Dictator of Peru, appointed Sucre as Marshal of Ayacucho.

There were, however, two further serious military matters. The fate of

Upper Peru had not been decided, and the port of Callao had not agreed to surrender. Bolívar ordered Sucre to invite the commander of royalist forces in Upper Peru, General Pedro Antonio de Olañeta, to join the patriot cause, failing which Sucre was to invade the region. Olañeta wavered and Sucre marched, first taking La Paz in February and then Potosí in March 1825. The battles were minor, and Upper Peru, soon named Bolivia, was incorporated into the patriot camp. Thus ended the wars for independence in Spanish America. In 12 months, Bolívar had defeated a royalist army of 18,000 soldiers. In early August a National Assembly declared the independence of Bolivia, and later in the month Bolívar entered La Paz to popular acclaim.

Sucre was given executive authority in Bolivia, having agreed to serve for two years. He was an honest and earnest administrator, but the problems confronting the new country were too great for him. The government's near bankruptcy was the most serious problem because it was difficult to pay the troops—always a touchy situation, but especially so in an infant state. In a military uprising, Sucre received a serious wound to his arm; and in 1828 he gave up his position and left the country he had helped to found. When Sucre had been in Quito, he met and fell in love with a woman of the aristocracy, a person of enormous wealth; and when he was president of Bolivia, he married her by proxy. The ceremony took place in Quito a few days after he was wounded in the military uprising. Upon leaving the presidency, he returned to Quito to join his wife and supervise her estates, but he was assassinated in 1830. When informed of Sucre's murder, Bolívar exclaimed, "My God, they have shed the blood of Abel!" Administrative changes in Bolivia for the next century and a half would be quite irregular, to say the least.

Callao was another story entirely, and its fate during the final moments of Spanish dominion in South America recalls the horror of war, the personal suffering of those who participated, and the frequent mindlessness of those who led. The Spanish governor of Callao, General José Ramón Rodil, refused to acknowledge the settlement of Ayacucho, which called for the surrender of Callao. In the forts of Callao, Rodil had 2,500 soldiers, well equipped with arms, munitions, artillery, and provisions. The forts also protected some 3,800 royalist civilians who had fled to Callao. Among them were many leading government officials, including former president Torre Tagle.

Callao's forts could not be breached by frontal assaults, so the patriots began a year-long siege. Within the forts, Rodil established a spy system to control both civilians and soldiers, and he executed some 200 people for conspiracy. When food supplies ran low, Rodil forced civilians without their own provisions into the buffer zone separating the forts from the patriot troops. At first the patriots allowed them to pass through their lines, but when they realized that Rodil was sending the civilians out of the forts to preserve his supplies they refused passage, and many starved to death. Soon supplies were so low in the forts that soldiers and civilians began to eat the remaining animals, including horses, mules, dogs, cats, and rats. An epidemic of scurvy and typhus struck the weakened population, and by the time Rodil surrendered in January 1826, few had survived. Rodil's official tally was that among his veteran soldiers 2,095 had died, with 444 surviving. It is difficult to estimate the civilian deaths, but it is safe to say that somewhere between three and four thousand perished.

There is a maddening irony in this sad ending to the campaign for Peruvian independence. The capitulation permitted the survivors their freedom. Rodil sailed for Spain, where he was greeted as a hero. Ferdinand VII later appointed him as captain general of Cuba. He went on to become the Spanish minister of war, and then president of the council of ministers. Ferdinand raised him to the rank of nobility, and when the king died Rodil became the guardian of his two daughters.[23]

Mexico

Mexico did not become involved in the second phase of the independence movement until quite late. However, the insurgency that began with the Hidalgo revolt endured for 10 years, and placed a great strain on the royal government and its treasury. The royalists developed an elaborate program of counterinsurgency, which included raising regional militia units especially for this purpose; granting amnesties; creating terror; and deploying *destacamentos volantes*—flying detachments—capable of pursuing guerrilla bands. Many Spanish officers serving in Mexico had learned the techniques of counterinsurgency from their French enemies in Spain, and they put their knowledge to good use against the Mexicans. Although the most spectacular insurgency occurred during the first years after the *grito de Dolores* in 1810, more insurgencies continued through 1820.[24]

The matter of insurgency changed dramatically in 1820, when Ferdinand proclaimed the Liberal constitution of 1812 and summoned a new *Cortes*. The viceroy was compelled to loosen the political restraints of the colonial government. Under the reinstated constitution, the militia and tax systems that had supported the counterinsurgency collapsed, and the royalist regime could no longer sustain a vigorous anti-guerrilla campaign.

The person who emerged to lead Mexico to independence during this stunning change in royal military policy was Agustín de Iturbide. Iturbide was born in 1783 to a prominent landowning family in western Mexico. During the first phase of the independence movement, he fought with the royalist forces against the patriots. As a reward for his military successes, in 1815 Colonel Iturbide was made commander of a district that included the provinces of Guanajuato and Michoacán. The brutality of his administration led to acute discontent among the residents in his district, who secured his recall in 1816. However, not enough evidence could be collected against Iturbide, and instead of being dismissed from the army he was relieved of his command and placed in a sort of military limbo. As late as 1820, there were still a few insurgent bands of guerrillas roaming the Mexican countryside. Attempts to defeat them did not go well, and the viceroy decided that Iturbide might be the person to do the job. In November 1820 Colonel Iturbide accepted the appointment as commander of the royalist forces charged with dealing with the insurgent bands, and immediately he marched against the most important rebel leader, the mestizo Vicente Guerrero, who later would be president of Mexico.

Instead of fighting the rebel leader, Iturbide made a deal with him. They agreed to join forces, and in February 1821 they issued the joint *Plan de Iguala*. The plan was entirely pragmatic and appealed to just about everyone in the colony. It declared the independence of Mexico from Spain based on three principles. First, the new government should be a monarchy, headed preferably by Ferdinand VII of Spain, a member of his family, or someone from another royal house. Second, the Roman Catholic religion would maintain its traditional position in society, and no other religion would be officially tolerated in the country. Third, the principle of racial equality was established. These three principles, taken together, won a broad spectrum of support throughout the colony, and the Army of the Three Guarantees was created from a combination of royalist and insurgent forces to carry out the plan.

Mexico also had secret lodges to which many in the military belonged, and at times they conspired to further their ends. The lodges supported the new movement, successfully inciting one military garrison after another to join the rebels. News of rebel successes roused soldiers in the capital to action and royalist officers pressured the captain general to resign. (The title of viceroy was abolished by the now reinstated Cádiz constitution.) But before Captain General Juan Ruíz de Apodaca resigned in early July, the liberal Spanish *Cortes* appointed Juan O'Donojú to replace him. Captain General O'Donojú arrived at Veracruz in August 1821 to find the former viceroyalty in a political shambles.

The new captain general was determined to govern with the support of the Mexican people. Thus, soon after arriving in Mexico, O'Donojú met with Iturbide in the town of Córdoba, where they signed the Treaty of Córdoba, which created the Mexican empire. The treaty confirmed, with modest alterations, the *Plan de Iguala*. In this way, Mexican independence was validated by the leading Spanish official in the realm. Toward the end of September 1821 Iturbide marched into Mexico City, where a junta, including O'Donojú, was selected, and it appointed Iturbide as its first president. A declaration of independence was then issued.

The governing junta soon appointed a regency to act as the executive branch of government until an emperor might be chosen. Iturbide became president of the regency and resigned his position as president of the junta. In February of the following year, a congress met to supersede the junta as the legislative body. According to the *Plan de Iguala* and the Treaty of Córdoba, the new Mexican government would offer a crown to European royalty. Before an exhaustive search could be made, a street crowd proclaimed Iturbide as the new emperor, and the following day, May 20, 1822, the congress did likewise. On May 21 Iturbide became Emperor Agustín I. Several provinces that were not part of the old viceroyalty—including the Captaincy General of Guatemala (Central America)—soon joined the new Mexican empire.

Opposition to the new emperor was quick to develop. Iturbide inherited an economy that could not support a national government. Neither the military nor the bureaucracy could be paid in a timely fashion. Furthermore, the provinces had their own critical financial needs, and they no longer felt compelled to funnel their taxes or their silver to a central treasury. Iturbide's program of government required markedly increased revenue, and while the provinces remained recalcitrant, the congress was unwilling to vote for new taxes. A formidable rebellion against Iturbide, led by Antonio López de Santa Anna and Guadalupe Victoria (two future presidents of Mexico), began before the end of 1822. In March 1823 Iturbide resigned, and in May he went into exile. The empire was dissolved and a republican form of government established. Iturbide later returned to Mexico and was captured and executed.

Central America

The independence of Guatemala (which included the 5 modern nations of Guatemala, El Salvador, Honduras, Nicaragua, and Costa Rica, and the Mexican province of Chiapas), was led by the captain general, the Spanish general Gabino Gaínza. It was proclaimed on September 15, 1821. In January 1822, independent Guatemala became annexed to the Mexican empire. With the fall of Iturbide and the empire, Central America declared its own independence on July 1, 1823, and, with the exception of Chiapas—which remained with Mexico—it became the United Provinces of Central America.

Actually, it was not quite so simple. Central American unity was undermined by political problems, but fundamentally these difficulties revolved around regional rivalries that were so prevalent in Spanish America. (These regional rivalries will be considered in the chapters to follow.)

Other Regions

By the middle of the 1820s Argentina, Mexico, Venezuela, Colombia, Ecuador, Bolivia, Peru, Chile, Central America, and Paraguay were independent, although Ecuador would not declare its independence officially until 1830.

Little has been said thus far about Paraguay, in several ways the most unusual country in early national Spanish America. A large landlocked province of the Viceroyalty of the Río de la Plata, Paraguay at the beginning of the nineteenth century was sparsely populated with approximately 120,000 people, mostly Guaraní Indians and mestizos. The province's main source of income was its highly regarded green tea, *yerba maté*, which was harvested in the wild and then largely sent downriver, ultimately reaching Buenos Aires, where much of it was reexported. This "backwater" of the Spanish empire was the only region to undergo a social revolution during the independence era. These changes were not the result of violent conflict between classes, however. The Paraguayan revolution was consummated by the most successful dictator of early national Spanish America.

Paraguay's initial steps toward independence were similar to those of other Spanish American colonies, except that Paraguay was a province under the political control of the viceroy of the Río de la Plata; and therein lay an insoluble problem. When Buenos Aires deposed the viceroy and established a junta, it intended to retain hegemonic control over the entire Plate River system. When, in July 1810, Paraguayans learned of the Buenos Aires junta and its intention to supersede viceregal jurisdiction, a *cabildo abierto* was convened in Asunción to advise the governor. It recognized the Regency in Spain, while making it clear that it would not recognize Buenos Aires's suzerainty. In response Buenos Aires blocked Paraguay's downriver trade, and sent a disciplined army under Manuel Belgrano to reestablish its self-proclaimed authority over the province. Belgrano entered Paraguay in late December 1810 and was defeated.

To this point, nothing radical had occurred in Paraguay. The royal governor continued to govern a royal province and in the name of the deposed king. But, in May 1811, a bloodless military coup reduced the governor's powers and created what amounted to a triumvirate to govern the province. The governor was soon jailed, and a congress of delegates from all parts of the province met and created a five-man junta that declared independence. The junta included Dr. José Gaspar Rodríguez de Francia, doctor of theology in canon law, lawyer by profession, and soon to be the most powerful and long-lived dictator in all of early national Spanish America. At the end of September 1813, a congress of 1,000 delegates again declared Paraguay's independence and replaced the junta with two alternating consuls, one of whom was Francia. A year later a new congress created a single executive, and named Francia as the Supreme Dictator. Representation in the congresses that elected Francia as consul and then as dictator was unusually broadly based, going beyond merely the elite. It is fair to say, therefore, that by 1814 Francia was the most popularly elected executive, albeit dictator, in Spanish America. The congress of 1814 also created a Superior Tribunal of Justice, but the tribunal was never convened. The next congress met in 1816 and elevated Francia to Perpetual Dictator of the Republic. It also provided for a congress to meet whenever Francia might think it was appropriate—which turned out to be never. For the next 26 years Francia ruled Paraguay, unaided or obstructed by any consultative body. Nor was there a federal judiciary. Francia even abolished the town council of Asunción, which might have interfered with his authority. Furthermore, Francia governed his country without a central administrative bureaucracy. At his disposal was a minister of treasury and assistant, a government secretary, and, remarkably, no one else. Although he wielded absolute control over his country's patrimony, Francia did not seek to enrich himself.

Between 1814 and Francia's death in 1840, Paraguay was at once the most autocratically governed and yet most egalitarian republic in the Americas, despite the persistence of slavery. Some scholars use Paraguay to demonstrate how effectively and equitably a country could develop during the nineteenth century when it was cut off from the intrusion of international capitalism. During the Francia dictatorship, the economy of Paraguay was largely cut off from international capitalism and became more diversified. The determination of Buenos Aires and the Littoral provinces to tax heavily and otherwise impede the transport of Paraguay's *yerba maté* caused the upriver republic to reduce vastly its dependence upon that staple and simultaneously increase its production of a wide variety of goods, such as livestock products. During the *Franciata,* Paraguay was able to supply its own food needs and even produce a surplus for export. It was a much more balanced and sound economy than those of its neighbors. Subsistence farming expanded, and there existed a limited but highly controlled international trade. It is almost certain that life for the average Paraguayan was better in 1840 than it had been in 1814.

For the development that did occur, there was a price to pay. Francia deprived Paraguay of foreign capital, technology, expertise, modern science, and modern medicine. Although he expanded the system of primary education, he terminated it at that level. There was no press or newspaper in the republic, and any criticism of the regime, even if only imagined by the dictator, might result in imprisonment or execution. The political influence of the remaining peninsulars was immediately neutralized, and any who chose to marry were required to do so with an Indian, a mestizo, or a person of color. Francia neutralized the power and presence of the creole elite by imprisoning or executing many of its leading members and confiscating their properties, including slaves and livestock. In fact, the state became the most important landholder and player both in agriculture and commerce. The Church's political and economic power was also neutralized. Francia permitted the secular and regular clergy no contact with their superiors outside the republic, not excepting the Vatican. In 1816 the government began to collect the Church tithe, and the clergy was thereafter placed on civil salary. Furthermore, all monastery property, slaves and livestock included, was secularized and turned over to the state patrimony.

What evolved in Paraguay was a form of proto-state socialism, which was underpinned by a military force that was large and well provided for. In fact, this was a society nearly without significant socioeconomic gradation (although much more research is necessary to go beyond this rather broad assertion), one that approached a Rousseauian democracy, especially as understood by Robespierre. From a purely theoretical perspective, it may be called a society governed by the *general will,* and from a purely practical perspective it may be characterized as a dictatorship of terror on behalf of the common man.[25]

It took Uruguay a little longer than the others to become independent. The Banda Oriental was conquered by Brazil in 1817, and then annexed into the Brazilian empire. In 1825 a small group of Uruguayan refugees crossed over from Buenos Aires and began a rebellion. The *porteños* supported these rebel efforts, and for the next three years Buenos Aires and Brazil were involved in a low-level conflict over the Banda Oriental. Finally, in 1828, Great Britain forced both countries to recognize the existence of Uruguay as an independent buffer state separating the two powers.

Of all the Spanish American colonies to strike out for independence, Santo Domingo had the most difficult time. The sparsely settled colony was ceded to France in 1795, and, as we have seen, invaded by Toussaint in 1801. In 1805, the colony was again invaded, this time by Dessalines. However, between 1809 and 1821 the colony again came under Spanish control. In 1821, Santo Domingo declared its independence, but the following year it was conquered by Haiti, a subjugation that endured more than two decades.

Cuba and Puerto Rico remained loyal, and for many reasons. These islands were heavily garrisoned; but perhaps as importantly, they had proportionately the largest populations of African descent among all the Spanish American colonies, which some whites found threatening. The horrors and excesses of the revolution in Saint-Domingue were well known in these colonies, now home to many refugees from that conflagration, who were often planters who arrived with capital, expertise, and stories. The Saint-Domingue debacle had another effect on Cuba and Puerto Rico. The devastation caused by the slave rebellion in the French colony led to a shortfall in the world's sugar and coffee supplies as well as higher prices. As a result, Cuba, and later Puerto Rico, greatly expanded production. By 1795–96 the price of sugar and coffee had increased markedly, and a new prosperity ensued, especially in Cuba. Spain responded to the islands' new economic potential—and loyalty—by liberalizing trade restrictions. The reforms, although disturbing to those who thrived within the restricted trading network, were also intended to militate against subversive agitation. And in fact, both colonies remained within the empire until late in the nineteenth century.[26]

Unlike Spanish America and Haiti, Brazil achieved independence with some elegance. As a result of the French invasion of Portugal in 1807, the king and royal court fled to Brazil, arriving early the following year. Brazil now enjoyed greater imperial status, along with more liberal trade and industrial policies. In 1815 Brazil was declared a kingdom, equal to Portugal. However, the liberal revolt in Portugal in 1820 altered the situation. The metropolitan reformers required the king to return to Portugal, and insisted upon a return, as well, to the traditional subordination of Brazil. The king returned home, leaving his son Pedro as regent of Brazil. In concert with mounting public pressure, Pedro declared the independence of Brazil on September 7, 1822, and later in the year he became emperor.

Three additional topics from the period require attention: the role of the Catholic Church; the question of foreign recognition; and the women of independence.

The Church and Independence

The reaction of the clergy to the independence movements varied greatly from colony to colony and region to region. It also varied sometimes according to whose army was in control. Recent research permits a more precise appreciation of the reaction of the clergy to independence than was possible only a few years ago. The lower clergy throughout Spanish America were punished particularly hard by the Bourbon reforms at the end of the colonial period. Curtailing the privilege of personal immunity in criminal cases aroused not only members of the local clergy, but also their supportive parishioners. Perhaps more important, however, were the economic reforms, especially the attack on the chantries and pious works (discussed on pp. 18–20). These reforms seriously undercut the modest economic position of the lower clergy, who were often dependent solely on these sources for their meager incomes. As a result, members of the lower clergy were involved in practically all of the early schemes for independence, but the following examples will demonstrate how varied their attitudes could be. In large numbers the lower clergy supported independence, and this was the case in the Río de la Plata. There the lower as well as the upper clergy in general favored independence from Spain, but tended to oppose the liberal religious reforms of the 1820s passed in the Río de la Plata after the break with Spain.[27]

On the other hand, in Mexico the situation was more complex. Most lower clergy in Mexico also appear to have supported the independence movement, and even apart from priests like Hidalgo and Morelos others bore arms in the patriot insurgency. Some clergymen remained neutral, an affront to the traditional royalist regime that also may have aided the patriot cause.[28] However, some lower clergy supported or even fought with the royalists.

With the establishment of the liberal government and the new *Cortes* in

Spain after Riego's revolt in 1820, the situation changed markedly. The *Cortes* passed laws so radical that they forced important members of the Mexican upper clergy to join the independence movement, but in the hope of preserving their privileges. Among other things, the laws of 1820 ended clerical immunity in civil cases, and prohibited ecclesiastical institutions from acquiring additional real estate.

Foreign Recognition

Great Britain and the United States engaged in a spirited rivalry over Spanish America. Both wanted to dominate the new and gigantic commercial market represented by the former colonies. Neither was interested in territorial aggrandizement, although some North Americans had a fancy for certain contiguous lands as well as for Cuba. The United States could more easily support the independence movement openly since it professed no sympathy for monarchy, as Great Britain did, of course. Yet the United States was restricted by the negotiations with Spain that led to the acquisition of Florida.

Spanish Americans thought that recognition by either of these two powers probably would bestow legitimacy, and therefore irrevocability, on their independence. The new nations concentrated their efforts on Great Britain and sent diplomats there, but these novices were in for tough times in London. The plight of the Chilean representative, José de Irisarri, was somewhat typical.

Irisarri arrived in London in 1818, displaying boundless optimism. Since his primary goal was to secure recognition, he set out to impress the London community. He quartered himself well, rode around town in a fine carriage replete with liveried coachmen, and invited influential people to his residence. All this was designed to suggest that many well-placed people had an interest in the future of Chile. Before the end of 1818, however, the limited funds that the Chilean government could afford to send him put an end to this grandiose scheme, and by 1819 he was relegated to life in a boardinghouse. Perhaps the knowledge that other Spanish American representatives with similar schemes already had ended up in debtors' prison induced him to reduce his expenditures. At any rate, his first diplomatic efforts were not successful. He focused his attention on the foreign minister, Lord Castlereagh, hoping to convince him of the advantageous nature of recognition to all concerned. But he was forced to do this indirectly, since Castlereagh continually refused to meet with the Chilean plenipotentiary because such a meeting would have been construed by some as tantamount to recognition. In 1819 the British government decided to maintain a policy of strict neutrality in the Spanish American wars, thus permitting the foreign minister to greet the Spanish American representatives officially without offending anyone. This change in policy was actually a form of *de facto* recognition.

It was the United States that first officially recognized the independence of the Spanish American nations. In March 1822, President Monroe sent a message to Congress in which he recognized the independence of Chile, Argentina, Peru, Colombia, and Mexico. Great Britain did not recognize the independence of any of the new nations until the very end of December 1824 (announced publicly early in the new year), when it recognized Mexico, Colombia, and Argentina. Recognition by the United States occurred prior to the final battles of independence, two years before the battle at Ayacucho. Recognition by Great Britain was less bold; it took place after Ayacucho and after the proclamation of Monroe's celebrated "hands-off" message of 1823. As the years passed, both the United States and Great Britain added other nations to the list of those they had recognized already as independent.

With Great Britain's recognition, the political independence of Spanish America was irreversible. Economic independence was another matter—in this arena, battles were still to be fought.

The Women of Independence

It was common for women to accompany military forces during campaigns. They served as cooks, menders, and nurses, and they helped to acquire essential supplies. Although historians have greatly expanded our knowledge of women and their place in Spanish American history, there has been too little research concerning the active role played by women during independence. Nor, unfortunately, has there been sufficient research concerning the ways in which independence improved women's political rights and raised their political consciousness.[29] Both sides relied on the support of women during the struggles for independence. Many were patriots, but there were also many royalists. Patriot women participated actively through their efforts in propaganda, by conveying secret messages, and, in the case of Mexico at least, by literally seducing royalist troops to desert to the patriots.[30] On one occasion in Mexico, patriot women under the cover of a picnic delivered a printing press to the patriot troops. For their efforts some patriot women in Mexico were imprisoned and even executed.

Patriot women came from all segments of society. In many aristocratic families of Spanish America, the husband was a peninsular and the wife a creole, and sometimes political tension disrupted family life. In fact, many families were split over the issue of independence. When the conspiracy at Querétaro in 1810 was discovered by the royalists, the wife of the *corregidor* of Querétaro, Doña María Josefa Ortiz de Domínguez, found out and warned the rebels. It was this alert that caused Hidalgo to call his parishioners to revolt in September 1810, months before originally planned. Doña María—*La Corregidora,* as she is known in Mexican history—was imprisoned.

The great heroine of Mexican independence was Doña Leona Vicario of Mexico City. Doña Leona was an orphan of great wealth who supported the patriot cause, even though her uncle and guardian was a royalist. Doña Leona gave money to the rebels, but she also provided arms, recruited patriot soldiers, and provided information, which she sent by secret code. In March 1813 she was imprisoned, and later her property was confiscated. Escaping from jail, she joined the rebel army of José María Morelos. Riding with the rebel army, she controlled its finances, while supervising the care of the ill and injured. She also married a rebel, her uncle's former law clerk, Andrés Quintana Roo, and in 1817 she gave birth to her first child, in a cave in Achipixtla. The rebel government declared her a national heroine, and the first congress of independent Mexico granted her a hacienda, along with several houses in Mexico City, both as a recognition of her great contributions and as a means to recompense her for financial losses on behalf of the patriot cause.

Doña Leona's activities were exceptional, but with regard to the patriot (and royalist) activities of women generally throughout Spanish America, we have only begun to scratch the surface of historical knowledge.

6

The Independence Leaders as Liberals

The Spanish American independence movements began as civil wars between the colonies and the mother country, although frequently internal civil wars erupted over such issues as control of territory, resources, and customs houses. In the long run, the civil wars for independence produced revolutionary changes for Indians, castes, slaves, and, indeed, whites.

There were, however, immediate social gains during the period of warfare, especially for people of color. Many male slaves were emancipated by both sides on the condition that they serve in the armies, usually for lengthy periods; many perished and many deserted, but thousands survived to become free. Free men of color found opportunities during the independence wars that had not existed under the colonial regime. A few free colored patriots became generals, and at least one an admiral (although he was executed for treason by the patriots), while hundreds became officers and noncommissioned officers. A few men of mixed blood later became the presidents of their countries. After independence, the possibilities for upward socioeconomic mobility and access to educational and bureaucratic opportunities for people of African descent were vastly greater than in Cuba and Puerto Rico, which remained Spanish colonies. Nevertheless, comprehensive social change for people of color and for the rest of the population was slow in coming, with the exception of Francia's long and deep Paraguayan dictatorship.

In fact, very few leaders of the independence movements advocated radical social change, even though the early constitutions incorporated universal manhood suffrage, a fundamental element of what we refer to as democracy in the twentieth century. The founding fathers of the Spanish American nations adopted a republicanism that, in theory, brought the entire free male population into the active citizenry—thus shattering a basic premise of colonial government, namely, rule by a small elite of aristocrats and other people of wealth and high accomplishment. After centuries

ATLANTIC

OCEAN

MEXICO

Mexco
City

Vera
Cruz

Acapulco

Guatemala

CUBA
(Sp.)

PUERTO RICO
(Sp.)

JAMAICA
(Br.)

HAITI
(Ind.)

CENTRAL
AMERICA

Caracas

Panama

VENEZUELA

GUIANAS

Bogotá

COLOMBIA

Quito

ECUADOR

BRAZIL

PACIFIC

PERU

Lima

OCEAN

Bahia

La Paz

BOLIVIA

Charcas

Rio De Janeiro

PARAGUAY

Asunción

ARGENTINE
PROVINCES

CHILE

URUGUAY

Santiago

Concepción

Buenos Aires

Montevideo

ATLANTIC

OCEAN

**SPANISH AMERICA
AT THE END OF
THE WARS OF INDEPENDENCE**

of colonial rule, all free adult males theoretically were permitted to vote and to participate in the political process for the first time. But an enormous gap existed between theory and reality.

All of the national constitutions of the time incorporated restrictions that could disqualify adult males from active citizenship, such as being unemployed or not having an independent source of income. At times, the franchise was denied to agricultural workers, domestic employees, and people in debt to the public treasury. Literacy was also usually required for full political participation, which meant generally that the early constitutions eliminated nearly the entire adult male population from active citizenship and, therefore, from the franchise itself. These were common restrictions throughout the Atlantic world, including the United States, Great Britain, and France, where very few adult males were permitted to vote in elections. Yet, in Mexico between 1820 and 1835 a larger percentage of adult males were permitted to vote than was the case in the United States, Great Britain, or France.[1]

Significantly, however, the Spanish American founding fathers had taken a momentous step forward in their definition of citizenship. No free adult male of sound mind was permanently excluded from citizenship or the franchise, regardless of race. Thus the Chilean constitution of 1822 and the Bolivian constitution of 1826 both established a literacy requirement for citizenship, but postponed the date that it would take effect for 10 years, presumably allowing enough time for all adult males to learn to read and write. Other constitutions allowed an even longer period of grace. Nineteenth-century Liberals were shaped by the Enlightenment, and therefore they were optimistic and confident about human potential: They believed that all free men could raise themselves to the level required for active citizenship and participation in public affairs. There was a dark side to this optimism, however, since early nineteenth-century governments did not possess the fiscal resources to provide adequate public education, and economies weakened by war could not provide opportunities to lift the masses above the level of perpetual impoverishment. Yet, even though social and economic progress occurred at glacial speed, more and more people joined the active citizenry and gained the franchise. By the last decades of the nineteenth century, a significant number of males had become enfranchised, thus making fundamental political reform possible.

Until universal manhood suffrage became a reality, people of wealth and standing would govern on behalf of the common good—the *bien común*. The justification of elite rule was based on traditional Spanish political theory modified to fit nineteenth-century realities. Local elites asserted this right during times of crisis, such as the 1765 Rebellion of the Barrios in Quito. Following independence, the establishment of high property and income qualifications for officeholding in the new republics artificially created the necessity for the elite to govern in the name of the "people." The founding fathers saw no contradiction in supporting republican ideals and limiting political participation.

Many of the new republics passed laws of free womb, which emancipated children who were born to slaves. It was common, however, for these freed children to serve long apprenticeships, a *de facto* bondage. Some nations ended the international slave trade and passed ameliorative legislation, while others abolished slavery altogether, as did Chile in 1823, Central America the following year, and Mexico in the 1830s. Uruguay abolished slavery in 1842, but Argentina, Bolivia, Peru, Colombia, Venezuela, and Ecuador did not fully emancipate all slaves until the 1850s. The most egalitarian republic, Paraguay, did not end the slave trade and pass a law of free womb until 1842, after Francia's death, and it did not abolish slavery until 1869.

The independence movements were led by the *ciudadanía activa,* the active citizenry: the oligarchy and people on the way up from the middle and lower ranges of society. Others fought for independence by generally doing what they were told, with little appreciation for the consequences of their actions. Though all sectors of society contributed to the political character of the new nations, the active citizenry wrote the constitutions and shaped the new polities. It is, therefore, important to know more about this group.

By and large, the leaders of Spanish American independence were Liberals, in the nineteenth-century sense of the term. It was Liberalism heavily influenced by Locke and Montesquieu, just like the Liberalism of Thomas Jefferson, James Madison, and Alexander Hamilton. Many Spanish American Liberals, like Pueyrredón of Argentina, Bello of Venezuela and Chile, and Mora of Mexico, were also influenced by Jeremy Bentham's utilitarianism. Utilitarianism is known to generations of students as the political philosophy that judged the value of legislation by the degree to which it brought the greatest good to the greatest number of people. It was also a political philosophy of individualism, which argued that individuals should be as unrestricted in their activities as possible since, as Bentham said, "they are the best judges of their own interest."[2] Utilitarianism was essential to the active citizenry and it informed their Liberalism. Some, like José María Luis Mora, found additional instruction for their Liberalism in the writings of the Frenchman Benjamin Constant, who was particularly concerned about protecting individual liberties by strengthening intermediate governmental agencies, such as provincial judiciaries. Mora strongly advocated trial by jury in criminal cases, which did not exist under Spanish rule. Nevertheless, Mora's Liberalism was based on the belief that only property owners should participate in the political process.

Nineteenth-century Liberals were clearly not democrats in the sense of Rousseau's general will, and in fact they wrote constitutions that, like the United States Constitution, carefully guarded against *democracy* in the eighteenth and early nineteenth-century meaning of the term. There were democrats or men with democratic leanings among them, like Carrera of Chile; but these men were quickly repressed and their ideas pushed aside for nearly a half century. Some Spanish American Liberals, like Mariano Moreno of Buenos Aires, invoked the name of Rousseau to justify their revolts for independence. However, they interpreted Rousseau's ideas about kings and the governed in terms that were strikingly similar to those expressed by the Spanish thinker Francisco Suárez. That is, fundamental elements of Rousseau's philosophy were quite similar to elements of traditional Spanish political theory. Even so, when Mariano Moreno translated and printed the *Social Contract* to justify the Buenos Aires revolt for independence, he did so selectively, deleting the religious sections that offended him. Moreno wrote: "Since Rousseau had the misfortune to rant and rave when he dealt with religion, I suppressed that chapter and the principal passages in which he has treated these matters."[3]

Moreno and countless other leaders throughout the colonies desired the establishment of what they considered to be freedom of the press. They had lived under an intolerable press censorship, and independence increased their desire for freedom of expression. As nineteenth-century Liberals their concept of freedom of expression was limited, but within the confines of their own conception of society, they undoubtedly thought they were advocating complete freedom of expression. Again, Moreno wrote: "At last we perceive that the masses of the people will exist in shameful barbarism if they are not given complete liberty to speak on any matter. . . . " This statement embodied unambiguous Liberal theory. But Moreno finished the sentence with the pragmatic qualification: "as long as it is not in opposition to the holy truths of our august religion and the decisions of the government, which are always worthy of our greatest respect."[4]

Under the broad umbrella of nineteenth-century Liberalism, there existed a wide and frequently eclectic range of practical political choice, from liberalism to conservatism. Usually, liberals favored free trade and low tariffs, a diminished role for the Catholic Church, including secular education, and militaries of modest and controllable size. The conservative elements favored a more restricted trade with higher tariffs, a strong presence for the Church, including Church-run education, and strong militaries. Conservatives were more likely to support presidential dictatorships and military rule, and in Mexico they advocated monarchy. It is important to bear in mind, however, that many politically active people were liberal in one area and conservative in another. Thus, some people were "liberal" about matters of trade and "conservative" when it came to Church privileges.

Landowners and merchants frequently found their economic needs in conflict with their general political preferences. Mariano Moreno represented the organization of large landowners, the *Junta de Hacendados,* in 1809; and on its behalf he wrote his now famous *Memorial of the Hacendados,* in which he argued for free trade with England. These large landowners needed free trade in order to sell their products, as did agrarians in many other parts of Spanish America. Nevertheless, there were landowners who favored low tariffs for some agricultural products and high protective tariffs for others. Similarly, there were merchants during the late colonial period who favored a freer trading system, but later desired the perpetuation of monopoly and restricted trade. There were also pragmatists who favored free trade as a means of gaining recognition by Britain or the United States. As in the greater Atlantic world, it was essentially a belief in the sanctity of private property and unfettered socioeconomic opportunity that brought coherence to the disparate parts of nineteenth-century Liberalism (and which accounted for the attractiveness of utilitarianism among the active citizenry).

In fact, the issue of monarchy during the early nineteenth century is really quite academic. The statesman irrevocably committed to either monarchy or republicanism was rare indeed. José Miguel Carrera of Chile was one of the few who clearly opposed monarchy. José de San Martín favored monarchy, although it does not appear that he became thoroughly convinced that it was the best form of government for Peru until fairly late. By that time Simón Bolívar had switched from his earlier monarchical leanings to republicanism, albeit autocratic republicanism. These were the extremes. Most of the early Spanish American statesmen seem to have preferred either the British system of limited monarchy or the United States variety of republicanism. Many leaders were pragmatic and would have functioned comfortably under either form of government.

The issue of monarchy was for many Spanish American leaders more a matter of diplomacy than of ideology. Bernardo O'Higgins, for example, supported both republicanism and monarchism at different times, in an effort to attract recognition from the United States or Great Britain. He would gladly have taken Chile in either direction if the decision guaranteed recognition from one or another of the great powers. As early as 1818 or 1820, British recognition might have led to a series of experiments with limited monarchies in Spanish America—any number that Britain would have deemed appropriate. After the initial period of constitution making, monarchism became attractive to some, especially to the "Conservatives" of Mexico, because it represented authoritarian government, continuity, and strong Church influence.

The Constitutions of Independence

The constitutions of the era of independence were expressions of nineteenth-century Liberalism. The economic character of this Liberalism was inspired by Adam Smith and his adroit popularizer and interpreter, Jean Baptiste Say, by the French physiocrats, and by the Spanish economic reformers of the late eighteenth century, especially Gaspar Melchor de Jovellanos. Politically, Liberalism found its sources in the examples of Great Britain and the United States as well as in revolutionary France. Spanish American Liberalism's most direct inspiration was the 1812 Liberal Cádiz constitution (to be discussed later). Almost all of the constitutions adopted during the first decades of independence were structurally consistent with the examples available from Europe and the United States.

However, a few Spanish American constitutions were exotic exceptions to the objectives sought by early nineteenth-century Liberalism. Francisco Miranda, veteran of the French and American revolutions, was an author of exotic constitutions. Two decades before the independence movement actually commenced in Venezuela, Miranda suggested to British officials the establishment of one independent government for all of Spanish America, including the territory from the Mississippi River to San Francisco Bay. At the head of the government would be an hereditary official, an Inca, called emperor. A bicameral legislature would include an upper house, or senate, comprised of lifetime appointees of the emperor (*caciques*); and a lower house, or chamber of communes, comprised of men appointed by the emperor for 5-year terms, with the possibility of reappointment. The emperor would also appoint the judiciary, all of whom would have life tenure. This constitution, however, was never seriously considered in Venezuela.

By 1808 Miranda had toned down his plan somewhat, proposing to British officials that 4 states be established on the "Colombian Continent." One state would include Mexico and Guatemala; a second, New Granada, Venezuela, and Quito; a third, Peru and Chile; and a fourth, the Río de la Plata. However, as already mentioned, by July Britain and Spain had signed a formal peace, and British troops were sent to the Iberian peninsula to aid the Spanish patriots against Napoleon's forces; the British, therefore, were not interested in Miranda's constitutional plan. Also in 1808, Miranda proposed a constitution for Venezuela that called for a unicameral legislature, and an elected dual executive, called Incas.

Sometimes foreign travelers and foreign diplomats suggested unsuitable constitutions that ignored local needs and culture. Especially notorious was the United States agent in Chile, Joel Roberts Poinsett, who achieved fame later as envoy to Mexico and perhaps even greater fame because of the flower named for him. A persistent and uncritical advocate of his country's form of government, he went out of his way to contact leading Chileans and convince them of the need for a constitution modeled on the United States example. He even drafted a constitution in July 1812, and presented it to José Miguel Carrera, the leader who was then in control of the Santiago government. True to his precepts, Poinsett's constitution called for an administration of three branches, with the executive being a *gran jefe* (great chief). Not surprisingly, the Chilean counterpart of the United States president would be at least 36 years old. It is remarkable that Poinsett displayed so little political acumen: Carrera was only 28 at the time! The document was not accepted.

Simón Bolívar: Writer of Constitutions

Simón Bolívar was the most famous proponent of exotic constitutions. He was also the most prolific writer of constitutions in the independence era, and he deserves special attention.

Bolívar was a nineteenth-century Liberal and a great admirer of the British constitutional system. He took his constitutional ideas from both the modern and ancient worlds; and although he firmly believed with Montesquieu (and traditional Spanish political theory) that laws should reflect the particular characteristics of the country in which they were formulated, he often grafted artificial limbs onto otherwise natural bodies. His views evolved and shifted as his military campaigns for independence progressed.

Bolívar's first public policy statement was given, as we have seen, in Cartagena in 1812, in the wake of Venezuela's failed First Republic. He now held the Republic's federalist constitution as mostly responsible for weakening its government. From that moment, Bolívar would be a dedicated advocate of central governments.

One of Bolívar's first substantial public statements on political theory and constitutions was his well-known Jamaica letter of 1815. In it he indicated a preference for paternalistic republics for Spanish America. He was not opposed to monarchy, but he considered the idea of a single monarch for all South America rather chimerical. In 1815 he thought that Mexico might become a constitutional monarchy, which later it did, for a while. "If any American republic is to have a long life," he wrote, "I am inclined to believe it will be Chile." Again he was correct as far as Chile was concerned, but other republics also endured. Bolívar added:

> Peru, on the contrary, contains two factors that clash with every just and liberal principle: gold and slaves. The former corrupts everything; the latter are themselves corrupt. The soul of a serf can seldom really appreciate true freedom. Either he loses his head in uprisings or his self-respect in chains. . . . I imagine that in Lima the rich will not tolerate democracy, nor will the freed slaves and *pardos* [the free colored of mixed ancestry] accept aristocracy. The former will prefer the tyranny of a single man, to avoid the tumult of rebellion and to provide, at least, a peaceful system. If Peru intends to recover her independence, she has much to do.[5]

He was not far wrong about Peru either.

In 1815 Bolívar elaborated his own ideas on governmental structure for New Granada. He thought that New Granada would unite with Venezuela if they both agreed to form a single republic. "Its government might follow the English pattern," he said, "except that in place of a king there will be an executive who will be elected, at most, for life, but his office will never be hereditary, if a republic is desired."[6] There would be an hereditary upper chamber, or senate, and a lower chamber modeled after the House of Commons. At this time Bolívar strongly desired a "*union*" of all the Spanish American states as a means of protecting and perpetuating the independence of all. He did not mean a single government for Spanish America, which he knew would fail. The ideal of unity would become one of Bolívar's favorite themes. At his insistence, a congress of representatives of American states met in Panama in 1826, but it was neither well attended nor popularly supported. In hindsight, it is clear that a "*union*" of Spanish American states required some sort of governmental apparatus, a confederation at the least, but this was merely a dream, even though support for a confederation went beyond Bolívar to include small but regionally important groups of articulate political leaders and bureaucrats.

As we have seen, by early 1819 Bolívar had established leadership over the various patriot bands, including the *llaneros* under Páez, and he had set up headquarters at Angostura, on the Orinoco River. He then called for a congress to meet at Angostura to draft a constitution for Venezuela, although much of the old colony remained under royalist control. In February he presented his constitutional objectives to the congress. He appeared to be a thoroughgoing republican, even arguing that frequent elections are necessary to prevent one person from gaining too much power. At the same time, he argued the apparently contradictory point that the executive in a republic required greater authority than a constitutional monarch. In fact, he declared, "let the entire system of government be strengthened. . . . Precisely because no form of government is so weak as the democratic, its framework must be firmer . . . " He suggested a legislature with an hereditary senate, following the British example of the House of Lords. An independent judiciary would be established, consistent with republican government. Bolívar lectured the delegates on the constitutional history of the world to justify the establishment of an Areopagus—a fourth branch that would be, in effect, a moral power—taken from the experience of Athens, Rome, and Sparta. This unique body which was not found in the English, United States, or French examples was to be a body of censors, with "jurisdiction over the youth, the hearts of men, public spirit, good customs, and republican ethics."[7]

The delegates at the Congress of Angostura were manifestly less under the Liberator's influence than one might imagine, considering his military importance at the time. They adopted his general plan for a constitution, but made important modifications. They dropped the idea of a fourth branch and modified Bolívar's suggestion for an hereditary senate, granting senators life terms. The presidency, however, was consistent with Bolívar's plan. Presidents would serve a four-year term and could be reelected for one term before having to step down for at least one term. The final constitution, without the Liberator's exotic trimmings, was very much like other Liberal codes of the period, and as such, it placed strong emphasis on the protection of private property and openly recognized two classes of citizens: active and passive. One of the qualifications for active citizenship, which meant the privilege of voting, was the ability to read and write. This qualification, however, would not go into effect until 1830; that is, the delegates, with their Liberal belief in the efficacy of legislation, were giving the uneducated a decade in which to become educated and thus participate in the suffrage.

As already noted, Bolívar was selected to be the first president, and then shortly afterward, he took his troops into New Granada, where he defeated the Spaniards at Boyacá. With this great success, Bolívar persuaded the Congress of Angostura—which already included delegates from parts of New Granada—to proclaim the creation of the Republic of Colombia, with Cúcuta as its provisional capital.

In 1821 a congress at Cúcuta wrote a constitution for the Republic of Colombia, superseding the preliminary constitution drafted at Angostura. The president was given a 4-year term, with one immediate reelection possible, and senators were given 8-year terms. From the results of the congress, it is difficult to gauge Bolívar's influence over the delegates, though it seems likely that Bolívar would have desired longer terms for the senators. The constitution was not burdened, however, by any of the Liberator's earlier exotic trappings. Francisco de Paula Santander was named vice president, and Bolívar became president, although he soon left his active post to continue his military campaigns.

From Colombia Bolívar carried the independence movement into Peru in 1823, but he did not become that country's president until 1826. Before this, he wrote his most celebrated constitution, the one for Bolivia. Since early 1825, Upper Peru had been under the control of the Liberator's most trusted general, José Antonio Sucre. In 1825, an assembly called by Sucre declared the independence of this region, which soon became known as Bolivia. Bolívar wrote the new country's constitution, and this document represents a second stage in the Liberator's political development. While he had strongly supported a powerful senate until about 1825, now he favored stronger presidential authority. He wanted the president to enjoy life tenure and the right to appoint his successor. The Bolivian constitution provided for a legislature of 3 houses: tribunes, senators, and censors. Again Bolívar wanted his Areopagus, and this time he got it. The censors were to preside over education and the press, and they were each given life terms. Tribunes were to serve for 4 years, and senators for 8. The country was divided into departments, each one administered by a prefect; the departments were divided into provinces, administered by governors, and provinces were subdivided into cantons, administered by *corregidores*. Notwithstanding the exotic frills, the Bolivian constitution was similar to other Liberal documents of the period, with a strong emphasis on individual freedoms and property rights. With only minor changes, the constitution was adopted by the delegates. As soon as he finished the document, Bolívar returned to Peru.

Bolívar wanted Peru to adopt the Bolivian constitution. The Peruvians agreed to do so, but only under the condition that Bolívar accept their presidency. The constitution was adopted with minor changes, and Bolívar became president of Peru. But again he left the scene without overseeing the implementation of a constitution, this time drawn away be the news of great political discord in Colombia.

The chamber of censors lasted only a few months in Peru before it was dismantled. Early in 1827 the Peruvian government was overthrown by the military, and a new constitution was proclaimed the following year. It established a 2-chamber legislature and a president who would be permitted a 4-year term, with the possibility of 1 immediate reelection.

By the time Bolívar reached Bogotá, the Republic of Colombia was already straining at the seams and nearly ready to break up. In Bogotá he actively assumed the presidency and tried to put things in order; and in 1827 he sought a new constitution. A constitutional assembly met at Ocaña in 1828, but the majority of the delegates were not under the Liberator's influence and refused to change the old constitution. Bolívar then withdrew his own delegates, and he soon broke with Santander. Ocaña marked the beginning of the end for the Liberator.

The Liberator's great political creation, the Republic of Colombia, could not be sustained. Because Peru had invaded Ecuador, Bolívar felt it necessary to leave Bogotá and travel to that troubled area; and by the time he returned, his position in Bogotá had grown tenuous. His authority was now being challenged on several fronts, and he could no longer hold the republic together. In late 1829, Páez took Venezuela out of the Republic of Colombia, and soon Juan José Flores did the same with Ecuador, becoming that country's first president. In March 1830 Bolívar resigned. Santander, exiled in 1828, returned to Bogotá in 1832, and he was elected president of New Granada, a post he held for four years.

The Liberator resigned, but it was clear to just about everyone that he was being exiled. His monumental achievement of independence for five countries was founded in his decision to form and lead a professional military, but in this is to be found the seeds of his ultimate failure. In prosecuting the wars of independence, Bolívar never remained in any capital long enough to build a political infrastructure with deep loyalties to him. The Liberator departed from Bogotá on his final journey on the morning of May 8, 1830. To accompany him during the initial moments of his journey were many military officers, diplomats, government officials, and civilians. As Bolívar rode off into the distance, the English minister observed, "He is gone, the gentleman of Colombia!" Bolívar left Manuela behind, but he wrote to her of his deep love: "My love, I love you very much. . . . I am always your most faithful lover" ("*Amor mío, mucho te amo. . . . Soy siempre tu más fiel amante*").

With his bodyguard of loyal soldiers, the Liberator made his way down the Magdalena River to the coast, where he expected to board a ship headed perhaps for England. His health was in fast decline. By the fall of 1830 his cough had severely weakened him; in the tropical heat, he wrapped himself in wool. On his deathbed he dictated his final message, telling the people of Colombia: "As I depart from your midst, my love for you tells me that I should make known my last wishes. I aspire to no other glory than the consolidation of Colombia."[8] His aspiration is a commentary on the tragedy of his public life. Shortly before, he had offered an even more stunning commentary: "We have ploughed the sea."[9] Bolívar died on December 17, 1830, at the age of 47, and he was buried in Colombia. There was such official hatred for him in Venezuela that his family was not able to transport his body to his homeland for 12 years. Eventually, however, his memory was honored, and he became the great hero of Venezuelan independence. In Venezuela today, Simón Bolívar enjoys a status similar to that of George Washington in the United States, and he is even more revered.

Constitutional Structures

Only a few of the constitutions written during the first decades following 1810 were burdened by exotic and irrelevant trappings. The others were clearly within the mainstream of late eighteenth and early nineteenth-century constitution making in the revolutionary Atlantic world. The leaders of Spanish American independence found inspiring examples in the United States Constitution and in the constitutions of the French Revolution. They drew on these sources, as well as on traditional Spanish political theory that had been updated by the Enlightenment and presented finally in the 1812 constitution of Cádiz.

The Cádiz constitution, which provided for limited constitutional monarchy, was the culmination of the Liberal movement in Enlightenment Spain. Its essence was notably Spanish, but its ideas were couched in the vocabulary of the French revolutionary constitutions. When the *Cortes* (parliament) met in 1812, very few written constitutions existed anywhere in the world, and four of them were French: those of 1791, 1793, 1795, and 1799. The French codes were undoubtedly influenced, in turn, by the United States Constitution (and the state constitutions of the United States), but the Cádiz delegates quite often took their wording directly from one or another of the French documents. Many clauses, in fact, were direct translations from the French constitutions. This does not mean that the Cádiz delegates were lifting ideas; rather they were simply and expeditiously seeking a guide for expressing their own views.

The 1812 constitution of Cádiz incorporated ideas that were progressive in their time. For instance, the constitution ended press censorship and restricted the activities of the Church. It also terminated the traditional all-powerful monarchy and replaced it with a limited monarchy. The liberal decrees of the constitutional convention fired up many marginal patriots in the colonies and turned them into active participants in the independence movement.

One step taken by the *Cortes* was a great boon to the independence movement. It had been estimated at the time of the *Cortes* that 15 to 16 million people lived in the Spanish American colonies and the Philippines and that only about 10.5 million lived in Spain itself. Thus, based on the one man, one vote principle, representation in the *Cortes* and in future parliamentary bodies would have given a majority of votes to colonial residents rather than to Spaniards. Spanish control was guaranteed by Article 22 of the constitution, which excluded the colored castes from the status of citizenship and therefore from the franchise. The article was passed after a vigorous debate by a vote of 108 to 36, at a time when there were more than 50 Spanish American delegates at the *Cortes*. The dilemma for some colonists was that the colonies could gain equal or majority representation in the *Cortes* only if the colored castes were granted citizenship and enfranchised, and apparently, some colonists chose to vote for the exclusionary Article 22. Racial discrimination against people of color was thus incorporated into the constitution. This turned out to be an effective propaganda tool for the independence leaders in the colonies; it served to encourage Spanish Americans of African descent to join the armies of independence.

The political ideas of the Spanish American founding fathers were expressed in both centralist and federalist constitutions. The federalist constitutions were usually more innovative, better attuned to the needs of new nations as a whole, and more nearly a reflection of the aspirations of regional (and not always marginal) power groups. They were natural reactions to the Spanish American colonial experience that favored central regions to the detriment of the provinces. Yet federalist constitutions were unable to satisfy the desires of controlling power blocs in the new nations, and they eventually failed everywhere. Centralist constitutions, on the other hand, sometimes proved more durable during the tumultuous years of early nationhood; strong central government, however, stunted local and regional institutions and inhibited provincial economic development. A discussion of some of the early constitutions will permit an appreciation of the character of the political thinking—the Liberalism—that informed the era. For the moment we shall concentrate on centralist constitutions.

Chile and Uruguay were the only two Spanish American nations whose constitutions written before the end of 1833 lasted until the twentieth century. Both were centralist. The Argentine constitution of 1853, which was not replaced until 1949, was the longest lived of all Spanish American constitutions, and although it had certain federalist trappings, it was effectively a centralist document, too.

Chile had its first constitution, a provisional document, as early as 1812. This short code gave executive authority to a 3-man junta, but the executive authority was sharply limited by a senate of 7 members. Here, then, appeared what would become one of the central characteristics of Chilean constitutional history: Strong executives were balanced by strong congresses.

Chile's next constitution was promulgated in 1818, after the country won its independence. It, too, was a provisional code. Until a congress was called (and as it turned out that would not be for several years), the legislative branch comprised a senate of only 5 members, selected by the chief executive, Supreme Director Bernardo O'Higgins. The primary purpose of the senate was to ensure the observance of the constitution. It was given the broad and effective powers that legislatures commonly possess in a republican form of government. Senate approval was required on all important matters, such as "imposing taxes, soliciting loans, declaring war, making peace, forming treaties of alliance, commerce, neutrality; sending ambassadors, consuls, deputies or envoys to foreign powers; raising new troops or sending them outside the State; undertaking public works and creating new authorities or employs." The senate could pass a law over the supreme director's veto, and provision was made for amending the constitution.

This constitution remains a frequently misinterpreted document. Since the senators were not elected, but appointed by the supreme director, it has seemed to many that the supreme director merely created a puppet legislature to lend respectability to his regime. It is often suggested that O'Higgins reserved unlimited powers for himself. This may have been his intent, but as it turned out, the Chilean senate proved to be a viable, energetic legislature.

The heart of the Chilean Liberal system was the senate, as in a few years it would be the congress. This was also true of the rest of republican Spanish America, with the exception of Paraguay. Far too much has been made of presidential power, perhaps because presidents sometimes ignored or suspended legislative and judicial institutions and bestowed on themselves extraordinary powers. As a result, the importance of congresses to the Liberal system is often overlooked. Strong congresses, like the one in Chile, contributed greatly to political stability. The strength and independence of the Chilean senate created by the constitution of 1818 reveals much about Chilean Liberalism. This body constantly reviewed the supreme director's actions, often overruling him on critical issues.

Chile's next constitution was drafted in 1822. The three familiar branches were established, with the legislature now bicameral—a chamber of deputies and a court of representatives. The chamber was granted broad powers and was clearly the more powerful of the two legislative houses, reminiscent of the unicameral legislative body created by the 1812 Cádiz constitution. To the Liberal mind, the court of representatives was an eminently logical agency of government. It was a permanent body of 7 members elected by the chamber, and at least 4 had to be deputies. While the chamber was not in session, the court of representatives was charged with safeguarding the constitution. The framers of the constitution were particularly concerned with protecting constitutional freedoms; and the court was an appropriate instrument to guarantee these freedoms.

After a provincial rebellion overthrew O'Higgins in January 1823, a new constitution was adopted. Additional constitutions appeared in 1826 and 1828, but the most important early constitution was accepted in 1833, and it endured until 1925.

Credit for the success of the constitution of 1833 is generally given to Diego Portales, the merchant son of the former superintendent of the royal mint in Santiago, who in 1829 organized the *pelucón* government (*pelucón* meant big-wig, a derisive term used by their political opponents). Many historians believe that Portales dominated the *pelucón* government and created an authoritarian presidential state based on an alliance of the landed oligarchy, the military, and the clergy. In reality, the core of the *pelucón* alliance was a large intermixed group of merchants, miners, and landowners. Portales himself was never president, and he had less influence in the *pelucón* government than is generally supposed. He had little to do with the drafting and passage of the constitution of 1833. In fact, the government did not draft a proposal for a constitution, nor did it offer unified support for any of the three drafts presented by different delegates at the constitutional convention. Yet Portales did set the pattern and tone of the new government shortly after the *pelucones* seized power. The new government was to be clearly civilian and impersonal. One of Portales's first steps was to reduce the size of the military officer corps and to create a civil militia as a counterweight to the professional army. Other merchants, such as Manuel Rengifo, became the heart of the new bureaucracy, placing their loyalty in the system, not in the president.

Although presidents, serving generally 2 consecutive 5-year terms, had considerable power and controlled patronage, until the end of the century the administration of government was generally characterized by the rule of law rather than by the personal whim of individual leaders or parties. The Chilean success was partly due to the strength of congress. In fact, congresses were empowered everywhere in Spanish America, except in Paraguay. When Spanish American chief executives became dictators, this usually happened in spite of constitutions, not because of them.

The Chilean constitutions were representative of the other Liberal codes of the period. Running through them was a vigorous emphasis on law and order, the protection of individual freedoms, and the sanctity of private property. Even when a constitution might aim to restrict large landed estates, it still emphatically protected private property rights in general. In one way or another, they all mentioned and were dedicated to the theme stated in the Argentine constitution of 1815: "*la Libertad, la Igualdad, la Propiedad y la Seguridad*" (Liberty, Equality, Property and Security).

Federalist constitutions were almost always advocated by the provinces (or later by states), but sometimes they also found support in central regions. Only one federalist constitution, however, was the creation of a central region. The Venezuelan code of 1811 was crafted in Caracas without representation by several provinces. Yet the constitution, which endured only about a year, granted the provinces extraordinary autonomy. There is little doubt that the federal constitution adopted in December of 1811 was considerably inspired by Francisco Miranda, but it is also clear that many delegates were influenced by the United States Constitution and the constitutions of several North American states. The delegates had in their hands Thomas Paine's *La Independencia de la Costa Firme...*, a Spanish translation done in Philadelphia in 1811, which included appendixes of the United States Constitution and the constitutions of Massachusetts, Pennsylvania, and Virginia. In addition to these sources, the delegates borrowed from the French revolutionary documents. It should be remembered, too, that this Venezuelan code was written prior to the Cádiz constitution of 1812.

The Venezuelan Federal Constitution of 1811 was a typically Liberal document, dedicated, like the 1815 Argentine constitution, to the preservation and enhancement of the fundamental rights of man: "*la libertad, la igualdad, la propiedad y la seguridad.*" Like so many other codes of the period, this one attempted to establish civil authority over the military—partly by emphasizing the importance of a civil militia: "A well regulated and trained militia, composed of the citizenry, is the most suitable and secure natural defense of a free State." But the constitution also provided for a three-man executive authority, perhaps because of Miranda's influence. The First Republic endured only a half-year after the completion of the constitution of 1811, and on more than one occasion, Bolívar later stated that the failure of the constitution was due to the provision for a plural executive. Yet when he returned to Caracas in 1813 Bolívar established an equally impermanent centralist regime.

There was another federalism more theoretical and sophisticated than the type that was adopted in Venezuela in 1811. Derived from the writings of Benjamin Constant, it was espoused perhaps especially by José María Luis Mora of Mexico. Mora sought to strengthen intermediate agencies like judiciaries and town councils, and to make these agencies the basis of a federalism that would limit the powers of the central government in favor of expanding individual liberties. But this was theoretical federalism, and while its logic may have been compelling, it was not regional federalism, the kind of federalism widely attempted in Spanish America.

The federalism most suited to Spanish America was the brand advocated by the provinces. Federalism was their way of establishing a government balanced between regional needs and central power—which is to say that the provinces attempted to neutralize the commanding power and influence held by the capital regions during the colonial period. Apart from Mora's theoretical federalism, this federalism in the provinces was the most interesting, most creative constitutionalism of the independence era. It failed everywhere because capital regions, with their vested interests and traditional authority, (though they often also had some federalists) were too powerful for the provincial leaders, who were not always united in their efforts and frequently depended on the capitals for revenue derived from foreign trade. In some countries, however, and perhaps most notably in Mexico, federalism failed partly because some states were determined not to send their tax revenues to the capital when they were sorely required within the states; and the national (that is, federal) congress would not legislate the new taxes necessary to meet the administrative and developmental needs of the country at large.

Federalists were found across the political spectrum. Many of them gravitated toward the more "liberal" side of nineteenth-century politics, since liberal politics generally permitted greater provincial or state autonomy than did conservative politics. This was especially true in Mexico, where between 1820 and 1835 federalists enfranchised a much larger percentage of the population than did the centralists, who succeeded them to political power. Mexican federalists also led the liberal attack on Church privilege. Yet federalism sometimes meant conservative reaction; this was the case in Argentina, where federalists led the fight in support of Church privileges, under the banner of *Religión o Muerte* (Religion or Death). To some, turning power over to the provinces created an opportunity for local one-man or family rule—as indeed was the case in Argentina—and when liberals understood this, they usually advocated centralism.

All three constitutional projects considered by the convention that drafted Chile's code of 1833 provided for provincial assemblies, and these assemblies were approved by the delegates. However, Manuel José Gandarillas—who was both the editor of the government's official newspaper, *El Araucano,* and an active public critic of the conservative point of view at the convention—proposed the abolition of provincial assemblies. The convention discussed the motion on one day, then adopted it the next day. Among government leaders, Gandarillas was something of an ultraliberal. More than any other active participant in the convention, Gandarillas held the line for the preservation of the truly liberal features of the constitution of 1828; and yet he was responsible for one of the most enduring characteristics of the new constitution—the organic basis of a strong central government. Gandarillas was a liberal who understood that provincial assemblies sometimes could be anything but liberal.

The controversies surrounding the federalist-centralist debate were among the gravest problems faced by many of the new nations. Some countries, like Chile, managed to resolve the issues fairly quickly and effectively; but others—Argentina, for example—experienced a difficult time. Even when the debate between federalism and centralism did not interrupt a country's stability for too long a time, as in Chile, a working formula had to be reached. Chile's central region generally dominated national politics, but to secure the allegiance of southern elites the government recruited many of Chile's early leaders, its supreme directors, and then its presidents from the south. Other countries, however, had a more difficult time in working out a solution. The relationship between the federalist–centralist controversy and stability will be discussed in Chapter 7; here, more must be said of the political ideas represented by federalism, and examples drawn from two different countries may provide a better understanding of these ideas.

Uruguay

In the colonial period, the Banda Oriental fell under the jurisdiction of the Viceroyalty of the Río de la Plata, whose capital was Buenos Aires. When Montevideo decided upon independence, it wanted a federalist confederation rather than a centralist nation to be created out of the old viceroyalty.

The leader of the federalist movement in the Banda Oriental was José Gervasio Artigas, who brought Montevideo and the Banda Oriental provinces together in the effort to gain independence from both Spain and Buenos Aires. In 1813, as a constituent assembly met in Buenos Aires to draft a constitution for the former viceroyalty, the Banda Oriental held its own congress to decide on the position its delegates would take toward the Buenos Aires assembly. To the Oriental representatives, Artigas presented a plan for a federalist confederation, which may be the most extreme statement of federalism made during the entire Spanish American independence period. The Banda Oriental would maintain an extraordinary degree of autonomy in what Artigas conceived of as a confederation. He took pains to ensure that Buenos Aires would not dominate trade in the Plate region.

Because Buenos Aires wanted centralism, the five Oriental delegates sent to the Buenos Aires convention were refused admittance. But for the moment, Buenos Aires's ambitions were doomed to failure. As we have seen, several Argentine provinces shared the federalist sentiments of Artigas; and they soon joined him in his *Liga Federal* and the fight against Buenos Aires's hegemony.

Mexico

The basis of Mexican federalism was fundamentally economic. Many Mexicans in the provinces sought a federalist state so that the overweening power of the capital city might be reduced, making regional economic development possible. For example, during the late colonial period a glaring rivalry existed between the merchants of Veracruz and Mexico City. There was also a rivalry between the residents of Veracruz and those of Tampico, since both wanted their respective ports improved and opened to international trade. In 1812 a Mexican delegate to the Cádiz convention, Miguel Ramos Arizpe, published a book (republished in Mexico in 1813) that advocated a federalist approach to Mexico's economic development; specifically, Arizpe called for improvements for the north–central region. Later, the crown took steps to improve regional facilities, including opening the port of Tampico to international trade. With the overthrow of Iturbide, however, the issue of federalism flared, and the result was the federalist constitution of 1824.

The Mexican constitution of 1824 granted considerable autonomy to the states. It provided for a republic whose primary inspiration was the Constitution of the United States. However, some Mexican federalists, like Mora, found the wellspring of their federalism in the writings of French theorists like Benjamin Constant. Furthermore, there had been a recent structural impulse toward federalism. The Cádiz constitution created Provincial Deputations to govern broad provincial regions. These bodies superseded previous authorities, including the viceroyalty itself. The former viceroy, whose title was now abolished, became technically the Political Chief of the Provincial Deputation of Mexico, which was one among 6 autonomous deputations created first, with others added later. Ferdinand's reinstatement of the 1812 constitution in early 1820 reaffirmed the Provincial Deputations. By the end of 1822, 17 Deputations were authorized for Mexico, and the unauthorized Deputation of New Mexico had also been created. By the end of the following year, 1823, 23 Provincial Deputations were functioning in Mexico. By the 1820s the authority and power of the Deputations had expanded well beyond their original sanction. In fact, by the end of 1823 some of the Deputations were politically autonomous.[10] Thus, the structural basis of a federal system was already in place before Mexicans sat down to write the constitution of 1824, which replaced the Deputations with states.

The federal constitution of 1824 was noticeably typical of other constitutions of the period, and with its emphasis on individual freedoms and property rights it was a lineal descendant of the Apatzingán constitution of 1814. The 1824 constitution endured only about a decade, when it was replaced by a centralist code; yet during this decade and even afterward under centralist regimes, many advocates of federalism became powerful national figures and attempted to attend to the needs of the provinces. Often leaders with profoundly liberal leanings, like Valentín Gómez Farías and Benito Juárez, received their start in national politics through their experience in regional governorships.

Many political theories were extolled during the era of Spanish American independence, and the constitutions they produced ranged from the exotic to the truly practical, and from federalist to centralist. Mostly, the constitutions were derivative, even when they were brilliant, but this is not meant as criticism, since the same can be said as well about constitutions in both the United States and Europe. Finally, there was no lack of intelligence or awareness among those who crafted the Spanish American constitutions. Yet why many of these constitutions proved to be short-lived needs to be considered, and this is the subject of Chapter 7.

7

The Problems of Independence

Many of the problems faced by the new nations of Spanish America are well known and have been described by a countless number of writers. For a long time, emphasis has been placed on the issues of geography, transportation, race, and praetorianism (government by the military); the lack of qualified administrative personnel and the lack of political experience; the disruptive church-versus-state question; and the problems caused by conflicts between centralism and federalism. During the last two or more decades, the issue of neocolonialism has been seized upon as a central cause of economic retardation and even political instability in the new nations.

For convenience, we may divide the problems confronting the new nations into two broad categories: those relating to the more current topic of neocolonialism and world capitalism, and those of a general administrative nature. This chapter examines some of the problems in both categories, in the hope of providing a better understanding of the texture of early national life in Spanish America and the difficulties of independence.

The New Nations and World Capitalism

The Spanish American countries were colonies for centuries. Then, with relatively little anticipation, they were thrust upon the world capitalist scene as independent nations. And at the moment, there was little alternative. They might have joined in some form of common market or formed a sort of economic league; but these were unrealistic options for countries often at odds, even at war, with each other, over boundaries, the control of strategic ports, and the general balance of power. At about the same time that the stultifying but stable Paraguay withdrew into its own isolation, the unity of Central America tore apart, and Peru and Bolivia went to war with Chile. The chance to form a common market—which would have increased interregional trade, expanded potential markets, and enhanced economic specialization (that is, the division of labor)—was lost, and this, perhaps more than any other single factor, diminished the chance for maturing economically. In fact, in most parts of Spanish America, more intercolonial trade existed before independence than in the decades after 1810. In many parts of Spanish America the colonial system of compelled purchases had more thoroughly integrated Indian communities within regional economies—through their manufacture and sale of textiles and their sale of grains and animals—than was true in the early national period. With independence, the purchasing power of these communities declined, which, in turn, diminished the potential growth of national markets.

For both internal economic development and their participation in the world capitalist marketplace, the Spanish American nations faced serious deficiencies. The topography made trade difficult and limited the range of markets during the early national period, just as it had done during the colonial period. Not until after midcentury, when the railroad was introduced in the independent nations, were the effects of this enormous obstacle compensated for here and there. Even where railroads were built, some regional economies suffered as the result of a new onslaught of cheaper foreign manufactures.

The wars of independence devastated regional and national economies. Silver mines were abandoned and many filled with water. This great motor of the colonial economy was, for the most part, stopped cold. In 1803 there were hundreds of silver mines in Potosí, in Upper Peru, while two decades later there were only about 50 mines in operation, producing roughly half the amount of silver. In Mexico, so great was the damage to silver mines that while more than 26 million pesos were minted in 1809, less than 6 million were minted in 1821. This dramatic blow fell upon a Mexican economy that was seriously flawed and fragile even before the warfare erupted.[1] Furthermore, in Mexico as well as in many other colonies, there was a flight of capital as Spaniards departed during the independence period. Indeed, the early national economies faced a severe shortage of developmental capital.

This was a matter of great consequence. Not only did silver production decline precipitously and ominously, and agricultural production drop in areas of depredation, but so too did textile manufacturing—workers fled, *obrajes* were destroyed, and cheaper foreign (especially English) textiles drove local textiles off the market. This does not mean that there was no developmental capital within the new national economies, for there certainly was some, but there was not enough for broadly based economic growth. Capital moved to sectors of the economy that favored lenders in safety and return, rather than to where it might most be needed. This would not have been deleterious had there been sufficient capital to support investment needs across the economy.

Thus, when silver production increased during the early national period in Mexico, merchants loaned money to the miners rather than to cotton textile manufacturers who desperately needed it. At such moments, with silver production increasing significantly, Mexicans were able to import cheaper and better cotton textiles than could be manufactured inside the country. During periods of downturn in silver production, or times of European warfare, when silver could not be exported normally or European manufactures could not be imported according to demand, local manufacturing increased and Mexican merchants were willing to provide developmental capital. The cotton textile manufacturers of Puebla, for instance, were able to import modern technology during the 1830s and 1840s and increase their output; at such times, Puebla enjoyed the benefits of sufficient capital, imported technology, and an ample labor supply.

There appears to have been no absence in Mexico of these central inputs for industrial development, including the necessary managerial skills.[2] But this applies only to specific sectors of the economy. Investment capital did not sustain the cotton manufacturers during the long term. Furthermore, while there was ample factory labor, even in the skilled areas, it is questionable whether there was enough technical skill or developmental capital for the machines of the textile revolution to be produced in Mexico, or, for that matter, anywhere else in early national Spanish America. The market was simply too small to warrant the necessary inventiveness and investment. In some countries, the market was too small simply because the population was small. In the early nineteenth century there were countries in Spanish America with fewer people than the city of London, and others with large land masses and as few people as lived in London and Paris combined. Where populations were fairly large (as in Mexico, where approximately 6 million people lived in 1810), extreme differences in the distribution of wealth, coupled with comparatively high transportation costs, rendered the effective market insufficient for a full industrialization.

Nowhere in Spanish America was there an industrial development comparable to that of Britain or the United States, where machine shops, skilled labor, and capital combined to produce the machines that would produce the standardized parts of industrialization. One of the reasons for this must have been the availability of developmental capital in Britain and in the northeastern United States. (Why else did Eli Whitney locate his factory for fabricating his cotton gins in New Haven, Connecticut, rather than in the south, where he had invented the gin and where they would be sold? In New England he could raise the capital and find the necessary skilled labor.) In Spanish America, capital was startlingly more expensive than in Britain, the United States, or many other places.

Certainly the political and, in some regions, social instability must have discouraged many Spanish American capitalists from long-term investment, the kind that might have contributed to a more fundamentally sound industrialization. Frequent changes in government, while they were often superficial, could not have been encouraging to investors. Between 1824 and 1857, 16 presidents governed Mexico, in addition to 33 provisional national governments. That is, during a 33-year period Mexico lived through 49 national administrations. Perhaps even more perplexing to the investing capitalist, during the same period the ministry of finance changed hands 87 times.[3] Between 1821 and 1845 Peru lived through a change in government, on average, once a year.[4]

Although our knowledge of the availability of capital, its cost, and its relationship to Spanish American industrialization is extremely limited, we may assume that such administrative instability discouraged a willingness to loan capital for long duration at low interest. Routinely, Spanish Americans paid 2 or 3 times as much for their capital as did the British or North Americans. During the late 1820s Venezuelan planters paid 2 or 3 percent a month on short-term capital, that is, somewhere between 24 and 36 percent interest at a time when agriculturalists in Britain or the United States paid only a fraction of that amount. This comparative disadvantage prevailed even at the end of the 1830s, when interest rates fell to about 1 percent per month in Venezuela.[5] In post-independence Peru, much agricultural credit was provided by merchants. When they acquired a *hacendado*'s future crop through a consignment contract, merchants routinely granted short-term credit at 18 to 24 percent annual interest. Peruvian merchants also extended agrarians straight loans without regard to a future crop, at an annual interest of 24 to 30 percent.[6] In many of the new nations, manufacturers were forced to borrow at rates of interest that alone greatly diminished their ability to compete with imports. In the high cost of capital in newly emergent Spanish America there is inscribed a legacy of political and social unrest.

In almost every case, public revenues could not meet public expenditures. To pay for the wars of independence, the new governments had to resort to forced loans and the expropriation of royalist property. No new Spanish American country possessed the tradition or the financial capacity to issue interest-bearing bonds on the domestic capital market. They also increased their national debts by taking on foreign loans, for which they had to pay premium interest rates. From 1822 through 1825, 5 Spanish American countries floated loans in Britain, ranging from £167,000 to £4,750,000. Mexico floated 2 loans of £3,200,000 each. Peru floated 3 loans for a total of £1,200,616, and Colombia floated 2 loans for a total of £6,750,000. All of the securities had to be discounted, anywhere from about 10 to 30 percent, in order to make them publicly attractive. Yet all sold originally for even less than their discounted prices. Furthermore, commissions had to be paid. This means that the emergent nations had taken on additional debt that ranged from modest to nearly overwhelming levels, but they received only a part of the total loan value. Still, all had to repay total interest and principal on the face value of the loan. The Mexican loan of 1824, for instance, sold in Britain at only 58 percent of its principal.[7] Not only were these loans serious financial burdens on national treasuries; but they also were used generally for operating expenses and to shore up financially weakened administrations, rather than for capital improvements. The emergent nations thus began their independence with national debts and with an inability to balance their operating budgets.

It was almost impossible for an emergent nation to enter the world capitalist market and to protect all sectors of its economy. A high universal protective tariff potentially reduced markets for that nation's exports, while raising the costs on imports. Furthermore, there were strong incentives to encourage trade. The new national leaders understood the importance of recognition from one of the great powers, which were eager to trade with Spanish America. In this regard, new tariffs could be protective only selectively, but a liability of selective protection was the transfer of potential investment capital sometimes to the least efficient sectors of the economy. Additionally, while the wars of independence were being fought, the new nations needed certain manufactures, especially armaments, and they could acquire these only from abroad. Finally, many of the emergent nations saw tariffs as likely sources of governmental income, which was desperately needed. For this reason, they sometimes taxed exports, a money-raising procedure that reduced the competitiveness of some Spanish American products in the international marketplace.

In fact, some sectors of these new national economies suffered sharp and irremediable damage. Most importantly, the woolen and cotton textile industries were undermined in many regions by cheaper and better European goods. Europe, especially Britain, enjoyed clear comparative advantages over Spanish American textile manufacturing. The Europeans enjoyed the benefits of modern technology and machinery, low-cost capital, a generally ample amount of skilled and unskilled labor, and the advantage of shipping their higher quality goods cheaply, by sea, from Europe to Spanish America. Once the Boston merchants began to transfer their commercial capital into the textile industry during and just after the War of 1812, the United States enjoyed similar comparative advantages. Spanish Americans, with their backward technology, shortage of capital, and high-cost capital, could not compete. Argentina, Bolivia, Mexico, and many other countries experienced economic dislocation and lost opportunities.

Could the new nations have protected their economies more efficiently—especially textile manufacturing, that sector so universally central to the process of industrialization? The problem is complex, and is only now being elucidated by historians. In Argentina, for instance, British cotton cloth had begun to inundate the country by 1810, when 3 million yards of cheap calico and muslin were imported. By 1824 Argentina was importing more than 15 million yards of these cotton cloths, and some provincial regions could not possibly have financed a successful competing industry, especially when they had to produce something salable to pay for the imports. Could Argentina have protected a local cotton textile industry in face of its broader needs and the benefits from cheap British and then other foreign textiles? It seems doubtful. And it should be added that through innovative selling techniques—auctions and the sale of surplus— the British made cotton textiles available to the greater population, thus raising the general standard of living.[8]

Ideologues apart, Spanish Americans often found themselves adherents of free trade or, alternatively, of protection, according to current personal or national economic needs. Additional complexity was thus added to the difficult task faced by the emergent nations in their attempt to industrialize. Mexico, for instance, had a large textile manufacturing sector during the colonial period, but it was based on antiquated technology, and it could not withstand the competition of cheaper and better British cottons. In 1823 the importation of ordinary woolen and cotton cloth was prohibited. However, the loss of the corresponding customs revenues caused the government to reverse itself and, in 1824, to permit again the importation of cheap cotton cloth. Even though textile-producing states like Puebla argued vociferously in favor of prohibition, the national government permitted the importation of cheap cottons because they contributed a large share of the government's revenues. During the 1820s, British cottons imported into Mexico perhaps amounted to between 30 and 60 percent of the new nation's production. Could Mexico have erected a tariff sufficiently high to

protect its national textile industry? Could the government afford to pro-
hibit foreign textile imports when, between 1822 and 1832, tariffs on textiles amounted on average to 45 percent of the national government's revenues?[9]

The problems faced by Mexico's textile industrialists, even as they purchased modern technology, were exacerbated by the producers of domestic
cotton, who exerted their own self-serving pressure on the national government. Consequently, Mexican textile manufacturers were legally compelled
to purchase their cotton exclusively from domestic producers. Because
domestic cotton was more expensive than imported raw cotton, it added
greatly to the cost of domestically manufactured cotton products and de-
graded the potential benefits of mechanization. Furthermore, because domestic growers could not always meet the needs of the manufacturers, some
productive mills were forced to cease operations. Foreign cotton sometimes
could be acquired by special license, but this *ad hoc* system favored specu-
lators and rendered such supplies expensive. The problem was that it was
politically difficult to justify the protection of many sectors of the economy, including cotton textiles as well as other agricultural products, and
not protect the cotton growers. The result was that the cotton textile industry, which, according to the example of Britain and the United States,
should have spearheaded an industrial revolution, did not do so.[10]

Foreign Domination and Exploitation

No aspect of independent life in Spanish America seems to arouse Spanish Americans and students interested in the area quite so much as the issue
of foreign domination and exploitation. Clearly, it was one of the gravest
problems faced by the new nations. The United States, Great Britain,
France, and other European nations saw Spanish America, and Brazil too,
as an infinite and enticing new market. British merchants enjoyed the initial advantage. Great Britain was more advanced industrially, its merchants
had greater credit and shipping facilities to offer the Spanish Americans,
and it enjoyed special trading privileges with Brazil that gave it advantages
in trading with the rest of the continent. The United States and the European nations found great economic leverage because the Spanish Americans needed and welcomed foreign merchants and their capital. More than
one Spanish American statesman suggested that his country grant one of
the major powers a long-term, exclusive trading privilege in return for diplomatic recognition and support. More than one statesman proposed the

ceding of national territory to a foreign power as a trading factory in return for recognition and support. One would expect such an atmosphere to have been highly attractive to foreign merchants.

And indeed they flocked in. Merchants from Great Britain, the United States, and elsewhere set up shop in all of the new nations, finding more success in some places than in others. They not only lodged themselves in the leading ports, but frequently also in the hinterland. They quickly became a powerful force, not only economically but politically. The new nations depended on them for arms and ammunition, for capital and credit; and they wanted diplomatic recognition from the home countries. This circumstance allowed the foreign merchants to exert a good deal of political pressure, especially when British merchants called on the commander of the British naval forces stationed in nearby waters to support their petitions.

Although the precise nature of the political relationship between the new nations and foreign merchants requires further study, the relationship between British merchants and the Chilean government between 1817 and 1823 argues that the foreigners were not as politically powerful as has often been suggested. The Chileans acquitted themselves quite well in their political dealings with the foreign merchant community. Similarly, in Peru foreign merchants attempted to force a policy of free trade upon the new national government. However, the protectionist sentiment in Lima, from the commercial and agricultural elite down to the artisan community, was so strong that foreign merchant and ministerial pressure came to no avail. Peru adopted a policy of protection, although in areas distant from Lima, this policy was viewed as economically detrimental and in fact undermined national unity. Furthermore, it usually goes unnoticed that many resident foreign merchants became Spanish American citizens, married Spanish Americans, and sired Spanish American families. By the middle of the nineteenth century many of the great foreign merchant and banking houses were, in a meaningful sense, Spanish American and not foreign.

Recognizing that indeed economic exploitation by foreigners existed— that many foreign merchants, for instance, arrived in Spanish America, stayed a short while, made fortunes (sometimes spectacular ones), and then departed for home—it would still be salutary to see the other side of the picture, to learn something of the contribution of foreign merchants and of foreign capital.

The case of a young Scotsman, John Parish Robertson, is particularly interesting. Robertson traveled to the River Plate region first in 1807, and again in the following year. For about two years he worked as a clerk in

Buenos Aires; then, at the end of 1811, he traveled over a thousand miles upriver to Asunción, the capital of Paraguay, where he awaited the arrival of a shipment of goods that he was supposed to sell. He was the first British subject to trade directly in the new country. Robertson was successful, and he remained in Asunción for three years. The costs of transportation, including insurance and credit charges, inflated the cost of goods shipped from Buenos Aires to Asunción, but scarcity in the upriver market made the greatest difference and accounted for the trade's profitability. Robertson did so well that in 1814 he had his younger brother William come over to join him in the business. But from that point things went bad. Returning from a trip to Buenos Aires, he was robbed and nearly killed. Worse, perhaps, he was no longer in favor with the Paraguayan dictator, Francia, and was expelled from Asunción. He and his brother then established themselves in the provincial town of Corrientes, in the Argentine province of the same name. The province of Corrientes had been one of Argentina's great cattle-producing regions during the colonial period, but the civil wars waged between the provinces and Buenos Aires during the independence period had seriously disrupted the pastoral economies of Corrientes and its neighbors. Dried hides could be purchased in Corrientes very cheaply and sold in Buenos Aires at considerable profit, and then again in Britain for another large profit.

The cattle provinces required two things in particular to revive their economies: an effective marketing system for cattle hides and an inducement to put the cattle estates back into shape. The Robertsons supplied both of these requirements through a simple but ingenious plan. They were aware that before the independence movement merchants paid the cattle raisers low prices for their hides and charged high prices for the goods they sold to them. "So we reversed the plan of the Old Spaniards," the Robertsons said, "we gave high prices for hides, and took low ones for goods." This was fundamental capitalism, brilliantly conceived and executed. Furthermore, because the rural estates of Argentina, the *estancias*, required very little capital investment, the Robertsons took the next step and supplied it. Through a partnership with another Scot in Buenos Aires, the Robertsons were able to provide credit to the cattle raisers, allowing them to rehabilitate their estates. Since relatively little credit was required by each cattle raiser, the Robertsons were able to supply credit to a large number; the credit was given as a *habilitación,* an advance on future production. Thus the Robertsons "induced many small and middling estancieros, or country gentlemen . . . to return to their estates, and collect hides, skins, horse-hair, and wool . . . to put their farm houses into repair; to get their corrales, or pens for cattle made good; to collect some milch cows and horses; and to gather together a flock of sheep." But this was only part of it. The Robertsons also supplied the cattle raisers "with tobacco, spirits, yerba, salt, and ponchos, the indispensable articles at once of necessity and luxury for the estanciero and his servants." In a while, the "higher class of estancieros, seeing the new order of things established, and knowing they now had a sure and profitable market for their hides, were gradually up and stirring . . . to re-organize their estancias, and to collect again their herds of cattle."[11] In a short time, both the province of Corrientes and the Robertsons were prospering. Early in 1817, John Parish Robertson returned to Britain and established a merchant house in Liverpool, while William set up shop in Buenos Aires.

What is one to make of the Robertsons? They were two young foreigners who, in a couple of years, not only contributed significantly to the economic restoration of Corrientes, but also made a tidy sum in the process. In so doing, they were not always well appreciated by local Argentine merchants. In both Paraguay and Argentina, the Robertsons supplied a valuable service that local merchants either were unwilling or unable to provide. They helped the economic development of Paraguay and Argentina and, in the latter instance, made fortunes for themselves.

But not all foreigners were quite so lucky. Some, like John Miers, invested small fortunes and lost them, in part due to a local approach to business to which their ventures would not adapt. Miers had brought 5 Englishmen and 40,000 dollars in machinery with him to Chile, for the refining of copper and its manufacture into sheets for the American market and the East Indian trade. According to his own account, he invested an equal amount in the venture once he arrived in Chile. After incessant problems with provincial officials, including a lawsuit that dragged on for 3 years and an earthquake, Miers gave up the whole project and emigrated to Argentina. Many foreigners lost capital invested in Spanish American mining. The British Real del Monte Mining Company, for instance, invested more than 16 million dollars in Mexican silver mining between the time the company was founded in 1824 and its ultimate failure in 1849, and during the period of operation, it lost more than 5 million dollars.

William Wheelwright was one of the most famous foreigners to work in Spanish America in the decades after independence. Born in Newburyport, Massachusetts, in 1798 to a family of established and wealthy merchants, he acquired a small fortune by working as a merchant in Guayaquil, during the late 1820s, and in 1829, he settled in Valparaíso, Chile. During the next decades, he introduced steam navigation to Pacific South America, built

Chile's first railroad, and provided several other important internal improvements. By 1860 he had shifted his attention to Argentina. His Chilean experience is highly instructive for an attempt to understand the phenomenon called foreign exploitation.

Funds for the establishment of the Pacific Steam Navigation Company (PSNC) had to be raised abroad—in this case, Great Britain—for two fundamental reasons. First, the Chilean government still functioned under the mercantilist logic of a balanced budget and did not have the money to finance such a company, however advantageous it might be to the country. Second, the financial energies of the private citizenry were turned elsewhere—to more profitable ventures.

We can learn something about British financial adventurousness and neocolonialism generally from the early life of the PSNC. In December 1844, at the company's second annual shareholders' meeting, the directors announced a loss of over £72,010 (a pound sterling equaled about 5 U.S. dollars or 5 Chilean pesos) during the first 4 years of operation, on a paid-up capital of £93,905. But from that moment things began to change. Although a breakdown of the steamer *Peru* during 1845 cost the company about 15,000 pesos and a lost coal freighter another 8,000 pesos, the new year saw the company develop a refreshing momentum, stimulated by a mail contract finally arranged with the British government. The contract provided for a regular mail service between Valparaíso and Panama, touching at many intermediary ports. A British government subsidy was fixed at £20,000 per year for 5 years. The British government was not concerned with any mail contract that the company might have with the Chilean government, but only with the service guaranteed by its own contract. The company was supposed to use the steamers *Chile* and *Peru,* but the contract induced the directors to order their first iron vessel. Later in the year, the iron steamer *Ecuador* was launched in England.

The new mail contract put Wheelwright as well as the company in a highly optimistic mood. The company's stock had fallen to below £9 from a high of £40, and in 1845 its capital was valued at less than £8,000. It was then that the mail contract was secured. Wheelwright later noted: "Without this contract the Company would not be in existence. The British government resolved to pay this sum because it understood the great public utility of the enterprise and saw that without this aid it would find it impossible to continue forward."[12] Furthermore, it is fair to conclude that there would have been no steam navigation along the Pacific coast of South America had it not been for British private capital and public subsidy. It is quite clear that the PSNC was not one of those legendary British colonialist companies that marched into Spanish America, used and abused its hospitality, made a quick and substantial profit, and sent the returns home. It proved to be quite the opposite; in fact, it was not until 1848 that the company really began to get on its feet. The shareholders were rewarded with their first dividend—2.5 percent!

Another Wheelwright venture is pertinent. He had become interested in the building of railroads in Chile even before the PSNC was established. The problem for him was how to raise the money. In 1833 the important newspaper the *Mercurio* of Valparaíso noted that capitalists were not eager to invest in low interest-yielding roads and canals when they could earn around 18 percent from personal loans and business investments. This is an extremely important point. Although Chileans and most other Spanish Americans possessed the capital to finance most of the necessary nineteenth-century internal improvements, they had to rely on foreign capital because national capitalists preferred to invest their money in more appealing enterprises. At first, governments were not willing to take a strong position in such financial ventures, partly because they lacked adequate tax structures and the collection techniques necessary to finance new obligations. This left them unable to produce the infrastructural requirements of maturing capitalist economies.

The matter of taxation deserves further consideration. The countries with large Indian populations faced a fundamental problem that tested their commitment to nineteenth-century Liberal principles. In colonial Spanish America, all adult male Indians were forced to pay a tribute to the crown—a regressive tax that placed a great burden on the Indian population. The question facing the new countries was how to end the insidious system of tribute and still ensure adequate state revenues.

One example of the problem and its resolution occurred in Ecuador. In 1830 Ecuador wrote a constitution that declared its independence as the State of Ecuador, a part of the Republic of Colombia. The first executive was the Venezuelan, General Juan José Flores. When the patriots gained control of the future Ecuador, they abolished tribute, thus ending the regressive tax that had burdened the Indian population for centuries. But overturning this cornerstone of the colonial system caused a shortfall in governmental revenues. Consequently, Simón Bolívar revived the tribute, but renamed it the *contribución personal de indígenas*. In 1830 this tax amounted to three and one-half pesos per adult male. The burden and iniquity of the tax was widely recognized in Ecuador, and in 1831 President Flores persuaded the congress to replace it with a general, graduated income tax, the *contribución ordinaria*. This tax was based on ability to pay, and it excluded Indians, the young, the old, and the impoverished. Of course, a graduated income tax was ahead of its time, and not surprisingly, the Ministry of Finance was unable to collect the new tax. It was soon replaced by the old tribute tax and by several additional regressive consumption taxes.[13] Liberal principles fell to the realities of governmental needs, as they did elsewhere and in similar circumstances.

General Administrative Problems

Some of the problems that challenged the ingenuity of even the most proficient government leaders during the early decades of the nineteenth century are well known and need only be mentioned briefly.

Topography and poor transportation facilities worked against national unity and economic growth. It was often cheaper to import agropastoral products by sea than to move them even short distances overland. During the decade of the 1820s, it sometimes took as much as a year for a United States minister to have his messages from Santiago, Chile, reach Washington. So little confidence did officials place in the shipping facilities that they made a practice of sending several copies of a dispatch, each by a different vessel. In 1836 a sailing ship set a new record of 87 days for the voyage between New York and Valparaíso. It was not until 1845 that a daily mail service was instituted between Santiago and Valparaíso, a distance of only 84 miles, which took about 13.5 hours in each direction. A letter sent from Santiago took 9 days to Concepción in the south, and about equal time to Copiapó in the north. And it should be noted that in this regard Chile was in much better shape than many other Spanish American nations. In Central America, the capital of Costa Rica was a thousand miles from Guatemala City. When conditions were good, it took at least a month and a half to travel the distance and to deliver a message. During the rainy season—nearly half the year—travel between the two capitals was almost impossible (as it was virtually impossible between Quito and Guayaquil, in Ecuador). It was even more difficult for the Central American capitals to communicate with Mexico City.

There were also fundamental social problems. Many of the new nations contained large Indian populations. During the colonial period, Indians normally resided in their own communities, the *repúblicas de indios,* created by the crown ostensibly to protect them from abuse by the white population. Aggregating Indians in this manner also made it easier for the crown to collect the tribute and other taxes owed by the Indians, and to supervise

Indian forced labor. On the other hand, the communities were governed by Indian notables who contributed to a general cohesiveness that somewhat protected the individual Indian from the harshness of the outside world. Many of these communities were highly litigious, often going into the courts successfully to redress grievances, as when large landowners encroached upon community lands.

With independence the situation changed dramatically. Early nineteenth-century Liberalism often brought about a dismantling of the colonial legislation that had protected the Indians. Where racial equality was legislated, as in Mexico, the separate Indian communities necessarily had to be declassified, although many continued to exist *de facto*. Nineteenth-century Mexican politics divided the active citizenry into two broad political alliances—Liberals and Conservatives. The Liberals mounted an attack on corporate privilege, and this included lands owned by the *de facto* Indian communities. Indians who had not already become small peasant proprietors and daily wage laborers now were set free to find their own way in the capitalist marketplace and defend themselves against the predations of large-scale commercial agriculture. While there is more to the story, and other factors need to be considered, it is clear that in their attempt to provide the benefits of private property ownership and to assimilate them into the broader society, the Liberals failed the Indians. Altogether, large segments of Mexican Indian society were relegated to impoverishment and illiteracy, a result that did not contribute to the maturation of the capitalist system. Where this occurred in the Andean countries, the results were similar.

And there was the matter of praetorianism, the militarism that triumphantly carried out the independence movement and often wanted a share of governmental power. Although the patriot armies owed their origins to the late colonial reorganization of the military, the praetorianism of the early nineteenth century evolved during the wars for independence. Now the military often wanted to govern the new nations. The Liberal constitutions of the period generally attempted to establish civilian authority over the military. They did so partly by establishing civil militia forces as a counterweight to the professional military establishment. Where the new governments were not successful, there often were *coups d'état* and military intervention. The military tradition that was nurtured and brought to maturity and fulfillment during the wars of independence seriously undermined the growth and development of many Spanish American nations.

Every nation had its *caudillo* problem. *Caudillos* were the local chieftains, whose charisma and physical prowess established them as the leaders of provincial bands and sometimes of regional and even national populations. *Caudillos* were often large landowners who had at their immediate service a band of retainers, usually horsemen; but, in all cases, they controlled local resources and acquired broader personal followings. Generally, they stood above governmental structures, securing their goals through the use or threat of physical force. During the wars for independence they became high military officers, and in the case of the most famous of them, like José Antonio Páez, generals. As a result of these positions, they normally acquired great wealth in the form of landed estates given to them by governments in appreciation of their contributions to independence. *Caudillos* were not professional soldiers, since professionalism was not consonant with the political culture of *caudillismo*. Some *caudillos* returned from the wars of independence to arbitrate the futures of regions or localities, while others became constitutional presidents or governors and functioned within the rule of law. However, there was always the possibility, demonstrated time and again during the early nineteenth century, that they would revert to the use of their personal power and govern arbitrarily. At both the regional and national levels, *caudillos* often disrupted economies and political structures, whether they held political office or not. At other times, they pursued agendas that served the needs of regional or national constituencies.

The example of Peru contributes to an appreciation of the range of possible action and impact of the *caudillo*. No Spanish American country suffered the political disruption of *caudillos* during the post-independence period more than Peru. There were dozens of regional *caudillos,* but Grand Marshal Agustín Gamarra, a mestizo from Cuzco, came to dominate them all, and through a coalition of lesser *caudillos,* he controlled national political life on and off between 1829 and his death in 1841. The central issue in Peru at the time was trade policy, and the country was divided broadly into northern protectionists and southern free traders. Gamarra represented northern interests, and once he controlled Lima, he set about undoing unfavorable trade policy and replacing it with policies favorable to his constituency. What he instituted was logical and effective for the north, but disruptive for the south. In this instance, we find a classic *caudillo* usurping national power on behalf of a rational, but regional, political and economic agenda. Had northern trade needs been those of all other Peruvian regions, Gamarra would have brought peace and stability with him to national politics; but such was not the case. Gamarra also provides an example of how regional *caudillos* could become enormously powerful once they gained control of national institutions such as the military, of which Gamarra took full advantage to enforce the north's economic agenda.[14]

One of the problems, constantly mentioned, that faced the new nations was the general lack of qualified governmental personnel. All the colonies possessed trained and effective administrative bureaucracies, and these might have made for an easy transition from colonialism to national government; but the wars of independence and the nature of early national government resulted in a shortage of qualified personnel in many places. At the outset of independence, some Spanish bureaucrats left the colonies for the security of Spain, while others were expelled by some of the new nations, even when they had sworn allegiance to the new governments and become citizens. To varying degrees, all the new nations politicized their civil bureaucracies, creating employment for patriots and personal clients in particular. What occurred at the national level was reproduced over and again at the provincial level, thus marking the beginning of the bloated and inefficient Spanish American bureaucracies of the national period. Even where qualified bureaucrats remained in their positions and others were added, depleted treasuries caused salaries to be paid erratically, and sometimes to be lowered to the point that many officials had to leave their positions or seek additional emoluments through corruption. Many nationals who might ordinarily have gone into the bureaucracy found that after the wars of independence it was necessary for them to remain in the private sector in order to repair their fortunes.

There was also the serious problem of finding men willing to serve in the new congresses and in provincial or state assemblies. These conspicuous republican bodies won the interest and attention of scores of talented men who, in colonial times, might have gone into the administrative bureaucracy and done a creditable job. Now, however, many potential congressmen had pressing financial or family reasons not to be away from home for half a year or more. In many of the new countries, service at the national level, even in very prestigious positions, could not compensate for arduous trips of a month or two in duration, in addition to several or many months of actual service. Some countries, like Chile, suffered very little from a lack of qualified bureaucrats and congressmen during the early national period; others, like New Granada, suffered noticeably.

It is often said that the new countries lacked political experience, sometimes even that they were not sufficiently prepared for independence. The new nations did not lack citizens with administrative experience; however, they did lack citizens with legislative experience. The two should not be confused: There is a world of difference between running a government and running a legislature. Even so, it took only a short time for Spanish Americans to understand the workings of legislative assemblies and to tolerate and manage dissent and opposition—hallmarks of republican government. The fact that some Spanish Americans did not pay much attention to the niceties of republican government does not mean that they lacked political experience. In some instances, it might be argued that this demonstrated their considerable political maturity—they had learned to manipulate the political process. It is a central point of this chapter that there are no simple answers to why the emergent nations developed along a continuum from stability to disrupting instability, why one witnessed an era of general progress and another an era of retardation.

Finally, there was the church-state problem. In countries like Chile, where the colonial Church had not become very wealthy and did not own much land, the issue of religion was decided without a great deal of disruption. In Chile, for instance, the major Church properties during the colonial period belonged to the Jesuits, and these were sold at auction after the Jesuits were expelled in 1767. During the first decades after independence, the Chileans did not have to face the power of an overly wealthy Church establishment; nor did they need to confiscate Church land. In Mexico the situation was reversed. There the Church was excessively wealthy and powerful. As part of a general attack on corporate privilege, and a specific desire to set Church lands free and into the economy, Mexican reformers undertook a long and disruptive confrontation with the Church. Furthermore, in order to establish civilian control over the Church, to curb Church abuses, and to establish secular education, the reformers of the 1830s and thereafter had to be willing to fight and to face the consequences (often insurmountable) of an antagonistic Church. In more than one nation, the alienation of the Church brought down governments.

Centralism and Federalism

No problem was more ruinous to many of the early national governments than the issue of centralism versus federalism. The examples of two regions will provide further insight into the complicated problems faced by the new national governments.

Central America

The first example is that of Central America. By the end of the colonial period there was wholesale provincial discontent over the power and influence exerted by the capital of the captaincy general, Guatemala City. The growing European textile industry during the eighteenth century caused the indigo produced in the captaincy general to be a highly prized commodity. It was produced primarily in El Salvador and Guatemala, and was sent through Guatemala City (where trade in the commodity could be controlled and taxes collected) to a gulf port. The dominant position of Guatemala City and her merchants in this trade resulted from natural advantages and political power. Other provinces also benefited from the indigo trade. While Guatemala and El Salvador produced indigo, Nicaragua and Honduras produced the agropastoral products needed by the indigo workers. The Central Americans had worked out their own preindustrial division of labor. The problem was that the Guatemala City merchants controlled the entire process through their advantageous location in the capital city; through their control of markets; and through the influence accrued from the distribution of European goods.

During the second half of the eighteenth century, provincial producers and merchants became highly dissatisfied with the system and petitioned the crown for reforms. The crown was impressed with the provincial position and took steps to end the virtual monopoly of the Guatemala merchants. New routes to the coast were established, and credit facilities were to be expanded to reduce the dependency of the provincial planters on the Guatemala City merchants. But the reforms were widely circumvented during the final decades of the colonial period, and provincial discontent did not abate.

Central American federalism also had its political origins. Provincial capitals were displeased with the political power exerted by Guatemala City, but even at the provincial level there was a conflict among urban centers for political ascendancy, or at least for relative autonomy. Between 1808 and the declaration of complete independence from foreign powers, including Mexico, in 1823, there were many local revolts, some of which pitted one provincial town against another. When Central America joined Iturbide's Mexican empire in 1822, it did so mainly because some of the provinces preferred to be under the political tutelage of distant Mexico City rather than Guatemala City. With Iturbide's fall from power in 1823, the Central American states declared their independence and drafted the constitution of 1824. The new organic code established the Federation of Central America.

What the Central Americans had done was to re-create the old Captaincy General of Guatemala, without the province of Chiapas, in such a way as to enjoy the benefits of unity while not suffering the dominance of the former province of Guatemala. The new republic was blessed with rich

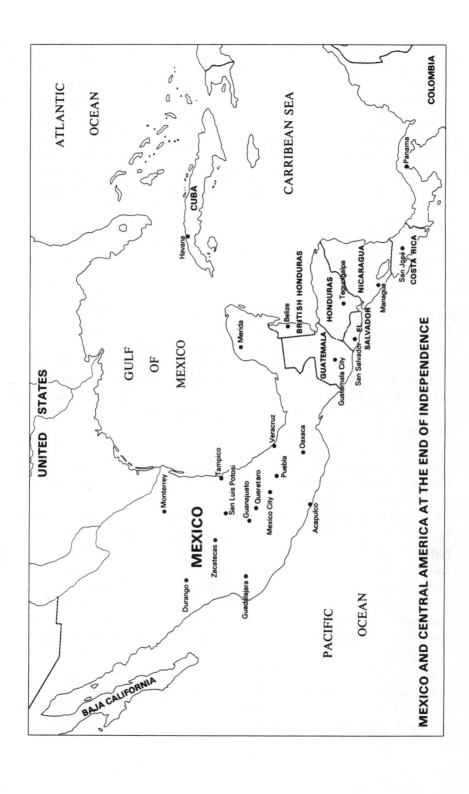

MEXICO AND CENTRAL AMERICA AT THE END OF INDEPENDENCE

economic resources and a benign climate, but its vast potential was to be unfulfilled. The first congress met in 1825, but in the following year there began a disruptive civil war that lasted three years, and after that, warfare ensued for another two years. By 1831 the economy of the republic had been seriously jeopardized, and its political structure threatened.

By the end of the decade, the Federation of Central America (which by then was really a loose confederation, rather than a tightly organized federation) ceased to exist, and a series of Central American nations superseded it. No other part of Spanish America needed unity, through some form of federated government and unified economy, more than Central America. The failure of the former captaincy general to achieve its potential—a consequence of many factors, several of which culminated in the enfeebling federalist-centralist controversy—is one of the most disheartening results of Spanish American independence.

Argentina

The second example is that of Argentina. The provinces of the former Viceroyalty of the Río de la Plata had almost as difficult a time in coming together as did those of Central America. It took them until after the middle of the nineteenth century to do so. But by the 1860s Argentina was functioning as a unified political and economic unit, although by then, the province of the Banda Oriental had long been independent as the Republic of Uruguay.

No country had a more difficult time in creating a national government than Argentina. For decades it appeared that the city and province of Buenos Aires would not be able to bring the other provinces into any sort of unified nation. The issues of federalism and centralism nearly Balkanized Argentina; the great economic potential of Argentina was almost lost.

The problem in Argentina was economic. Leaving aside the Banda Oriental, the former viceroyalty was divided into three distinct economic regions. First and foremost was the city and province of Buenos Aires. The city (and port) of Buenos Aires was the region's commercial entrepôt and controlled the tariff revenues from goods passing through it. The city was an important market for goods produced by the other provinces, but it was not dependent on them since its needs could be supplied easily and often more cheaply from abroad. The city's merchants distributed European goods, as well as domestic items such as *yerba,* hides, textiles, and wine.

The rest of the former viceroyalty (with the exception of Upper Peru) comprised the Interior provinces, including Córdoba, Tucumán, Santi-

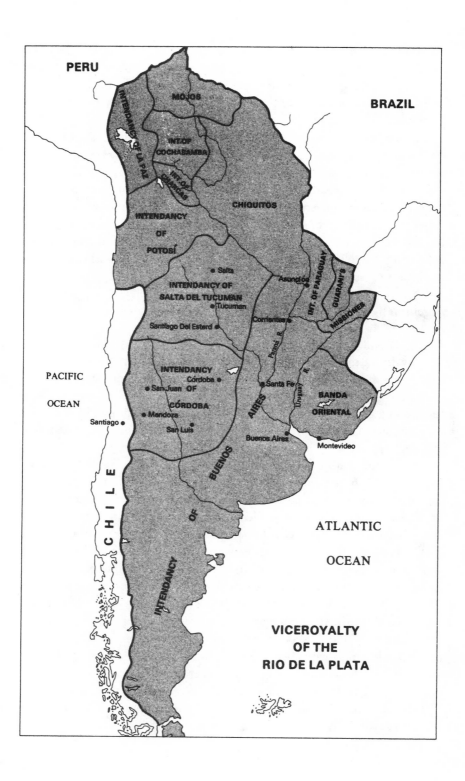

PERU

BRAZIL

INTENDANCY OF LA PAZ

MOJOS

INT. OF COCHABAMBA

INT. OF CHARCAS

CHIQUITOS

INTENDANCY OF POTOSÍ

• Salta

Asunción

INT. OF PARAGUAY

GUARANIS

INTENDANCY OF SALTA DEL TUCUMAN

• Tucuman

Corrientes •

MISSIONES

Santiago Del Estero •

PACIFIC

OCEAN

INTENDANCY OF CÓRDOBA

Córdoba •

San Juan •

• Mendoza

• San Luis

Santiago •

BUENOS

Santa Fe •

Paraná R.

Uruguay R.

BANDA ORIENTAL

AIRES

Buenos Aires •

Montevideo •

C H I L E

INTENDANCY OF BUENOS

ATLANTIC

OCEAN

INTENDANCY

VICEROYALTY
OF THE
RIO DE LA PLATA

ago del Estero, San Juan, and Mendoza; and the Littoral provinces of Corrientes, Santa Fe, and Entre Ríos. The Interior provinces produced a wide range of goods, including hides, textiles, cotton, and fruits in Córdoba; wines and dried fruits in Mendoza; hides, leather, cotton, timber, cheese, dried fruits, wines, and many other items in Tucumán and San Juan. These products were shipped to Buenos Aires, where they were consumed or transshipped to other provinces and abroad. In turn, Buenos Aires sent back products produced in its province (hides, salted meat, and wool) and from abroad.

There was a genuine conflict of interest here. Buenos Aires needed relatively free trade. It wanted to sell its pastoral products and import foreign goods. Its pastoral products sold well abroad and did not have to be protected at home against foreign pastoral products. Nor did Buenos Aires desire to protect local industry—of which the province possessed little—at the risk of restricting the influx of foreign commodities, the source of its economic prosperity. On the other hand, the Interior provinces sorely needed protection, not only for their local industries, which could not compete with cheaper foreign goods, but also for some of their agricultural products, most especially wine, which also faced foreign competition. There were exceptions to this general attitude, however. Some people in the Interior provinces preferred lower tariffs, but they did not carry the day.

The relationship between the Littoral provinces and Buenos Aires was fundamentally one of conflict. The products produced in the river provinces essentially competed with those produced in the province of Buenos Aires—pastoral products that were highly competitive in the world marketplace. The Littoral provinces also desired relatively free trade and opposed protection for industries they did not possess, at the risk of seeing tariffs raised abroad against their production. Their conflict with Buenos Aires centered around who should control foreign trade and customs duties. The port of Buenos Aires controlled the entrance to the Paraná River, along which lay the provinces of Corrientes, Entre Ríos, and Santa Fe. Oceangoing vessels could travel up the Paraná almost as easily as they could stop at Buenos Aires. Thus the Littoral provinces could have traded directly with Europe and collected their own customs duties. To protect their interests, the Interior and Littoral provinces desired a federal system. The battle lines were drawn; it took a half-century to resolve these fundamental issues.

Attempts to arrive at a working solution to the problems between the province of Buenos Aires and the other provinces were made even before independence was officially declared in 1816, but they were to no avail. The centralist constitution of 1819 naturally favored the province of Buenos Aires and was repudiated by the other provinces; and a succeeding constitution of 1826 produced the same outcome. During the next decades the provinces generally went their own ways, united among themselves sometimes formally and sometimes informally in a confederation.

The federalist question frustrated both political and economic progress in the former viceroyalty. Even the province of Buenos Aires witnessed political disruption over its own version of the federalist-centralist controversy, with the port in economic (and therefore political) conflict with the livestock interests of the greater province. None of the Interior or Littoral provinces had an easy time achieving economic prosperity. The main source of public revenues almost always was customs duties, and the amounts collected often did not meet public expenditures. These provinces well understood that their best interests lay in a mutually cooperative federalist government that treated their local economic and political interests fairly.

It is clear that Argentina would have fared much better both economically and politically if all the provinces had been able to arrive at an equitable solution to their federalist-centralist problems during the early years after independence. The solution finally reached in 1862 was to depoliticize the port of Buenos Aires by nationalizing the customs house, as well as other bureaucratic offices. Then, in 1880, Buenos Aires became a federalized district.

The Practical Problems of Daily Government

No picture of the many disturbing and debilitating problems faced by the early national governments would be complete without including at least some of the more ordinary, mundane complications of everyday government. These problems often were as disruptive to the growth and development of independent Spanish America as more complex problems such as foreign influence and federalism.

The early national governments had to support two costly institutions unknown to the colonial period. Each country (except Paraguay) had its own congress, often with two branches and provincial counterparts, and its independent judiciary. There were judges in the colonial period, but the system of courts in the republican period was far more imposing and demanding. Judges, congressmen, and staffs had to be paid, and this placed additional strain on the already precarious financial structures.

And having these congresses and judiciaries was both awkward and perplexing. It was not at all clear which colonial laws should apply to independent nationhood. A whole compendium of new legislation had to be written (or adopted), sometimes leading to procrastination and confusion. And it was not clear how a congress should function. Especially obscure was the appropriate relationship between the senate and president. As we know, the senate usually considered itself the special guardian of Liberalism, an attitude that often put it in direct conflict with the executive branch. It was not unusual for presidential powers to be curtailed, which sometimes led to ineffectual executive leadership or to a *coup* headed by the president or by the military.

There were so many problems—from the merely mischievous to the pernicious—confronting the newly independent nations of Spanish America that there is little wonder so few of them were even fairly successful at meeting the challenges of independence and a changing world economy. There was no single cause of the political instability or retrograde stability that often followed independence, or of the unstable and ineffectual economies. It was not foreign influence, or federalism, or the Church, or topography, or the lack of political experience that caused instability; it was a complex of factors. In each nation different issues were paramount, but commonly a combination of several problems contrived to limit the possibilities of progress—of growth and development—in the new nations.

Out of these conditions and problems evolved a political culture that tolerated outdated technology, the flight of domestic capital, bureaucratic corruption, and a dependence on foreigners for technical and financial resources; that is, a culture of underdevelopment.

8

Conclusion

These independence movements, which disrupted one of the world's great empires and gave rise to 16 independent nations, were monumental in scale and often violent and cataclysmic. Major military expeditions were undertaken, and sometimes they were brilliantly conceived and executed expeditions, but they often benumbed entire regions. At times the individual could hardly fathom the purpose of it all, could hardly see the reason for the hardship that followed so naturally upon the rhetoric. These were civil wars, not only because the colonies were fighting against the mother country for home rule, but also because the wars split the colonists into royalists and patriots. Even families were split; famous Spanish American family groups were often shocked to their very foundations. How it must have been for those patriarchs who saw their relatives at each others' throats! They were civil wars also because factions within the patriot coalition sometimes fought each other, and with extreme brutality. They were civil wars, and ugly ones.

They were also revolutions. They did not start out as wars for a radical change of government or a vast alteration in social structures. The masses fought with one side or another, at times according to no recognizable pattern. Although common people paid for independence with their lives—tens of thousands of them—most benefited very little in the short term for their efforts. Yet legal barriers to full citizenship were breached during and immediately after the wars, promising future revolutionary change.

In early independent Spanish America, republicanism came to mean something more than the structure of government. It embodied a fundamental principle of what we call democracy—the right of every man to cast a ballot and vote his conscience and to participate in the political process. In the early nineteenth century, this meant only those sane free adult males, who, generally speaking, could read and write, were not in debt to the public treasury, and were not domestic servants. Those who wrote the Spanish American constitutions and ran the governments, like those in the United States, Britain, and France, understood that these restrictions eliminated most of the free male population from active citizenship and the right to vote. Nowhere were these disqualifications peremptory; that is, the optimism of nineteenth-century Liberalism allowed its adherents to believe that large numbers of the disqualified would raise themselves above their station in life and become part of the voting citizenry. Spanish American Liberalism failed in its promise, and for decades citizenship was narrowly defined and greatly circumscribed. But with the passing of decades, increasing numbers managed the ascent to full citizenship and fundamental reform became possible. The process began with independence.

Nineteenth-century Liberalism provided its major political benefits to men, although fundamental civil rights—those of life, liberty, and estate, in Locke's famous locution—applied to women also. The current wisdom among historians is that women gained practically nothing politically or legally as a result of independence. From the perspective of a modern observer this is certainly true. But this picture of early nineteenth-century Spanish American women is founded upon the barest of information. We have done far too little research in this significant area of women's history. Where women have been studied in great depth, we see a modest but important difference between their rights in the colonial period and after independence. In independent Mexico the age of majority of single female daughters was lowered, and therefore the age at which they could control their own legal affairs. Widows, who already were in control of their own affairs under Spanish law, now were given control over the legal affairs of their children after independence.[1] These were limited but important advances in women's rights, and they reflect a changing attitude toward women in independent Mexico. As historians study the comparative status of women in other Spanish American countries, we almost certainly will see these and other advances for women elsewhere, if not everywhere.

With independence the burdens of slavery were sometimes ameliorated, and steps were taken toward eventual emancipation. Where broad assimilation and miscegenation had blurred the line separating whites from the society of castes, as in Mexico, racial classification was ended. Men of the castes became generals and presidents. For those who suffered discrimination in the colonial period, society would never again be as restrictive.

Progress was slow, frequently exasperatingly slow, and *de facto* racism often made a mockery of well-intended statutory reforms. For Indians, the overthrow of the crown's paternalistic government often left their communities less protected than previously.

Independence most clearly benefited the active citizenry, the oligarchy and the people on the way up, the people, that is, who were socially positioned to take full advantage of the economic (and political) advantages of capitalism. The active citizenry determined the rationale of government, economics, and society in these new nations. It was a citizenry confident of its capabilities, but confronted by debilitating problems. This citizenry was often divided, over issues of trade, the Church, and internal improvements. Thus the need to modernize textile manufacturing in Puebla, Mexico, was impeded by the high costs of protected cotton and the limitations of an insufficient infrastructure. Almost everywhere, regionalism undermined the logic and promise of the broader marketplace. In early national Argentina, provinces fought each other with arms and with internal customs barriers. In Peru the economic interests of north and south were so divergent that the emergence of a strong national government had to await decades of fraternal feuding. It was not until the impetus of a powerful export product, bird manure (*guano*), propelled the Peruvian economy deep into the world marketplace that a strong and unifying government could evolve, but, ironically, this very circumstance rendered the country more susceptible to foreign influence.

There were too many problems for the active citizenry, and it failed to arrest the long slide into underdevelopment. Sometimes the problem was foreign influence and exploitation; at other times, it was the conflict between federalism or centralism, topography, a fight with the Church, a lack of political experience and qualified personnel, the absence of a good money crop or a product that could compete effectively in the international marketplace, or, paradoxically, the very presence of such a crop or product, which itself could cause a country to be vulnerable to foreign influence. Beyond these problems, it is clear that the active citizenry did not do enough to educate the greater population, and therefore raise both their skills and purchasing capacity to ever higher levels. In so many ways, Spanish American capitalism was fundamentally flawed.

And, finally, it seems almost mournful to suggest how much greater Spanish America's potential would have been had it overcome its systemic regionalism and formed a common market. A much larger market would have encouraged specialization and increased manufacturing. A larger proportion of resources would have remained within the market to be consumed by Spanish American manufacturing. Expansion of the industrial base would have resonated throughout the Spanish American economy and raised the standard of living more broadly and rapidly than occurred.

But this is not what happened.

Notes

Preface

1. Hernán Ramírez Necoechea, *Antecedentes económicos de la independencia de Chile,* 2d ed. (Santiago, 1967). The first edition was published in 1959. The new research has further eroded the theory of patrimonialism, which relied on a European model of royal bureaucracy that was grossly, if understandably, inaccurate.

2. See, for instance, Wallace Brown, *The Good Americans. Loyalists in the American Revolution* (New York, 1969), 97; 227–28.

3. The book was first published in 1926.

4. Gordon S. Wood, *The Radicalism of the American Revolution* (New York, 1992).

5. "Bando del General Prim contra la raza africana," Cayetano Coll y Toste, *Historia de la esclavitud en Puerto Rico* (San Juan, 1969), 79–85.

Chapter 1

1. Many scholars would generally agree that the colonial economy was essentially capitalist. For instance, two historians argue that "colonial Mexico functioned as an emerging capitalist society within the worldwide economic system that developed in the fifteenth and sixteenth centuries. . . . Although geographically New Spain [Mexico] was on the periphery of the world system, we maintain that it was neither a dependent nor an underdeveloped region." Colin MacLachlan and Jaime E. Rodríguez O., *The Forging of the Cosmic Race: A Reinterpretation of Colonial Mexico* (Berkeley, 1980), 1. See also John K. Chance, who sees "the early development of a capitalist socioeconomic system in central Mexico." Chance studied colonial Oaxaca, Mexico, "within the context of a developing system of commercial capitalism." *Race and Class in Colonial Oaxaca* (Stanford, 1978), 197.

2. This emphasis on the structural flaws of the colonial economy is based on the penetrating analysis of the problem by John H. Coatsworth, in "Obstacles to Economic Growth in Nineteenth-Century Mexico," *The American Historical Re-*

view 83, 1 (February 1978), 80–100, and other essays cited in the bibliographical essay.

3. Quoted in ibid.

4. Jonathan C. Brown, *A Socioeconomic History of Argentina, 1776–1860* (Cambridge, 1979), 19–20.

5. James R. Scobie, *Revolution on the Pampas* (Austin, 1964), 11. Several additional excellent examples are to be found in Richard L. Garner, *Economic Growth and Change in Bourbon Mexico* (Gainesville, 1993), 181–82.

6. This discussion is based on the pathbreaking work of Alfonso W. Quiroz, *Domestic and Foreign Finance in Modern Peru, 1850–1950* (Pittsburgh, 1993), 15–23.

7. John E. Kicza, *Colonial Entrepreneurs: Families and Business in Bourbon Mexico City* (Albuquerque, 1983), 19–24.

8. Eric Van Young, "Islands in the Storm: Quiet Cities and Violent Countrysides in the Mexican Independence Era," *Past and Present*, no. 118, 130–55.

9. Nils Jacobsen, "Livestock Complexes in Late Colonial Peru and New Spain: An Attempt At Comparison," in *The Economies of Mexico and Peru During the Late Colonial Period, 1760–1810,* ed., Nils Jacobsen and Hans–Jürgen Puhle, (Berlin, 1986), 113–42, 131. Jacobsen also notes that there were "at least nine cities of this size further distant from the market. . . . This represented, for the eighteenth century, a large aggregation of urban demand which favored an extension of trade networks for wool, tallow, live animals and hides and required a complex commercial structure" (131).

10. Jay Kinsbruner, *Petty Capitalism in Spanish America: The Pulperos of Puebla, Mexico City, Caracas, and Buenos Aires* (Boulder, 1987), 50. All further references to the grocers in Spanish America and in New York are from this book.

11. Not everyone would agree. For instance, the distinguished historian Ruggiero Romano considers the Spanish American economy feudal because it was "*essentially a natural economy.*" Ruggiero Romano, "American Feudalism," *Hispanic American Historical Review* 64, no. 1 (February 1984), 121–34 (hereafter cited as *HAHR*). The emphasis is Romano's. My own view is different from Romano's. However, there is good reason to consider the economy of Spanish America as centrally one of commercial capitalism distracted by remnants of the feudal system. This is essentially the view of the widely read Enrique Semo. To Semo, the colonial Mexican economy was one of tributary despotism, feudalism and embryonic capitalism. Enrique Semo, *The History of Capitalism in Mexico* (Austin, 1993). Of great importance to understanding the colonial economy is the work of Carlos Sempat Assadourian. See, for instance, his *El sistema de la economía colonial* (México, D.F., 1983). Because Spanish American labor was not entirely free, and in some instances was indeed coerced, some Marxist and near-Marxist scholars consider the economy to have been precapitalist until later in the nineteenth century. Marx considered capitalism as a mode of production that came into existence with industrialization and the formation of a wage-earning proletariat. This defini-

tion would date Spanish America's capitalism as of a very late origin, and there is no need to do so. Marx both recognized and declaimed that an economic system evolves over a long period of time and out of the system that it is in the process of replacing. Thus, he located "the dawn of the era of capitalist production" ("die Morgenröthe der kapitalistischen Produktionsära") in the sixteenth century, with the "discovery of gold and silver in America . . . " Karl Marx, *Capital: A Critique of Political Economy* (Eng. trans.; New York, 1977), 1:915). The German quote is from *Das Kapital* (Hamburg, 1867), 1:734.

12. Presumably, Marx meant *incipient* class in the first instance, and *mature* class in the second. The quotes are from excerpts of *The Eighteenth Brumaire of Louis Bonaparte*, in Lewis S. Feuer, *Marx and Engels: Basic Writings on Politics & Philosophy* (New York, 1959), 318–91; and Nicos Poulantzas, *Political Power and Social Classes* (Eng. trans.; London, 1973), 79. Poulantzas presents a sustained theoretical discussion of Marx's use of classes and fractions of classes. The most prominent applied example of this logic among Latin Americanists is perhaps Maurice Zeitlin, *The Civil Wars in Chile (or the bourgeois revolutions that never were)* (Princeton, 1984). For a fuller appreciation of this approach to class, one should see Frank Parkin, *Marxism and Class Theory: A Bourgeois Critique* (New York, 1979).

13. E. J. Hobsbawm, "Class Consciousness in History," in István Meszaros, *Aspects of History and Class Consciousness* (New York, 1972), 5–21.

14. The use of stratification theory holds analytical promise. As Magnus Mörner has observed, stratification theory is a "multidimensional way of organizing society according to the variables of wealth—income, occupation, ethnicity, education, kinship, status, and power . . . " (Mörner, "Economic Factors and Stratification in Colonial Spanish America with Special Regard to Elites," *HAHR*, 63, no. 2 (May 1983), 335–69.

Chapter 2

1. Quoted in Arthur P. Whitaker, "Enlightenment and Spanish American Independence," in Academia Nacional de la Historia, *El Movimiento emancipador de Hispanoamérica*, 4 vols. (Caracas, 1961), 4: 55–67.

2. I am here following O. Carlos Stoetzer, *The Scholastic Roots of the Spanish American Revolution* (New York, 1979), 16–26 and passim, although Stoetzer sees the Enlightenment as less influential in Spanish America than I do.

3. John Fisher, *Commercial Relations between Spain and Spanish America in the Era of Free Trade, 1778–1796* (Liverpool, 1985), 45–61.

4. I have here followed, in paraphrase, the important essay by Susan Deans-Smith, "The Money Plant: The Royal Tobacco Monopoly Of New Spain, 1765–1821," in Jacobsen and Puhle, *Economies of Mexico and Peru*, 361–87. For an important and informative discussion of another *estanco*, this one on sugarcane

brandy (*aguardiente*) in New Granada, see Gilma Mora de Tovar, *Aguardiente y conflictos sociales en la Nueva Granada durante el siglo XVIII* (Bogotá, 1988). New Granadan sugarcane producers were hurt by the influx of cheaper brandy from Catalonia, a direct consequence of the 1778 freedom of trade decree. For a further thoughtful example of the role and consequence of Spain's manipulation of the economy, see Kendall W. Brown, "The Spanish Imperial Mercury Trade and the American Mining Expansion under the Bourbon Monarchy," in Kenneth J. Andrien and Lyman L. Johnson, eds., *The Political Economy of Spanish America in the Age of Revolution, 1750–1850* (Albuquerque, 1994), 137–67.

5. Mark A. Burkholder and D. S. Chandler, *From Impotence to Authority: The Spanish Crown and the American Audiencias, 1687–1808* (Columbia, Mo., 1977), Appendix 1 and passim.

6. An excellent discussion of the successes and failures of the Bourbon Reforms is the introduction to Jacobsen and Puhle, *Economies of Mexico and Peru,* 1–25. The comment about Buenos Aires is from Lyman L. Johnson, "The Price History of Buenos Aires during the Viceregal Period," in *Essays on the Price History of Eighteenth-Century Latin America,* eds., Lyman L. Johnson and Enrique Tandeter (Albuquerque, 1990), 137–171.

Chapter 3

1. For this discussion of the Quito revolt, I have followed the important and perceptive work of Anthony McFarlane, "The Rebellion of the *Barrios:* Urban Insurrection in Bourbon Quito," in *Reform and Insurrection in Bourbon New Granada and Peru,* eds. John R. Fisher, Allan J. Kuethe, and Anthony McFarlane (Baton Rouge, 1990), 197–254. The following paragraphs dealing with Quito are also from McFarlane.

2. Information about Guanajuato and the quote are from David Brading, *Miners and Merchants in Bourbon Mexico, 1763–1810* (Cambridge, 1971), 233–34.

3. For this discussion of Saint-Domingue, I have relied extensively on the excellent work of Carolyn E. Fick, *The Making of Haiti: The Saint Domingue Revolution from Below* (Knoxville, 1990); and Michael Duffy, *Soldiers, Sugar and Seapower* (Oxford, 1987), 332–33.

Chapter 4

1. For this discussion of events in Mexico, I have closely followed Timothy E. Anna, *The Fall of the Royal Government in Mexico City* (Lincoln, 1978), 35–63. The insights are Anna's.

2. This quote is from the standard and masterful English-language biography

of Bolívar by Gerhard Masur, *Simón Bolívar* (Albuquerque, 1948). Unless otherwise noted, all further Bolívar quotes are from this source. My discussion of Bolívar comes essentially from the Masur biography, and from Daniel F. O'Leary, *Bolívar and the War of Independence: Memorias del General Daniel Florencio O'Leary. Narración,* (abridged version); trans. and ed. Robert F. McNerny, Jr. (Austin, 1970).

3. O'Leary, *Bolívar,* 17.

4. For this discussion of Miranda, I have followed William Spence Robertson, *The Life of Miranda,* (2 vols. repr. ed.; New York, 1969), and Robertson's *Rise of the Spanish–American Republics, As Told in the Lives of Their Liberators,* (paperback ed.; New York, 1965).

5. O'Leary, *Bolívar,* 36.

6. The example relies on Fisher, Kuethe, and McFarlane, *Reform and Insurrection,* 3–4.

7. These interesting points are made by David Rock, *Argentina, 1516–1982* (Berkeley, 1985), 73–76.

8. The material about Bernardo O'Higgins and the quotes are from Jay Kinsbruner, *Bernardo O'Higgins* (New York, 1968).

9. This discussion of the origins of Indian participation, or lack of it, in the Hidalgo uprising is taken from John Tutino, *From Insurrection to Revolution in Mexico: Social Bases of Agrarian Violence, 1750–1940* (Princeton, 1988), 3–212. Space has permitted me only to suggest the extraordinary richness of Tutino's research and argument.

10. For this discussion of Hidalgo and his revolt, I have followed Hugh M. Hamill, Jr., *The Hidalgo Revolt: Prelude to Mexican Independence* (Gainesville, 1966), a book that has aged very well and was a pleasure to reread after many years.

Chapter 5

1. Again I have followed my own book, *Bernardo O'Higgins.*

2. From 1777 the Peruvian government collected loans from various individuals at 3 to 6 percent interest, backed by funds collected by the *consulado* (the merchant tribunal) from new commercial taxes. Many merchants held these loans. Alfonso Quiroz offers the tantalizing observation that the possession of such interest-bearing loans tied merchants to the crown and helps to explain the extraordinary loyalism in Peru. Quiroz, *Domestic and Foreign Finance in Modern Peru,* 19; 21–22. In fact, the later republican governments never repaid these colonial loans.

3. Timothy E. Anna, *The Fall of the Royal Government in Peru* (Lincoln, 1979), 174.

4. Lecuna and Bierck, eds. *Selected Writings of Bolívar,* 2 vols. (New York, 1951), I, 222–23).

5. Quoted in Masur, *Simón Bolívar,* 283.

6. O'Leary, *Bolívar*, 139.

7. Ibid.

8. Ibid., 145.

9. Ibid., 150.

10. Ibid., 154.

11. Ibid.

12. Quoted in ibid., 157.

13. Ibid., 158–59, and following quote.

14. This account of the battle, as with all further battles, follows O'Leary, *Bolívar*, primarily, but also Masur, *Simón Bolívar*, who used many sources, but normally relied heavily upon O'Leary.

15. O'Leary, *Bolívar*, 172.

16. Morillo is quoted in ibid., 183. The further quotes are O'Leary's words from the same page. The final comment is from p. 184.

17. These are from letters in Vicente Lecuna, ed., *Simón Bolívar: Cartas del Libertador*, 10 vols. (Caracas, 1929–30).

18. The English version is from Masur, *Simón Bolívar*, 497. The Spanish version is from Lecuna, *Simón Bolívar*, 4:315–16.

19. Lecuna, *Simón Bolívar*, 6:3. My translation.

20. Essentially, I have followed Manuela's letter to O'Leary, which is in Daniel Florencio O'Leary, *Memorias del General O'Leary*, 32 vols. (Caracas, 1879–88), 3:333–38.

21. O'Leary, *Bolívar*, 251.

22. Ibid., 257–58.

23. For the siege of Callao and comments about Rodil, I have followed Anna, *Fall of the Royal Government in Peru*, 234–37.

24. Christon I. Archer, "'La Causa Buena': The Counterinsurgency Army of New Spain and the Ten Years' War," in *The Independence of Mexico and the Creation of the New Nation*, Jaime E. Rodríguez O., ed. (Los Angeles, 1989), 85–108.

25. For this discussion of Paraguay, I have navigated my way through Richard Alan White, *Paraguay's Autonomous Revolution, 1810–1840* (Albuquerque, 1978), who permits his theory to implode upon his facts; John Hoyt Williams, *The Rise and Fall of the Paraguayan Republic, 1800–1870* (Austin, 1979); and Thomas Whigham, *The Politics of River Trade: Tradition and Development in the Upper Plata, 1780–1870* (Albuquerque, 1991).

26. Most recently, Pedro Fraile Balbín, Richard Salvucci, and Linda K. Salvucci have argued that, in fact, it was the expansion of the Cuban economy that accounts for the island's loyalty. See their interesting contribution to the discussion of independence and loyalism, "El caso cubano: Exportaciones e independencia," in *La independencia americana: consecuencias económicas* eds. Leandro Prados de la Escosura y Samuel Amaral (Madrid, 1993), 80–101.

27. Fidel Iglesias, "A Collective Biography of the Río de la Plata Clergy, 1806–

1827," 33, no. 2 (1998) *LARR*, 166–83, and *A Prosopography of the River Plate Clergy During Independence and the Rivadavian Reforms, 1806–1827* (Lewiston, NY, forthcoming).

28. William B. Taylor, *Magistrates of the Sacred: Priests and Parishioners in Eighteenth-Century Mexico* (Stanford, 1996), 451 and passim.

29. Two important exceptions are Janet R. Kentner, "The Socio-Political Role of Women in the Mexican Wars of Independence" (Ph.D. diss., Loyola University of Chicago, 1957); and Silvia M. Arrom, *The Women of Mexico City* (Stanford, 1985). Arrom bases her discussion of the role of women during the Mexican independence movement essentially on Kentner's study. For an interesting discussion of the breakdown of the colonial Mexican patriarchal family during independence, see John Tutino, "The Revolution in Mexican Independence: Insurgency and the Renegotiation of Property, Production, and Patriarchy in the Bajío, 1800–1855," *HAHR* 78, no. 3 (August 1998), 368–418.

30. Arrom, *Women of Mexico City,* 32–33.

Chapter 6

1. Peter F. Guardino, *Peasants, Politics, and the Formation of Mexico's National State: Guerrero, 1800–1857* (Stanford, 1996), 90.

For a provocative study of the change from largeholding wheat production to smallholding maize production in Mexico as a result of the insurgency, and some of the economic consequences, see Tutino, "The Revolution in Mexican Independence."

2. Quoted in Charles A. Hale, *Mexican Liberalism in the Age of Mora, 1821– 1853* (New Haven, 1968), 150. For the discussion of utilitarianism here, I have followed Hale; see specifically, 148–151. Hale's book is one of the best works of intellectual history ever done by a Latin Americanist, and after a quarter-century I find that it has aged like a fine wine.

3. Quoted in José Luis Romero, *A History of Argentine Political Thought* (Stanford, 1963), 70. My thoughts about Liberalism have been greatly influenced by Hale's *Mexican Liberalism in the Age of Mora*. Comments about Mora and Constant in this chapter are from Hale, passim.

4. Romero, *History of Argentine Political Thought,* 70. The Moreno quotes also appear in Nicolas Shumway, *The Invention of Argentina* (Berkeley, 1991), 28, 30. Shumway locates Moreno's "authoritarianism" in the Argentine's seminary training, which contributed to an amalgam of scholastic and enlightened thought. This may have been so in Moreno's case, but we must not consider this to be a model possessed of explanatory power since there were other Spanish Americans, with similar religious training, who were more tolerant both of Rousseau's writings and of freedom of the press. On the other hand, there were many with more secular training who suppressed Rousseau and a liberal press.

5. Quoted in David Bushnell, ed., *The Liberator, Simón Bolívar* (New York, 1970), 11–21.

6. Ibid., 23–36.

7. Ibid.

8. Lecuna and Bierck, eds., *Selected Writings of Bolívar,* (New York, 1951), II, 765.

9. Actually, Bolívar said, "Those who have served the Revolution have ploughed the sea." Masur has translated this as "We have ploughed the sea," which involves a bit of dramatic license. In the circumstance of Bolívar's demise Masur's seems a fair translation, and I have adopted it in the text.

10. This discussion about the Provincial Deputations is from Nettie Lee Benson, *The Provincial Deputation in Mexico: Harbinger of Provincial Assemblies, Independence, and Federalism* (Austin, 1922), passim.

Chapter 7

1. This view of the weakness of the late colonial economy follows the innovative, and, for me, convincing work of John J. TePaske. See, for instance, his "The Financial Disintegration of the Royal Government of Mexico during the Epoch of Independence," in Rodríguez O., *Independence of Mexico,* 63–83.

2. With regard to cotton textile production in Puebla, I have followed the important work of Guy Thomson, "The Cotton Textile Industry in Puebla during the Eighteenth and Early Nineteenth Centuries," in Jacobsen and Puhle, *Economies of Mexico and Peru,* 169–202, and the comment by John H. Coatsworth, 233–39.

3. Donald F. Stevens, *Origins of Instability in Early Republican Mexico* (Durham, 1991), 59. This is practically a quote from Stevens's thought-provoking work.

4. Paul Gootenberg, *Between Silver and Guano* (Princeton, 1991), 11.

5. John V. Lombardi, *The Decline and Abolition of Negro Slavery in Venezuela, 1820–1854* (Westport, Conn., 1971), 99.

6. Quiroz, *Domestic and Foreign Finance in Modern Peru,* 31.

7. Rodríguez O., *Independence of Mexico,* 223.

8. Tulio Halperín-Donghi, *Politics, Economics and Society in Argentina in the Revolutionary Period* (Eng. trans.; Cambridge, 1975), 89. But in the Littoral provinces it was not Argentine cloth, but rather cheap Peruvian cloth that was being displaced. This was the result of political decisions that limited trade between Upper Peru and Argentina during the early independence period (ibid.).

9. Guy P. C. Thomson, *Puebla de Los Angeles: Industry and Society in a Mexican City, 1700–1850* (Boulder, 1989), 203–5; Richard J. Salvucci, *Textiles and Capitalism in Mexico* (Princeton, 1987), 163–68. See also the quantified discussion in Richard J. Salvucci, Linda K. Salvucci, and Aslán Cohen, "The Politics of Protection: Interpretating Commercial Policy in Late Bourbon and Early National

Mexico," in Andrien and Johnson, eds., *The Political Economy of Spanish America in the Age of Revolution, 1750–1850* (Albuquerque, 1994), 95–114.

10. David W. Walker, *Kinship, Business, and Politics: The Martínez del Río Family in Mexico, 1824–1867* (Austin, 1986), 155–63.

11. J. P. and W. P. Robertson, *Letters on South America*, 3 vols. (London, 1843), 1:175–79.

12. Quoted in Jay Kinsbruner, "The Business Activities of William Wheelwright in Chile, 1829–1860" (Ph.D. diss., New York University, 1964), 113.

13. Mark J. Van Aken, *Knight of the Night: Juan José Flores and Ecuador, 1824–1864* (Berkeley, 1989), 61–62. See also Magnus Mörner, *La corona española y los foráneos en los pueblos de indios de América* (Stockholm, 1970), 373–76, and more broadly, 337–84.

14. Gootenberg, *Between Silver and Guano*, 12, 69–74.

Chapter 8

1. Arrom, *Women of Mexico City,* 53–97.

✠

Selected Bibliography

This selected bibliography is designed to suggest further readings and to indicate some of the sources used in writing the present book. Space does not permit an exhaustive listing. Many older books familiar to generations of Latin Americanists are not included. Contributions well known to specialists—by Lucas Alamán, Bartolomé Mitre, Ricardo Levene, Ricardo Donoso, Eugenio Pereira Salas, and a host of others—therefore are not included. Also not included are scores of more recent books and articles that in their own right are valuable but that did not seem to fit the constraints of a selected bibliography.

For the sake of brevity, I have not repeated here several of the works cited in the notes. From the early 1970s through the summer of 1998, more than a hundred articles have appeared in English that are important to the topic of Spanish American independence. They have appeared in journals such as the *Hispanic American Historical Review* (hereafter *HAHR*), *The American Historical Review* (hereafter cited as *AHR*), *The Americas, Journal of Latin American Studies* (hereafter cited as *JLAS*), *Latin American Research Review* (hereafter cited as *LARR*), and *Past & Present*. These journals are available in many college libraries. I have included in the bibliography a representative sample of these articles.

During the past few years a large number of edited collected essays dealing with the independence period have appeared to our benefit. Of great importance is John R. Fisher, Allan J. Kuethe, and Anthony McFarlane, eds., *Reform and Insurrection in Bourbon New Granada and Peru* (Baton Rouge, 1990). Also important are Leslie Bethall, ed., *The Independence of Latin America* (Cambridge, 1989); and Bethall, ed., *Spanish America after Independence, c.1820–c.1870* (Cambridge, 1989). See also Robert Detweiler and Ramón Ruiz, eds., *Liberation in the Americas: Comparative Aspects of the Independence Movements in Mexico and the United States* (San Diego, 1978). Important essays by Coatsworth, MacLeod, TePaske, Klein, Carmagnani and the Villamaríns appear in Karen Spalding, ed., *Essays in the Political, Economic and Social History of Colonial Latin America* (Newark, Delaware, 1982); and by Coatsworth, Fisher, Van Young, Jacobsen, Larson, Thomson, Barbier, TePaske, O'Phelan Godoy, Deans-Smith, and others in Nils Jacobsen and Hans-Jürgen Puhle, eds., *The Economies of Mexico and Peru during the Late Colonial*

Period, 1760–1810 (Berlin, 1986). A challenging contribution is Leandro Prados de la Escosura and Samuel Amaral, eds., *La independencia americana: consecuencias económicas* (Madrid, 1993). Several important essays dealing with credit in the colonial Mexican economy are in Marie-Nöelle Chamoux et al., *Prestar y pedir prestado: Relaciones sociales y crédito en México del siglo XVI al XX* (México, D.F., 1993). A marvelous collection is Inge Buisson et al., eds., *Problemas de la formación del estado y de la nación en Hispanoamérica* (Cologne, 1984). Important essays appear in Brooke Larson and Olivia Harris with Enrique Tandeter, eds., *Ethnicity, Markets, And Migration In The Andes* (Durham, 1995). Valuable information and interpretation is in Steve J. Stern, ed., *Resistance, Rebellion, and Consciousness in the Andean Peasant World . . .* (Madison, 1987); and Friedrich Katz, ed., *Riot, Rebellion, and Revolution* (Princeton, 1988). Excellent essays appear in Richard L. Garner and William B. Taylor, eds., *Iberian Colonies, New World Societies . . .* (University Park, Pa., 1985); Jacques A. Barbier and Allan J. Kuethe, eds., *The North American Role in the Spanish Imperial Economy, 1760–1819* (Manchester, 1984); Arij Ouweneel and Cristina Torales Pacheco, eds., *Empresarios, indios y estado: Perfil de la economía méxicana (Siglo XVIII)* (Amsterdam, 1988); Reinhard Liehr, ed., *América Latina en la época de Simón Bolívar . . .* (Berlin, 1989); Joseph L. Love and Nils Jacobsen, eds., *Guiding the Invisible Hand: Economic Liberalism and the State in Latin American History* (New York, 1988); Lyman L. Johnson and Enrique Tandeter, eds., *Essays on the Price History of Eighteenth-Century Latin America* (Albuquerque, 1990); and Kenneth J. Andrien and Lyman L. Johnson, eds., *The Political Economy of Spanish America in the Age of Revolution, 1750–1850* (Albuquerque, 1994); Oscar Cornblit, *Power and Violence in the Colonial City: (Oruro from the Mining Renaissance to the Rebellion of Tupac Amaru (1740–1782)* (trans.; Cambridge, 1995); Leonor Ludlos and Carlos Marichal, eds., *Banca y poder en México (1800–1925)* (México, D.F., 1985); and Mark D. Szuchman, ed., *The Middle Period in Latin America* (Boulder, 1989); Antonio Annino et al., *America Latina: Dallo Stato Coloniale Allo Stato Nazione* (Milan, 1987); Germán Colmenares et al., *La independencia: Ensayos de historia social* ([Bogotá], 1986). A series of valuable bibliographic essays are in Robert M. Maniquis et al., *La Revolución Francesa y el mundo ibérico* (Madrid, 1990). Several older collections have held up well. See Heraclio Bonilla et al., *La independencia en el Perú* (Lima, 1972); Arthur P. Whitaker, ed., *Latin America and the Enlightenment*, 2d ed. (Ithaca, 1961). Still of importance are Congreso Hispanoamericana de Historia, *Causas y carácteres de la independencia* (Madrid, 1953); and Consejo Superior de Investigaciones Científicas, *Estudios sobre la emancipación de Hispanoamérica* (Madrid, 1963).

Important sources are the multivolume studies done by the Academia Nacional de la Historia, *El movimiento emancipador de Hispanoamérica*, 4 vols. (Caracas, 1961), *El pensamiento constitucional hispanoamericano hasta 1830*, 5 vols. (Caracas, 1961), and *El pensamiento constitutional de Latinoamérica, 1810–1830*, 5 vols. (Caracas, 1962). The latter two contain many significant articles and the constitutions of the period. An excellent constitutional study is Glen Dealy, "Prolegomena on the Spanish American Political Tradition," *HAHR* 48, no. 1 (February 1968). For the study that inspired much social and economic investigation, see Charles C. Griffin, "Economic and Social Aspects of the Era of Spanish-American Independence," *HAHR* 29, no. 2 (May 1949), 170–87, which was the core of his later *Los temas sociales y económicos en la época de la independencia* (Caracas, 1962).

On the Church see Pedro de Leturia, *Relaciones entre la Santa Sede e Hispanoamérica, 1493–1835,* 3 vols. (Caracas, 1959); John Lloyd Mecham, *Church and State in Latin America,* rev. ed. (Chapel Hill, 1966); and Nancy Farriss's especially important *Crown and Clergy in Colonial Mexico, 1795–1821* (London, 1968). On the role of the clergy during the independence period, see the monumental and defining work by William B. Taylor, *Magistrates of the Sacred: Priests and Parishioners in Eighteenth-Century Mexico* (Stanford, 1996). Also important are Sister Maria Consuelo Sparks, "The Role of the Clergy During the Struggle for Independence in Peru" (Ph.D. diss., University of Pittsburgh, 1972); and Fidel Iglesias, *A Prosopography of the River Plate Clergy During Independence and the Rivadavian Reforms, 1806–1827* (Lewiston, NY, forthcoming); and his "A Collective Biography of the Río de la Plata Clergy, 1806–1827," *LARR* 33, no. 2 (1998), 166–83; Luisa Zahino Peñafort, *Iglesia y Sociedad en México, 1765–1800* (México, D.F., 1996); and Carlos Antonio Heyn Schupp, SDB, *Iglesia y Estado en el Proceso de Emancipación Política del Paraguay (1811–1853)* (Asunción, 1991). The role of the Church in Mexico's colonial economy is clarified in Ma. del Pilar Martínez López-Cano, ed., *Iglesia, Estado y Economía: Siglos XVI al XIX* (México, D.F., 1995). The essay by John F. Schwaller is particularly important.

Many of the topics indicated in the remainder of this bibliography are covered by essays in the collections mentioned above. Furthermore, many of the items mentioned could be cited under various subject headings. On the late colonial revolts see Lillian Estelle Fisher, *The Last Inca Revolt, 1780–1783* (Norman, Okla., 1966); Scarlett O'Phelan Godoy, *Rebellions and Revolts in Eighteenth Century Peru and Upper Peru* (Cologne, 1985); Boleslao Lewin's provocative *La insurrección de Túpac Amaru,* 2nd ed. (Buenos Aires, 1967); Carlos Daniel Valcárcel, *Túpac Amaru: Precursor de la independencia* (Lima, 1977); Pablo E. Cárdenas Acosta, *El movimiento comunal de 1781 en el Nuevo Granada,* 2 vols. (Bogotá, 1960); John Leddy Phelan, *The People and the King: The Comunero Revolution in Colombia, 1781* (Madison, 1978); Alberto Flores Galindo, ed., *Sociedad colonial y sublevaciones populares: Túpac Amaru II. 1780* (Lima, 1976); the same author's *Independencia y revolución, 1780–1840,* 2 vols. (Lima, 1987); Alfredo Moreno Cebrián, *El corregidor de indios y la economía peruana del siglo XVIII . . .* (Madrid, 1977); Joseph Pérez, *Los movimientos precursores de la emancipación en Hispanoamérica* (Madrid, 1977; repr., 1982); Segundo E. Moreno Yáñez, *Sublevaciones indígenas en la Audiencia de Quito . . .* 3d ed. (Quito, 1985); Jürgen Golte, *Repartos y rebeliones: Túpac Amaru y las contradicciones de la economía colonial* (trans.; Lima, 1980); Edberto Oscar Acevedo, *Rebelión de 1767 en el Tucumán* (Mendoza, Argentina, 1969); and William B. Taylor, *Drinking, Homicide and Rebellion in Colonial Mexi-*

can Villages (Stanford, 1979). Several articles are particularly important: Anthony McFarlane, "Civil Disorders and Popular Protests in Late Colonial New Granada," *HAHR* 64, no. 1 (February 1984), 17–54; McFarlane, "The 'Rebellion of the Barrios': Urban Insurrection in Bourbon Quito," *HAHR* 69, no. 2 (May 1989), 283–330; Kenneth J. Andrien, "Economic Crisis, Taxes and the Quito Insurrection of 1765," *Past and Present*, no. 129 (November 1990), 104–31; Leon G. Campbell, "The Army of Peru and the Túpac Amaru Revolt, 1780–1783," *HAHR* 56, no. 1 (February, 1976), 17–54; and Campbell, "Social Structure of the Túpac Amaru Army in Cuzco," *HAHR* 61, no. 4 (November, 1981), 675–93. For an excellent discussion of the Maya during the late colonial period, see Robert. W. Patch, *Maya and Spaniard in Yucatan, 1648–1812* (Stanford, 1993). For a challenging consideration of the repartimiento in Oaxaca, a place much in the news these days, see, Jeremy Baskes, "Coerced or Voluntary? The *Repartimiento* and Market Participation of Peasants in Late Colonial Oaxaca," *JLAS* 28, no. 1 (February 1996), 2–28.

On the late colonial period and the Bourbon reforms see Robert J. Shafer's classic *The Economic Societies in the Spanish World, 1763–1821* (Syracuse, 1958); Thomas F. Glick, "Science and Independence in Latin America (With Special Reference to New Granada)," *HAHR* 71, no. 2 (May 1991), 307–34; Janet R. Fireman, *The Spanish Royal Corps of Engineers in the Western Borderlands. Instrument of Bourbon Reform, 1764–1815* (Glendale, Calif., 1977); Rose Marie Buechler, *The Mining Society of Potosí, 1776–1810* (Ann Arbor, l981); Jacques A. Barbier, *Reform and Politics in Bourbon Chile, 1755–1796* (Ottawa, 1980); Barbier's "The Culmination of the Bourbon Reforms, 1787–1792," *HAHR* 57, no. 1 (February 1977), 51–68; Leon G. Campbell, "A Colonial Establishment: Creole Domination of the Audiencia of Lima During the Late Eighteenth Century," *HAHR* 52, no. 1 (February 1972), 1–25; and Nancy M. Farriss's remarkable *Maya Society Under Colonial Rule* (Princeton, 1984). Many issues relating to mining and Indian labor in Upper Peru (which became Bolivia) are elucidated in Enrique Tandeter's *Coercion and Market: Silver Mining in Colonial Potosí, 1692–1826* (Albuquerque, 1993).

An excellent and essential study of the Bourbon period in New Granada is Anthony McFarlane, *Colombia Before Independence: Economy, Society, and Politics Under Bourbon Rule* (Cambridge, 1993). Very important also are Rafael Gómez Hoyos, *La Revolución Granadina de 1810: Ideario de una generación y de una época, 1781–1821* 2 vols. (Bogotá, 1962); and Margarita Garrido, *Reclamos y representaciones: Variaciones sobre la política en el Nuevo Reino de Granada, 1770–1815* (Bogotá, 1993). An interesting article is Victor M. Uribe, "Kill all the Lawyers!: Lawyers and the Independence Movement in New Granada, 1809–1820," *The Americas* 52, no. 2 (October 1995), 175–210. Uribe puts the matter of creole grievance over bureaucratic participation in clearer context. It was not the central reason that many creole lawyers started on the road to independence. Uribe adds further information about the lawyers in "The Lawyers and New Granada's Late Colonial State," *JLAS* 27, no. 3 (October 1995), 517–549.

With regard to the Bourbon reforms several important studies have appeared that deal with the issue of commerce. Among them are Geoffrey J. Walker, *Spanish Politics and Imperial Trade, 1700–1789* (Bloomington, 1979); Antonio García-Baquero González, *Comercio colonial y guerras revolucionarios. La decadencia económica de Cádiz a raíz de la emancipación americana* (Seville, 1972); García-Baquero, *Cádiz y el Atlántico (1770–1778) . . .* 2 vols. (Seville, 1976); Javier Ortiz De La Tabla Ducasse, *Comercio exterior de Veracruz, 1778–1821: Crisis de dependencia* (Seville, 1978); and John Fisher, *Commercial relations between Spain and Spanish America in the Era of Free Trade, 1778–1796* (Liverpool, 1985); Fisher, *Trade, War and Revolution: Exports from Spain to Spanish America* (Liverpool, 1992); Carmen Parrón Salas, *De las Reformas borbónicas a la República: El consulado y el comercio marítimo de Lima, 1778–1821* (San Javier, Spain, 1995); Stanley J. Stein, "Bureaucracy and Business in the Spanish Empire, 1759–1804: Failure of a Bourbon Reform in Mexico and Peru," *HAHR* 61, no. 1 (February 1981), 1–28; Juan Carlos Garavaglia, "Economic Growth and Regional Differentiations: The River Plate Region at the End of the Eighteenth Century," *HAHR* 65, no. 1 (February 1985), 51–89; Susan Deans-Smith, *Bureaucrats, Planters, And Workers: The Making of the Tobacco Monopoly in Bourbon Mexico* (Austin, 1992); Asunción Lavrin, "The Execution of the Law of *Consolidación* in New Spain: Economic Aims and Results," *HAHR* 53, no. 1 (February 1973), 27–49; Margaret Chowning, "The Consolidación de Vales Reales in the Bishopric of Michoacán," *HAHR* 69, no. 3 (August, 1989), 451–78; and José Cuello, "The Economic Impact of the Bourbon Reforms and the Late Colonial Crisis of Empire at the Local Level: The Case of Saltillo," *The Americas* 44, no. 3 (1988), 301–23.

On the workings of the colonial system see John Leddy Phelan's significant *The Kingdom of Quito in the Seventeenth Century: Bureaucratic Politics in the Spanish Empire* (Madison, 1967). Phelan presents a stimulating conceptual discussion, part of which is aimed at Richard M. Morse's "The Heritage of Latin America," a chapter in Louis Hartz, ed., *The Founding of New Societies* (New York, 1964). Morse presented a major interpretative essay, with which I disagree on several central points. A follow-up to the Morse essay is Magali Sarfati, *Spanish Bureaucratic-Patrimonialism in America* (Berkeley, 1966). Since then we have had excellent studies on the bureaucracy. See Linda Arnold, *Bureaucracy and Bureaucrats in Mexico City, 1742–1835* (Tucson, 1988); and Susan Migden Socolow, *The Bureaucrats of Buenos Aires, 1769–1810: Amor al Real Servicio* (Durham, 1987). Also of interest is José M. Mariluz Urquijo, *Orígenes de la burocracia rioplatense . . .* (Buenos Aires, 1974).

An important study of the colonial government is John Lynch, *Spanish Colonial Administration, 1782–1810: The Intendant System in the Viceroyalty of the Rio de la Plata* (London, 1958). Also important is John Fisher, *Government and Society in Colonial Peru: The Intendant System, 1784–1814* (London, 1970). See also Edberto Oscar Acevedo, *La Intendencia de Salta del Tucumán en el virreinato del Río de la Plata* (Mendoza, 1965). Of extraordinary importance is Mark A. Burkholder and D. S. Chandler, *From Impotence To Authority: The Spanish Crown and the American Audiencias, 1687–1808* (Columbia, Mo., 1977); and their *Biographical Dictionary of Audiencia Ministers in the Americas, 1687–1821* (Westport, Conn., 1982). Good also is Alí Enrique López Bohórquez, *Los ministros de la audiencia de Caracas (1786–1810)* (Caracas, 1984). Many important topics are treated in Reinhard Liehr, *Ayuntamiento y oligarquía en Puebla, 1787–1810*, 2 vols. (trans.; México, D.F., 1971). An important and informative book about the late colonial period is Charles R. Cutter's *The Legal Culture of Northern New Spain, 1700–1810* (Albuquerque, 1995). Also worthwile is D. S. Chandler, *Social Assistance and Bureaucratic Politics. The Montepíos of Colonial Mexico, 1767–1823* (Albuquerque, 1991), which, among other things, helps elucidate the Spanish logic of patriarchy.

The pioneering study of the military in late colonial Spanish America is Lyle N. McAlister, The *"Fuero Militar" in New Spain, 1764–1800* (Gainesville, 1957). Four important studies followed upon McAlister's initiative: Christon I. Archer, *The Army in Bourbon Mexico, 1760–1810* (Albuquerque, 1977); Leon G. Campbell, *The Military and Society in Colonial Peru, 1750–1810* (Philadelphia, 1978); Allan J. Kuethe, *Reform and Society in New Granada, 1773–1808* (Gainseville, 1978); and his *Cuba, 1753–1815: Crown, Military, and Society* (Knoxville, 1986). The following articles are important: Christon I. Archer, "The Royalist Army in New Spain: Civil-Military Relationships, 1810–1821," *JLAS* 13, no. 1 (May 1981), 57–82; and Brian Hamnett, "Royalist Counterinsurgency and the Continuity of Rebellion: Guanajuato and Michoacán, 1813–1820," *HAHR* 66, no. 1 (February 1982), 19–48. On the Spanish army, see Margaret L. Woodward, "The Spanish Army and the Loss of America, 1810–1824," *HAHR* 48, no. 4 (November, 1968), 586–607; and Gary M. Miller, "Status and Loyalty of Regular Army Officers in Late Colonial Venezuela," *HAHR* 66, no. 4 (November 1986), 667–96. Regarding women in the military campaigns, see Elizabeth Salas, *Soldaderas in the Mexican Military* (Austin, 1990); and Evelyn May Cherpak, "Women and the Independence of Gran Colombia, 1780–1830" (Ph.D. diss, University of North Carolina, Chapel Hill, 1973).

On the Cádiz *Cortes* see Nettie Lee Benson, ed., *Mexico and the Spanish Cortes, 1810–1822* (Austin, 1966); María Isabel Arriazu et al., *Estudios sobre Cortes de Cádiz* (Pamplona, 1967); Marie Laure Rieu-Millán, *Los diputados americanos en las Cortes de Cádiz: igualdad o independencia* (Madrid, 1990); and Mario Rodríguez, *The Cádiz Experiment in Central America, 1808–1826* (Berkeley, 1978), which should be read also to understand the Central American effort at unity. On the fall of the empire, see Timothy E. Anna, *Spain and the Loss of America* (Lincoln, 1983); Anna, "Spain and the Breakdown of the Imperial Ethos: The Problem of Equality," *HAHR* 62, no. 2 (May 1982), 254–72; Anna, "The Last Viceroys of New Spain and Peru," *AHR* 81, no. 1 (February 1976), 38–65; and Michael P. Costeloe, *Response to Revolution: Imperial Spain and the Spanish American Revolutions, 1810–1840* (Cambridge, 1986). The studies by Anna and Costeloe add greatly to our knowledge of attitudes and actions in Spain as the empire crumbled.

See also Juan Friede, *La otra verdad. La independencia americana vista por los españoles* (Bogotá, 1972).

Under the broad heading of social and economic history, the following are particularly important: Magnus Mörner, *The Andean Past: Land, Societies, and Conflicts* (New York, 1985); Walter Howe, *The Mining Guild of New Spain and its Tribunal General, 1770–1821* (Cambridge, 1949); Pedro Pérez Herrero, *Plata y libranzas. La articulación comercial del México borbónico* (México, D.F., 1988); Richard B. Lindley, *Haciendas and Economic Development: Guadalajara, Mexico, at Independence* (Austin, 1983); John C. Super, *La vida en Querétaro durante la colonia, 1531–1810* (México, D.F., 1983); David A. Brading, *Miners and Merchants in Bourbon Mexico, 1763–1810* (Cambridge, 1971) and his *Haciendas and Ranchos in the Mexican Bajío: León, 1700–1860* (Cambridge, 1978); Brian R. Hamnett, *Politics and Trade in Southern Mexico, 1750–1821* (Cambridge, 1971), and his *Roots of Insurgency: Mexican Regions, 1750–1824* (Cambridge, 1986); Linda Greenow, *Credit and Socioeconomic Change in Colonial Mexico . . .* (Boulder, 1983); Michael M. Swann, *Tierra Adentro: Settlement and Society in Colonial Durango* (Boulder, 1982), and his *Migrants in the Mexican North . . .* (Boulder, 1989); Claude Morin, *Michoacán en la Nueva España del siglo XVIII . . .* (trans.; México, D.F., 1979); John Tutino, *From Insurrection to Revolution in Mexico: Social Bases of Agrarian Violence, 1750–1940* (Princeton, 1988); John E. Kicza, *Colonial Entrepreneurs: Families and Business in Bourbon Mexico City* (Albuquerque, 1983), and his "Life Patterns and Social Differentiation Among Common People in Late Colonial Mexico City," *Estudios De Historia Novohispana* 11 (1991), 183–200; Eric Van Young, *Hacienda and Market in Eighteenth-Century Mexico: The Rural Economy of the Guadalajara Region, 1675–1820* (Berkeley, 1981); Cheryl English Martin, *Rural Society in Colonial Morelos* (Albuquerque, 1985); and Martin's *Governance and Society in Colonial Mexico: Chihuahua in the Eighteenth Century* (Stanford, 1996), for a fascinating and informative view of life for women on the Mexican frontier; Cynthia Radding, *Wandering Peoples: Colonialism, Ethnic Spaces, and Ecological Frontiers in Northwestern Mexico, 1700–1850* (Durham, 1997); Ramón María Serrera Contreras, *Guadalajara ganadera. Estudio regional novohispano, 1760–1805* (Seville, 1977); Richard J. Salvucci, *Textiles and Capitalism in Mexico . . .* (Princeton, 1987); Charles H. Harris, III, *A Mexican Latifundo: The Economic Empire of the Sánchez Navarro Family, 1765–1821* (Austin, 1975); Jorge González Angulo Aguirre, *Artesanado y ciudad a finales del siglo XVIII* (México, D.F., 1983); Patrick J. Carroll, *Blacks in Colonial Veracruz* (Austin, 1991); Richard L. Garner, *Economic Growth and Change in Bourbon Mexico* (Gainesville, 1993); Alberto Flores-Galindo, *Arequipa y el sur andino . . .* (Lima, 1977); Kendall W. Brown, *Bourbon and Brandy: Imperial Reform in Eighteenth-Century Arequipa* (Albuquerque, 1986); Martin Minchom, *The People of Quito, 1690–1810* (Boulder, 1994); Kenneth J. Andrien, *The Kingdom of Quito, 1690–1830: The State and Regional Development* (Cambridge, 1995); John R. Fisher, *Silver Mines And Silver Miners In Colonial Peru, 1776–1824* (Liverpool, 1977); Fisher, "Royalism, Regionalism, and

Rebellion in Colonial Peru, 1808–1815," *HAHR* 59, no. 2 (May 1979), 232–57; Alfonso W. Quiroz, *Domestic and Foreign Finance in Modern Peru, 1850–1950* (Pittsburgh, 1993); Thomas Millington, *Debt Politics after Independence: The Funding Conflict in Bolivia* (Gainesville, 1992); Ann Twinam, *Miners, Merchants, and Farmers in Colonial Colombia* (Austin, 1982); Miles Wortman, *Government and Society in Central America, 1680–1840* (New York, 1982); Ralph Lee Woodward, Jr., *Class Privilege and Economic Development: The Consulado de Comercio of Guatemala, 1793–1871* (Chapel Hill, 1966); Richmond F. Brown, *Juan Fermín de Aycinena: Central American Colonial Entrepreneur, 1729–1796* (Norman, 1997); Lowell Gudmundson and Héctor Lindo-Fuentes, *Central America, 1821–1871: Liberalism before Liberal Reform* (Tuscaloosa, 1995); Mercedes M. Alvarez, *Comercio y comerciantes* (Caracas, 1963), and her *El Tribunal del Real Consulado de Caracas,* 2 vols. (Caracas, 1967); Sergio Villalobos, *El comercio y la crisis colonial* (Santiago, 1968); Carlos S. A. Segreti, *Temas de historia Colonial . . .* (Buenos Aires, 1987); Juan Carlos Garavaglia, *Economía, sociedad y regiones* (Buenos Aires, 1987); Gilma Lucía Mora de Tovar, *Aguardiente y conflictos sociales en la Nueva Granada durante el siglo XVIII* (Bogotá, 1988); Robson Brines Tyrer, *Historia demográfica y económica de la Audiencia de Quito. Población indígena e industria textil, 1600–1800* (Quito, 1988); Thomas Whigham, *The Politics of River Trade: Tradition and Development in the Upper Plata, 1780–1870* (Albuquerque, 1991).

Important books that deal with the independence era and later in Argentina are Jonathan C. Brown, *A Socioeconomic History of Argentina, 1776–1860* (Cambridge, 1979); Mark D. Szuchman, *Order, Family, and Community in Buenos Aires, 1810–1860* (Stanford, 1988); Miron Burgin, *The Economic Aspects of Argentine Federalism, 1820–1852* (Cambridge, Mass., 1946); Marcello Carmagnani, ed., *Federalismos latinoamericanos: México/Brazil/Argentina* (México, D.F., 1993); and David Bushnell, *Reform and Reaction in the Platine Provinces, 1810–1852* (Gainesville, 1983). Several books by Tulio Halperín-Donghi are significant. Among them are *Politics, Economics and Society in Argentina in the Revolutionary Period* (trans.; Cambridge, 1975); *Guerra y finanzas en los orígenes del estado argentino (1791–1850)* (Buenos Aires, 1982); and, in a broader sense, his *The Aftermath of Revolution in Latin America* (trans.; New York, 1973). On the origins of Argentine nationhood, see Nicolas Shumway, *The Invention of Argentina* (Berkeley, 1991).

Among the important books on Mexico are Doris M. Ladd, *The Mexican Nobility at Independence, 1780–1826* (Austin, 1976); Sylvia M. Arrom, *The Women of Mexico City, 1790–1857* (Stanford, 1985); Brian R. Hamnett, *Revolución y contrarevolución en México y el Peru . . . (1800–1824)* (trans.; México, D.F., 1978); Guy P. C. Thomson, *Puebla de los Angeles: Industry and Society in a Mexican City, 1700–1850* (Boulder, 1989); David W. Walker, *Kinship, Business, And Politics: The Martínez del Río Family in Mexico, 1824–1867* (Austin, 1986); Robert A. Potash, *Mexican Government and Industrial Development in the Early Republic. The Banco De Avío* (Amherst, 1983); Barbara Tenenbaum, *The Politics of Penury* (Albuquerque, 1986); John Coatsworth, "Obstacles to Economic Growth in Nineteenth Century Mexico," *AHR* 83, no. 1 (February 1978), 80–100; Eugene L. Wiemers, Jr., "Agriculture and Credit in Nineteenth-Century Mexico: Orizaba and Córdoba, 1822–1971," *HAHR* 65, no. 3 (August 1985), 519–46; John Tutino, "The Revolution in Mexican Independence: Insurgency and the Renegotiation of Property, Production, and Patriarchy in the Bajío, 1800–1855," *HAHR* 78, no. 3 (August 1998), 367–418; Michael P. Costeloe, *La primera república federal de México (1824–1835)* . . . (trans.; México, D.F., 1975); Charles W. Macune, Jr., *El Estado de México y la Federación Mexicana* (México, D.F., 1978); Stanley C. Green, *The Mexican Republic: The First Decade, 1823–1832* (Pittsburgh, 1987); Anna Macías, *Génesis del gobierno constitucional en México: 1808–1820* (trans.; México, D.F., 1973); Harold Dana Sims, *The Expulsion of Mexico's Spaniards, 1821–1836* (Pittsburgh, 1990); Timothy E. Anna, *The Fall of the Royal Government in Mexico City* (Lincoln, 1978); and Romeo Flores Caballero, *Counterrevolution: The Role of the Spaniards in the Independence of Mexico, 1804–38* (trans.; Lincoln, 1974). The English edition of Nettie Lee Benson's *The Provincial Deputation in Mexico* (Austin, 1992) will bring this important study the wide readership it deserves. Interesting essays are in Josefina Zoraida Vásquez, ed., *Interpretaciones de la Independencia De México* (México, D.F., 1997). A brilliant analysis of federalism and liberal politics in the state of Guerrero is Peter F. Guardino's *Peasants, Politics, and the Formation of Mexico's National State: Guerrero, 1800–1857* (Stanford, 1996). Guardino also adds significantly to our understanding of early national republicanism, seen especially at the regional level. Also valuable is the above mentioned edited work by Marcello Carmagnani.

Other countries are well treated in John V. Lombardi, *The Decline and Abolition of Negro Slavery in Venezuela, 1820–1854* (Wesport, Conn., 1971); and his *People and Places in Colonial Venezuela* (Bloomington, 1976); Miguel Izard, *El miedo a la revolución: La lucha por la libertad en Venezuela (1777–1830)* (Madrid, 1979); P. Michael McKinley, *Pre-Revolutionary Caracas: Politics, Economy and Society* (Cambridge, 1987); Roger M. Haigh, *The Formation of the Chilean Oligarchy, 1810–1821* (Salt Lake City, 1972); Sergio Villalobos, *Tradición y reforma en 1810* (Santiago, 1961); Jaime Eyzaguirre, *Ideario y ruta de la emancipación chilena* (Santiago, 1957); Mary Lowenthal Felstiner, "Kinship Politics in the Chilean Independence Movement," *HAHR* 56, no. 1 (February 1976), 58–80; Lincoln Machado Ribas, *Movimientos revolucionarios* (Montevideo, 1940); Juan Uslar Pietri, *Historia de la rebelión popular de 1814* (Caracas, 1972); Timothy E. Anna, *The Fall of the Royal Government in Peru* (Lincoln, 1979); Nelson de la Torre et al., *La revolución agraria artiguista (1815–1816)* (Montevideo, 1969); Paul Gootenberg, *Between Silver and Guano: Commercial Policy and the State in Postindependence Peru* (Princeton, 1991); Peter Blanchard, *Slavery and Abolition in Early Republican Peru* (Wilmington, Del., 1992); E. Bradford Burns, *Patriarch and Folk: The Emergence of Nicaragua, 1798–1858* (Cambridge, 1991); John Hoyt Williams, *The Rise and Fall of the Paraguayan Republic, 1800–1870* (Austin, 1979); Mario Pastore, "Taxation,

Coercion, Trade and Development in a Frontier Economy: Early and Mid Colonial Paraguay," *JLAS* 29, no. 2 (May 1997), 329–54. Also good is Pastore's, "Trade Contraction and Economic Decline: The Paraguayan Economy under Francia, 1810–1840," *JLAS* 26, no. 3 (October 1994), 539–95. Interesting is Vera Blinn Reber, "Small Farmers in the Paraguayan Economy: The Paraguayan Example, 1810–1865," *The Americas* 51, no. 4 (April 1995), 495–524.

Also worthwhile are Carlos Marichal, *A Century of Debt Crisis in Latin America* . . . (Princeton, 1989); Frank Griffith Dawson, *The First Latin American Debt Crisis: The City of London and the 1822–25 Loan Bubble* (New Haven, 1990); and Reinhard Liehr, (ed.), *The Public Debt in Latin America in Historical Perspective* (Frankfurt am Main, 1995).

For an excellent discussion of the independence period in Brazil, see Roderick J. Barman, *Brazil: The Forging of a Nation, 1798–1852* (Stanford, 1988). Also useful is Kenneth Maxwell, *Pombal: Paradox of the Enlightenment* (Cambridge, 1995).

For Marxist interpretations see, for instance, Hernán Ramírez Necoechea's *Antecedentes económicos de la independencia de Chile*, 2d ed. (Santiago, 1967); Luis Vitale's *Interpretación marxista de la historia de Chile: La colonia y la Revolución de 1810* (Santiago, 1969); and M. S. Alperovich, *Historia de la independencia de México (1810–1824)* (trans.; México D.F., 1967).

On political thought and intellectual history, see O. Carlos Stoetzer, *The Scholastic Roots of the Spanish American Revolution* (New York, 1979); José Luis Romero, *A History of Argentine Political Thought* (trans.; Stanford, 1963); Eugene M. Wait, "Mariano Moreno: Promoter of Enlightenment," *HAHR* 45, no. 2 (August 1965), 359–83; Simon Collier, *Ideas and Politics of Chilean Independence, 1808–1833* (Cambridge, 1967); Jonathan Harris, "An English Utilitarian Looks at Spanish American Independence: Jeremy Bentham's "*Rid Yourselves of Ultramaria*" *The Americas* 53, no. 2 (October 1996), 217–33; Charles A. Hale, *Mexican Liberalism in the Age of Mora, 1821–1853* (New Haven, 1968); Luis Villoro, "The Ideological Currents of the Epoch of Independence," in Mario de la Cueva, ed., *Major Trends in Mexican Philosophy* (Notre Dame, 1966); Dorothy Tanck Estrada, *La educación ilustrada, 1786–1836: Educación primaria en la ciudad de México* (México, D.F., 1977); John V. Lombardi, *The Political Ideology of Fray Servando Teresa de Mier: Propagandist for Independence* (Cuernavaca, 1968); David A. Brading, *The Origins of Mexican Nationalism* (2d. ed.; Cambridge, 1983), and his *Prophecy and Myth in Mexican History* (Cambridge, [1984]). To Brading the independence movements in Mexico and Venezuela were revolutions rather than rebellions. See also Peggy K. Liss, *Atlantic Empires: The Network of Trade and Revolution, 1713–1826* (Baltimore, 1983).

Many good books deal with the personalities of the period. Among them are William Spence Robertson, *Rise of the Spanish-American Republics: As Told in the Lives of Their Liberators* (New York, 1961); John J. Johnson, ed., *Simón Bolívar and Spanish American Independence, 1783–1830* (New York, 1968); David Bushnell, ed., *The Liberator Simón Bolívar* (New York, 1970); and the standard biography in

English, Gerhard Masur, *Simón Bolívar,* 2d ed. (Albuquerque, 1969). For Bolívar's political thought, see Victor Andrés Belaunde, *Bolívar and the Political Thought of the Spanish American Revolution* (Baltimore, 1938). Of great value is the February 1983 issue of the *HAHR* (63, no. 1), in which the four articles consider Bolívar. See also Timothy E. Anna, "Economic Causes of San Martín's Failure in Lima," *HAHR* 54, no. 4 (November 1974), 657–81. An interesting study is Antonio Cussen, *Bello and Bolívar: Poetry and Politics in the Spanish American Revolution* (Cambridge, 1992). However, Cussen's book is an example of how seemingly difficult it is for scholars in other disciplines to read widely in the pertinent historical literature.

There is much recent interest in the life of Manuela Saenz. A selection of her letters, as well as some poems about her, are in Ligia Elena Rojas, *Manuela: Mujer Republicana* (Caracas, 1994). An interesting study is Manuel Espinosa Apolo, *Simón Bolívar y Manuela Saenz: Correspondencia íntima* (Quito, 1996). Here Manuela, like many other women, fights alongside the men, and is even raised to the rank of Capitan and then Colonel of Hussars. Probably such commissioning was honorific. Several fascinating portraits of Manuela are in Arturo Valero Martínez, ed., *En defensa de Manuela Saenz, Libertadora del Libertador* (Guayaquil, 1988).

Other important works are Hugh M. Hamill, Jr., *The Hidalgo Revolt* (Gainesville, 1966); Eric Van Young, "Islands in the Storm: Quiet Cities and Violent Countrysides in the Mexican Independence Era," *Past and Present,* no. 118 (February 1988), 130–55, and his "Millennium on the Northern Marches: The Mad Messiah of Durango and Popular Rebellion in Mexico, 1800–1815," *Comparative Studies in Society and History,* 28, no. 3 (July 1986), 385–413; William H. Timmons, *Morelos: Priest, Soldier, Statesman* (El Paso, 1963); Timmons, "Los Guadalupes: A Secret Society in the Mexican Revolution," *HAHR* 30, no. 4 (November 1950), 453–99; Timothy E. Anna, *The Mexican Empire of Iturbide* (Lincoln, 1990); Louis E. Baumgartner, *José del Valle of Central America* (Durham, 1963); Philip F. Flemion, "States' Rights and Partisan Politics: Manuel José Arce and the Struggle for Central American Union," *HAHR* 53, no. 4 (November 1973), 600–18; Nettie Lee Benson and Charles R. Berry, "The Central American Delegates to the First Constituent Congress of Mexico, 1822–1823," *HAHR* 49, no. 4 (November 1969), 679–702; Mario Rodríguez, *A Palmerstonian Diplomat in Central America* (Tucson, 1964); David L. Chandler, *Juan José del Aycinena. Idealista conservador de la Guatemala del siglo XIX* (South Woodstock, Vt., 1988); Benjamin Keen, *David Curtis DeForest and the Revolution of Buenos Aires* 2d ed. (Westport, Conn., 1970); John Lynch, *Argentine Dictator: Juan Manuel De Rosas, 1829–1852* (Oxford, 1981); John Street, *Artigas and the Emancipation of Uruguay* (Cambridge, 1959); David Bushnell, *The Santander Regime in Gran Colombia* (Newark, Del., 1954); Thomas Blossom, *Nariño: Hero of Colombian Independence* (Tucson, 1967); Jaime E. Rodríguez O., *The Emergence of Spanish America: Vicente Rocafuerte and Spanish Americanism, 1808–1832* (Berkeley, 1975); Mark J. Van

Aken, *King of the Night: Juan José Flores and Ecuador, 1824–1864* (Berkeley, 1989); Germán Carrera Damas, *Boves: Aspectos socioeconómicos de la Guerra de Independencia* 3d ed. (Caracas, 1972); Stephen K. Stoan, *Pablo Morillo and Venezuela, 1815–1820* (Columbus, Ohio, 1974); William Lee Lofstrom, *La presidencia de Sucre en Bolivia* (trans.; Caracas, 1987); Mark A. Burkholder, *Politics of a Colonial Career: José Baquíjano and the Audiencia of Lima* 2d ed. (Wilmington, Del., 1990); and William Lofstrom, *Dámasao De Uriburu, Un empresario minero de principios del siglo XIX en Bolivia* (trans.; La Paz, 1982).

Several articles and books deal with the elusive matter of *caudillismo*. See, for example, Robert L. Gilmore, *Caudillism and Militarism in Venezuela, 1810–1910* (Athens, Ohio, 1964); Glen C. Dealy, *The Public Man . . .* (Amherst, 1977); John Lynch, *Caudillos in Spanish America, 1800–1850* (Oxford, 1992); Mark D. Szuchman's above mentioned book, *Order, Family, And Community in Buenos Aires, 1810–1860,* especially his concluding remarks about Juan Manuel de Rosas, 218–24; C. Parra Pérez, *Mariño y las guerras civiles* 3 vols. (Madrid, 1959–60); Paul Gootenberg, "North-South: Trade Policy, Regionalism and *Caudillismo* in Post-Independence Peru," *JLAS* 23, no. 2 (May 1991), 273–308. Because of his much-deserved distinguished reputation, his vast knowledge of the independence period, and the authority with which he presents his arguments, Lynch's book will be the point of departure for discussions of *caudillismo* during the next years. It would be unfortunate if this caused students to overlook Dealy's important cultural interpretation. Dealy is one of the few political scientists ever to have successfully understood nineteenth-century Spanish American history. For many insights into the matter of regionalism and *caudillismo,* see the brilliant analysis in Magnus Mörner, *Region and State in Latin America's Past* (Baltimore, 1993). The books by Carrera Damas, Lynch, and Gootenberg mentioned in the preceding paragraph are extremely important to an understanding of *caudillismo.*

The role and status of women during independence are covered well in Janet R. Kentner, "The Socio-Political Role of Women in the Mexican Wars of Independence" (Ph.D. diss., Loyola University of Chicago, 1957); and Silvia M. Arrom, *The Women of Mexico City* (Stanford, 1985). John Tutino has begun an exploration of the undermining of patriarchy and the increased role of women in Mexican agriculture as a result of the Mexican insurgency, in "The Revolution in Mexican Independence: Insurgency and the Renegotiation of Property, Production, and Patriarchy in the Bajío, 1800–1855," *HAHR* 78, no. 3 (August 1998), 367–418.

A modest contribution to our understanding of royalism is Eduardo Pérez O., *La guerra irregular en la independencia de la Nueva Granada y Venezuela, 1810–1830* (Tunja, 1982). The author brings together standard information about bands and factions, but it was not his goal to analyze royalism.

In addition to many travel accounts, several books describe daily life in Spanish America during the independence period. See Jean Descola, *Daily Life in Colonial Peru, 1710–1820* (trans.; London, 1968); Alberto Crespo R. et al., *La vida cotidiana en la Paz durante la guerra de la independencia, 1800–1825* (La Paz,

1975); and M. D. Démelas and Y. Saint-Geours, *La vie quotidienne en Ameríque du Sud au temps de Bolívar, 1809–1830* (Paris, 1987).

The standard studies of diplomacy during the independence period are C. K. Webster, *Britain and the Independence of Latin America, 1812–1830* . . . 2 vols. (Oxford, 1938); William W. Kaufmann, *British Policy and the Independence of Latin America, 1804–1828* (New Haven, 1951); William Spence Robertson, *France and Latin-American Independence* (Baltimore, 1939); Arthur P. Whitaker, *The United States and the Independence of Latin America* (Baltimore, 1941); and John Street, *Gran Bretaña y la independencia del Río De La Plata* (trans.; Buenos Aires, 1967). See also Robert N. Burr, *By Reason or Force: Chile and the Balancing of Power in South America, 1830–1905* (Berkeley, 1965); and Ron L. Secklinger, "South American Power Politics during the 1820s," *HAHR* 56, no. 2 (May 1976), 241–67. Of interest also is María Teresa Berruezo León, *La lucha de Hispanoamérica por su independencia en Inglaterra, 1800–1830* (Madrid, 1989); and Celia Wu, *Generals and Diplomats: Great Britain and Peru, 1820–1830* (Cambridge, 1991).

Two attempts to apply social science theory to the independence movement are Jorge I. Domínguez, *Insurrection or Loyalty: The Breakdown of the Spanish American Empire* (Cambridge, Mass., 1980); and George Reid Andrews, "Spanish American Independence: A Structural Analysis," *Latin American Perspectives*, 12, no. 1 (Winter 1985), 105–32.

For an attempt to place the period of Latin American independence in a broad spatial framework, see Lester D. Langley, *The Americas in the Age of Revolution, 1750–1850* (New Haven, 1996).

A useful study of recent literature is Brian R. Hamnett, "Process and Pattern: A Re-examination of the Ibero-American Independence Movements, 1808–1826" *JLAS* 29, no. 2 (May 1997), 279–328.

Studies of my own cited in the notes are not repeated here; nor are my books on Bernardo O'Higgins and Diego Portales.

✠

Index

Page numbers in italics are illustrations.

Agustín I (Agustín de Iturbide), 98, 99,
    128, 147
Alvear, Carlos de, 59–60
Anzoátegui, José Antonio, 84–86
Apodaca, Juan Ruíz de, 99
Aranda, Count of, 9
Argentina, 151–52; abolition of slavery
    by, 111; Buenos Aires, 57–61; con-
    stitution of, 122; Bernardo O'Higgins
    in, 73; trade in, 16–17, 149
Arizpe, Miguel Ramos, 128
Army of the Three Guarantees, 98
Artigas, José Gervasio, 60–61, 127

Barreiro, José María, 87
Becker, Carl, 9
Belgrano, Manuel, 59, 72, 101
Bello, Andrés, 46, 48, 50
Bentham, Jeremy, 50, 111
Beresford, William Carr, 44
Berney, Antonio, 24–25
Bolívar, Juan Vicente, 46
Bolívar, Simón, *39,* 50–56, 82–83, 89,
    113, 119–120; assassination attempt
    on, 91–92; Cartagena Manifesto by,
    53, 115–16; in Colombia, 83, 88, 90–
    91, 119; foreign legion under, 82, 89–
    90; in Great Britain, 48; in Haiti, 78,
    80; Indian tax under, 141; influences
    on, 46–47; in military, 51–52, 53–54,
    226; and Pablo Morillo, 89; in New

Granada, 53–54, 56, 84–87; in Peru,
    77–78, 93, 94–95; political beliefs of,
    115–20; as public official, 54–56, 83,
    88, 93, 119; and José de San Martín,
    77; slavery opinion of, 78–79; in
    Venezuela, 47–48, 50–52, 54–56, 79–
    81, 87
Bolivia, 96, 110, 111, 118–19
Bonaparte, Joseph, 36, 43, 45
Bonaparte, Napoleon, 34–36, 47
Borja, Francisco de, 29
Bourbon reforms; causes of, 12–13;
    church reforms under, 18–20; eco-
    nomic reforms during, 22–23; govern-
    ment officials during, 37–38; inten-
    dancy system under, 17–18; military
    reforms under, 13–14; protests against,
    27, 30; trade under, 14–17
Boves, José Tomás, 55–56
Brazil, 36, 103–4
British Legion, 82, 89–90
Brown, William, 61

Cádiz; constitution of, 120–21; Council
    of Regency of, 46, 48; trade monopoly
    of, 14–15
Cagigal, Juan de, 48–49
Cagigal, Manuel, 55
Campomanes, Count of, 9–10, 18
Canterac, José, 92–93, 95

Capitalism, 1–3, 160–61n. 11 (ch. 1)
Caroline reforms. *See* Bourbon reforms
Carrera, José Miguel, 63, 65–66, 112,
    113, 115
Carrera, Juan José, 65–66
Carrera, Luis, 65
Cartagena Manifesto, by Simón
    Bolívar, 53
Caste system, 5–6
Castlereagh, Viscount, 105–6
Caudillo, 143–44
Central America, *148;* Federation of, 147,
    149; trade in, 146–47; United Prov-
    inces of, 100
Centralism; in Argentina, 151–52; consti-
    tutions of, 122; in Mexico, 128–29; in
    Spanish America, 126–27
Charles III, 9, 35
Charles IV, 35, 36, 45
Chile, 62–66, 73–74; abolition of slavery
    by, 111; church in, 146; constitutions
    of, 110, 122–24, 126; Masonic lodge
    in, 75; Bernardo O'Higgins in, 64–65,
    74–75, 122–23; railroad in, 140–41;
    revolts in, 24–25, 30–32; trade in, 16
Christophe, Henri (King Henri I), 35
Church, 18–20, 30, 104–5, 146
Cisneros, Balthasar de, 58
Cochrane, Lord Thomas, 76
Colombia, 111; Bogotá, 45; Republic of,
    83, 87–91, 118, 119
Constant, Benjamin, 111–12, 125, 128
Costa Rica, 100
Council of Regency of Cádiz, 36, 46, 48
Creoles, 13–15, 18, 20–21
Cuba, 12, 103, 164n. 26 (ch. 5)

Descartes, René, 11
Dessalines, Jean-Jacques (Jacques I), 34–
    35, 103
Domínguez, María Josefa Ortiz de, 107

Ecuador, 90–91, 111, 119, 141–42;
    Quito, 27–29, 45
El Salvador, 100, 146–47
Elhuyar, Fausto, 10–11
Elhuyar, Juan José, 10–11

Enlightenment, 7–8; in Spain, 9–10; in
    Spanish America, 10–12
España, José María de, 25

Farías, Valentín Gómez, 128–29
Federalism, 125–29, 147, 149, 151–52;
    constitutions of, 121–22, 124
Feijoó, Benito Jerónimo, 9
Ferdinand VII, 36, 43, 88, 97–98; re-
    stored to throne, 7, 37, 56–57
Flores, Juan José, 119, 141
Floridablanca, Count of, 9, 18
France; influence of, 120–21, 125; Span-
    ish American trade with, 136–37
Francia, José Gaspar Rodríguez de, 101–2
Freire, Ramón, 73
Fretes, Juan Pablo, 19

Gaínza, Gabino, 65, 100
Gálvez, José de, 21–22, 30
Gamarra, Agustín, 144
Gandarillas, Manuel José, 126
García, José Ancelmo, 4
Garibay, Pedro, 44
Giraldes, Nicolás, 4
Giraldes, Tomás, 4
Godoy, Manuel de, 35, 36
Government officials, 20–22; problems
    with, 145–46; professionalization of,
    37–38
Gramusset, Antonio, 24–25
Great Britain, 48–50; governing Río de la
    Plata, 44–45; on independence move-
    ment, 93–94, 105–6; Spanish Ameri-
    can trade with, 136–37
Gual, Manuel, 25
Guatemala, 100, 146–47
Guerrero, Vicente, 98

Haiti, 32, 34–35, 78, 80
Hamilton, Alexander, 49
Henri I (Henri Christophe), 35
Hidalgo revolt, 66–70, *71,* 97
Hidalgo, Miguel, 20, 66–69
Honduras, 100, 146–47

Indians, vii, 142–43; revolts by, 25–27, 66–70; tax to, 141–42
Industrialization, in Spanish America, 132–33
Irisarri, José de, 105–6
Iturbide, Agustín de (Emperor Agustín I), 98, 99, 128, 147
Iturrigaray, Viceroy, 43–44

Jacques I (Jean-Jacques Dessalines), 34–35, 103
Jefferson, Thomas, 49
Jesuits, 18, 30, 146
Joáo (Prince Regent of Portugal), 36
Jovellanos, Gaspar Melchor de, 9, 10, 114
Juárez, Benito, 129
Junot, Andoche, 36
Juntas, 26, 36–37, 45–46, 52–53, 62–63

Knox, Henry, 49

La Carrera, Ignacio de, 62, 63
La Pezuela, Joaquín de, 76
La Plata, Fernando Márquez de, 62
La Serena, José de, 76–77, 94–95
La Torre, Miguel de, 89–90
Lancaster, Joseph, 50
Las Heras, Juan Gregorio de, 73
Leclerc, Victor-Emmanuel, 34
Letter to Spanish America, by Juan Pablo Viscardo, 18
Liberalism, 111–15
Liniers, Santiago de, 44–45, 58
Locke, John, 10
Louverture, Toussaint, 33–34, 103

MacGregor, Gregor, 80–81
Machado, Josefina, 79–80
Mackintosh, John, 84
Madison, James, 49
Mangino, Fernando José, 37
María (Spain), 35
María I (Portugal), 36
Mariño, Santiago, 54–56, 81
Martínez, José Antonio, 62
Masonic lodge, 50–51, 60, 61, 64, 75–76

Memorial of the Hacendados, by Mariano Moreno, 113
Mexico, 37–38, 127–29, 131–32, *148;* abolition of slavery by, 111; capitalism in, 159n. 1 (ch. 1); church in, 104–5, 146; constitution of, 128–29; Dolores, 67–68; Guanajuato, 29–30; Hidalgo revolt in, 66–70, *71,* 97; independence movement in, 97–100; revolts in, 45; suffrage in, 110; Viceroyalty of, 43–44; women in independence movement in, 106–7
Miers, John, 139
Military, 143; creoles in, 13–14; free people of color in, xvi–xvii; merchants in, 13–14
Miranda, Francisco, 7, 48–52, 64–65, 124–25; constitution under, 114–15
Monopoly; agricultural, 161–62n. 4 (ch. 2); in colonial Spanish America, 5; effects of, 2, 14–15
Monroe Doctrine, 93
Monroe, James, 93, 106
Monteagudo, Bernardo, 59–60, 77
Monteverde, Domingo, 51–52, 54, 55
Mora, José María Luis, 111–12, 125, 128
Morales, Francisco, 56
Morelos, José María, 69–70, 107
Moreno, Mariano, 112–13
Morillo, Pablo, 57, 81, 84, 85, 89

Napoleon, 34–36, 47
Nariño, Antonio, 53, 56
New Granada, 53–54, 84–87; in Colombia, 83; as colony, 56–57; juntas in, 52–53; Francisco de Paula Santander in, 119; Viceroyalty of, 17, 27–29, 30
Newton, Isaac, 11
Nicaragua, 100, 146–47
Noguera, José Gabriel Condorcanqui (Túpac Amaru II), 25–27

O'Donojú, Juan, 99
O'Higgins, Ambrosio, 63–64
O'Higgins, Bernardo, 7, 19, *41,* 50, 63–65, 73–75, 113–14, 122–23

O'Leary, Daniel Florencio, 82–83, 84–85, 86, 89, 90, 91–92, 94, 95
Olañeta, Pedro Antonio de, 96
Osorio, Mariano, 65–66

Pacific Steam Navigation Company (PSNC), 140–41
Páez, José Antonio, 80–81, 84, 85, 89–90, 119, 144
Paine, Thomas, 49
Paraguay, 100–102, 111
Patriotic Society (Sociedad Patriótica), 60
Peru, 63, 65–66, 94–95, 133; abolition of slavery by, 111; Simón Bolívar in, 77–78, 93, 94–95; Callao, 96–97; caudillos in, 144; Colombian army in, 92–93; independence of, 77; revolts in, 25–27; José de San Martín in, 72–73, 76–78, 92; Antonio José de Sucre in, 92–93; taxes in, 163n. 2 (ch. 5)
Pétion, Alexander, 35, 78, 80
Piar, Manuel, 54–55, 80–81
Piñeres, Juan Francisco Gutiérrez de, 30
Pitt, William, 49
Poinsett, Joel Roberts, 115
Polignac Memorandum, 93
Popham, Home, 44
Portales, Diego, 123–24
Portales, José Santiago, 16, 37
Portugal, 36, 103–4
Puerto Rico, 103
Pueyrredón, Juan Martín, 60

Railroad, 131, 140–41
Rebellion of the Barrios, 27–29
Reina, Francisco Javier, 62
Rengifo, Manuel, 124
Riaño, Juan Antonio, 68–69
Riego, Rafael, 88
Río de la Plata, 60, 104; Viceroyalty of, 17, 44–45, 150
Riquelme, Bernardo. See O'Higgins, Bernardo
Riquelme, Isabel, 64
Riva Agüero, José de la, 92
Rivadavia, Bernardino, 59
Robertson, John Parish, 137–39

Robertson, William, 138–39
Rodil, José Ramón, 96–97
Rodríguez, Simón, 46–47
Rojas, José Antonio de, 24–25
Roo, Andrés Quintana, 107
Rosales, Juan Enrique, 62
Roscio, Juan Germán, 88
Rozas, Juan Martínez de, 37, 62

Sáenz, Manuela, 91–92, 120
Saint-Domingue, 32–35; under Spanish rule, 103
San Martín, José de, 40, 50, 59–60, 66, 72–74, 76–78, 92, 113
Santa Anna, Antonio López de, 99
Santa Domingo, 103; under French rule, 32–35
Santander, Francisco de Paula, 84–88, 118–19
Say, Jean Baptiste, 114
Seven Years' War, 12–13
Seville; junta of, 36, 45
Slavery; abolition of, 108, 111
Smith, Adam, 10, 114
Sobremonte, Marquis de, 44–45
Social Contract, translated by Mariano Moreno, 112
Sociedades Económicas de Amigos del País, 9–10, 11
Soublette, Carlos, 80, 85
Spanish American colonies, 8
Suárez, Francisco, 12
Sucre, Antonio José de, 42, 90–91, 92–93, 95–96, 118

Thorne, Manuela Sáenz de, 91–92, 120
Toro Zambrano, Mateo de, 61–62
Toro, Marqués de, 51
Torre Tagle, Marqués de, 93, 96
Torres, Camilo, 53, 54
Toussaint Louverture, 33–34, 103
Trade, 14–17, 134–136; in Argentina, 149, 151–52; economic burdens of, 2; international, 48, 136–37; monopoly of, 146–47
Tres Antonios, 24–25

Túpac Amaru II (José Gabriel Condorcanqui Noguera), 25–27

United States; constitution of, 120–21,
124, 128–29; and independence move-
ment, 93–94, 105–6; Spanish Ameri-
can trade with, 136–37
Upper Peru, 17, 45, 58–59, 96, 131–32
Uruguay, 103, 111, 122, 127
Utilitarianism, 111–14
Uztáriz, Jerónimo de, 9

Venegas, Francisco Javier, 44
Venezuela, 46, 50–52, 54–57, 133; abolition of slavery by, 111; Simón Bolívar
in, 47–48, 79–81, 87; and Colombia,
83, 119; constitution of, 117–18, 124–
25; independence of, 89–90; junta in,
46; revolt in, 25
Vicario, Leona, 107
Victoria, Guadalupe, 99
Vinoni, Francisco, 87
Viscardo, Juan Pablo, 18

Wellesley, Arthur (Duke of Wellington),
50
Wheelwright, William, 139–41
Whitelock, John, 44–45
Wilberforce, William, 50

Yermo, Gabriel de, 44

Zea, Francisco Antonio, 83, 88